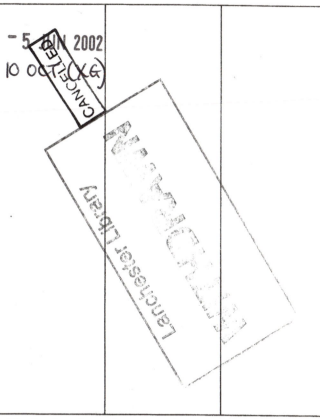

Studies in Musical Genesis and Structure

General Editor: Lewis Lockwood, Harvard University

Studies in Musical Genesis and Structure

Webern and the Lyric Impulse

Songs and Fragments on Poems of Georg Trakl

ANNE C. SHREFFLER

CLARENDON PRESS · OXFORD

Oxford University Press, Great Clarendon Street, Oxford OX2 6DP
Oxford New York
Athens Auckland Bangkok Bogota Bombay
Buenos Aires Calcutta Cape Town Dar es Salaam
Delhi Florence Hong Kong Istanbul Karachi
Kuala Lumpur Madras Madrid Melbourne
Mexico City Nairobi Paris Singapore
Taipei Tokyo Toronto Warsaw
and associated companies in
Berlin Ibadan

Oxford is a trade mark of Oxford University Press

Published in the United States by
Oxford University Press Inc., New York

© Anne Shreffler 1994

First published 1994

British Library Cataloguing in Publication Data
Data available

Library of Congress Cataloging in Publication Data
Shreffler, Anne Chatoney.
Webern and the lyric impulse: songs and fragments on poems of
Geog Trakl / Anne C. Shreffler.
(Studies in musical genesis and structure)
Includes bibliographical references.
1. Webern, Anton, 1883-1945. Lieder, instrumental ensemble acc.,
op. 14. I. Title. II. Series.
MT145.W38S5 1994 782.42168—dc20 93-45941
ISBN 0-19-816224-3

10 9 8 7 6 5 4 3 2

Printed in Great Britain
on acid-free paper by
The Ipswich Book Company, Suffolk

Editor's Preface

THIS series provides a number of monographs, each dealing with a single work by an important composer. The main focus of each book is on the compositional process by which the work developed from antecedent stages, so far as these can be determined from the sources. In each case the genesis of the work is connected to an analytical overview of the final version. Each monograph is written by a specialist, and, apart from the general theme of the series, no artificial uniformity is imposed. The individual character of both work and evidence, as well as the author's special critical viewpoint, dictates differences in emphasis and treatment. Thus some studies may stress a combination of sketch evidence and analysis, while others may shift the emphasis to the position of the work within its genre and context. Although no such series could possibly aim at being comprehensive, it will deal with a representative body of important works by composers of stature across the centuries.

Among the established master composers of the twentieth century, none remains a greater mystery to the common listener and reader than Anton Webern. His reputation is still framed by what Anne Shreffler rightly calls the 'sparseness, severity, and control' of his music, as well as by the celebrated brevity and density of so many of his mature works. Of the three leading composers of the so-called 'Second Viennese School'—Schoenberg, Berg, and Webern—Webern is still the most distant, most cerebral, and, for many listeners, the most difficult to comprehend.

In this monograph Anne Shreffler brings into view a new sense of Webern, through a close study of his settings of six poems by Georg Trakl (1887–1914), published as Opus 14. Written between 1915 and 1921, well before the twelve-tone system came into being, these songs show Webern primarily as a lyric composer, working intensively to use vocal composition as a way out of the impasse created by the radical brevity of his previous instrumental works. They show us a Webern imbued with concern for vocal qualities, declamation, and fine shadings of sonority in both voice and instruments—all this in music of great refinement and compression, but not the extreme concentration of material found in previous works. Shreffler has been able to locate further unpublished and fragmentary Trakl settings that help to place the published set in better perspective; to which she adds a thorough study of the surviving sketches for the songs. Beyond this, the book also gives us a well-defined picture of the cultural milieu in which both poet and composer were working—the troubled Europe of the later and final phases of the First World War; the death-throes of the Austro-Hungarian Empire; and the atmosphere of intellectual crisis and self-questioning in the Viennese artistic circles to which Webern and Trakl belonged.

Still, the main thrust of Shreffler's work is to throw a sharp new light on Webern's working procedures as composer—his use of various instrumental combinations, approaches to the blending of language and tone, his remarkable sense of texture and detail. It shows us a master engaged in the realization of his innermost thoughts, with lyric impulses tempered at every step by concerns with coherence and structure. At a time when Webern could compare the abandonment of tonality to the extinguishing of the light—'the most important means of building up longer pieces was lost'—these works emerge as milestones in the career of a master whose reputation is unshakeable but whose inner character and individuality remain to be much better known. To that end this book is a very substantial contribution.

Lewis Lockwood

Harvard University

Preface

THIS book grew out of a long-standing interest in music of the Second Viennese School, a repertory I have always found powerfully expressive as well as intellectually challenging. Webern's music in particular strikes me as passionately lyrical, even if its utterances sometimes emerge compressed or fragmented. This disjunct lyricism lies at the heart of Webern's vocal works, especially of the middle-period songs Opp. 12–18. These songs, many based on significant contemporary poetry, do not conform to the stereotype of pianissimo brevity that we have of Webern's music. Their thick textures and often forceful vocalism seem quite removed from the more 'classical' twelve-tone sonata and variation movements to come. Yet rather than articulating a substantially different aesthetic from the later Webern, the relatively neglected atonal vocal works provide a way to understand the consummate lyricism of all his music.

In the case of Webern, study of the compositional process takes on even more importance than usual. Whether because of the anxiety of creating a new musical language, or because of an innate hyperperfectionism (or both), Webern rejected most of what he composed. He either excluded a piece outright or, more often, simply did not complete it. The situation is especially convoluted with the Lieder, which make up almost half of his published output. After the First World War, Webern began to compose a series of songs on texts by Trakl, Goethe, Karl Kraus, Hans Bethge (translations from the Chinese), and Peter Rosegger ('folk-poems'). What could have become several song cycles, each based on a single author, instead turned out to be miscellanies with texts by several authors (in Opp. 12, 13, 15, 17, and 18). Only the Trakl cycle, Op. 14, was based on a single poet. This work, its genesis, and its cultural context form the subject of this book.

I began the project by examining Webern's manuscripts of both finished and unfinished pieces (the results were first presented in my dissertation, 'Webern's Trakl Settings', upon which this book is based).[1] I was extremely fortunate to have had access to the sources; this would have been nearly impossible for anyone working earlier

[1] (Ph.D. diss., Harvard University, 1989).

than I, since Webern's sketches and manuscripts were largely inaccessible until recently. Hans Moldenhauer collected much of the manuscript material himself, and allowed only very limited access to it. In 1984, The Paul Sacher Foundation in Basel acquired most of Moldenhauer's Webern archive; more followed in the next few years. (The remainder, a handful of important manuscripts, only became available after Moldenhauer's death in 1988; this material is now in the Library of Congress.) In the autumn of 1986 and again during the year 1987–8, I was able to examine there all the manuscripts—fragments, sketches, and fair copies—for Webern's middle-period songs. I therefore owe my greatest debt to Dr h.c. Paul Sacher and the Paul Sacher Foundation for financial support during my residencies in 1987–8 and the summer of 1990. I would also like to thank the staff of the Paul Sacher Foundation for their patience, helpfulness, and courtesy on my many visits to Basel. To Dr Felix Meyer, the curator of the Webern archive, I owe my deepest gratitude; without his broad knowledge of the Webern sources and many other things, this project (and several subsequent ones!) would have suffered greatly.

Professor Reinhold Brinkmann, my *Doktorvater* for the original dissertation, continued to provide invaluable assistance in this phase: his close readings of a succession of drafts were indispensable. I am also grateful to Professor Lewis Lockwood and Professor Richard Cohn for their detailed and helpful comments. I was fortunate to be able to work through many questions relating to Webern and the Second Viennese School in two graduate seminars at the University of Chicago; to the students who participated I owe a great debt for their enthusiasm and thoughtful work. The American Philosophical Society and the Chicago Humanities Institute provided additional financial support. Presenting my work to the CHI during my residency there in the autumn of 1991 helped me to articulate the broader issues surrounding the topic; conversations with Professor Norma Field were especially valuable. Throughout the whole project, I enjoyed the benefit of John Shreffler's wide knowledge of poetry and music (and also, since he is my husband, his fine library of poetry books and recordings!).

I deeply appreciate the help given me by Wayne Shirley at the Library of Congress, Rigbie Turner at the Pierpont Morgan Library, Dr Michael Ochs and Robert Dennis at the Eda Kuhn Loeb Library at Harvard University, and Dr Martina Sichardt at the Arnold Schoenberg Gesamtausgabe. I am grateful to Lawrence Schoenberg, Maria Halbich-Webern, and James Pruett of the Library of Congress for permission to include a facsimile of the letter from Webern to

Schoenberg. I would also like to thank the Otto Müller Verlag, Salzburg, for permission to reprint the sixteen Trakl poems that Webern set. My translations of the poems are based on those of Lucia Getsi, in *Georg Trakl: Poems*;[2] they are used here with her kind permission.

An earlier, shorter, version of Chapter 8 appeared as 'Webern, Trakl, and the Decline of the West: Webern's Setting of "Abendland III"', in a volume of Houston German Studies.[3] I treated the topic of Chapter 10 earlier (and rather differently) in a brief paper, 'Webern's Compositional Process: Origins of "Gesang einer gefangenen Amsel"', read at the XIVth Congress of the International Musicological Society, Bologna, 1987.[4]

Finally, I would like to thank Bruce Phillips, the music editor of Oxford University Press, and David Blackwell, for their assistance in innumerable matters large and small during the preparation of this book.

A NOTE ON MUSICAL EXAMPLES

The musical examples were prepared with great skill and care by Dr Murray Steib; I am very grateful to him for taking on this mammoth job (and I take full responsibility for any errors that remain). I am also grateful for the financial support provided for the preparation of the examples by the College of the University of Chicago. Musical examples and facsimiles from the Paul Sacher Foundation are reproduced here with their kind permission. Examples drawn from the published works of Webern are reprinted by permission of the publishers, Universal Edition in Vienna. The following acknowledgement applies to each example drawn from the music of Op. 14:

Webern SECHS LIEDER
Copyright 1924 by Universal Edition
Renewed copyright 1952 by Anton Webern's heirs
All Rights Reserved
Used by permission of European American Music Distributors Corporation,
    sole US and Canadian agent for Universal Edition.

Since the score of Webern's Op. 14 is easily available, few citations from that are reprinted here; most of the musical examples are from unpublished material. Because it is not possible to obtain photocopies

    [2] (Athens, Oh.: Mundus Artium Press, 1973).
    [3] Claus Reschke and Howard Pollack (eds.), *German Literature and Music: An Aesthetic Fusion: 1890–1989* (Munich: Fink, 1992), 145–57.
    [4] Published in *Atti del XIV Congresso della Società Internazionale di Musicologia*, iii (Turin: Edizioni di Torino, 1990), 369–80.

of manuscripts from the Sacher Foundation, all examples have been copied from my transcriptions of the original manuscripts. Though I exercised great care in copying from the manuscripts, and checked each transcription at least twice after copying, errors are still possible. It is also possible that there might be differences of opinion about readings of certain notes or passages. Webern's handwriting is normally quite clear and precise, but there are occasional crossings-out and ambiguities in notation. In the examples, I have tried to present something as close to Webern's original as possible. Unless otherwise noted, all stem directions, beaming, dynamics, accidentals, and instrumental indications appear as Webern wrote them.

For readers who are able to see the manuscripts in Basel, I have provided microfilm numbers for each page of manuscript cited. For others, I can only counsel patience; the forthcoming *Gesamtausgabe* of Webern's music—now only in the planning stages—will probably include all the songs and fragments related to this topic. The musical examples of unpublished material presented here are not intended to represent a critical edition.

A.C.S.

Contents

List of Plates

(appear between pages 130 and 131)

Plates 2–10 are provided by courtesy of the Paul Sacher Foundation,
Basel, Switzerland.

List of Musical Examples

(all Webern with Trakl texts unless otherwise noted)

Ex. 3.1. 'Schien mir's . . .' (Strindberg), Op. 12/3, mm. 1–7.

Ex. 3.2. 'Die Sonne', Op. 14/1 (1918), mm. 11–12. Contrabass part
  (PSS, film 104:0423).
Ex. 3.3*a* and *b*. 'Verklärung' (No. 3). Two opening gestures (PSS,
  film 103:0745).
Ex. 3.4. 'In der Fremde' (Bethge), 1915 sketch, mm. 1–2 (PSS, 'new
  sketches').
Ex. 3.5. 'Gegenwart' (Goethe), mm. 1–5 (PSS, film 103:0767).
Ex. 4.1*a* and *b*. 'Abendland II', Op. 14/3, c.d. sketch, two stages of
  mm. 7–9 (PSS, film 101:0569–0572).
Ex. 4.2. 'Die Sonne', Op. 14/1, c.d. sketch (PSS, film 101:0558).
Ex. 4.3. Voice parts as notated in piano/vocal score used in first
  performance (Library of Congress, Moldenhauer Collection): (*a*)
  'Abendland I', Op. 14/2, mm. 4–5; (*b*) 'Nachts', Op. 14/5, mm.
  2–3.
Ex. 5.1. 'In der Heimat', entire fragment (PSS, film 103:0736).
Ex. 5.2. 'In der Heimat'. Musical metre and poetic foot in 1st stanza.
Ex. 5.3. 'Die Einsame' (Bethge), Op. 13/2. Musical metre and poetic
  foot (2 lines).
Ex. 5.4. 'In der Heimat'. Schema of opening bars.
Ex. 5.5. 'Die Einsame' (Bethge), Op. 13/2. Development of 'cello
  figure'.
Ex. 5.6. 'In den Nachmittag geflüstert', entire fragment (PSS, film
  103:0739).
Ex. 5.7. 'In den Nachmittag'. Musical metre and poetic foot in 1st
  stanza.
Ex. 6.1. 'Verklärung' No. 3, vocal line, mm. 1–5 (PSS, film 103:
  0745).
Ex. 6.2. Orchestra song, no text, mm. 1–6 (PSS, film 103:0827).

CHAPTER 8   EXAMPLES: ALL OP. 14 NO. 4
('ABENDLAND III')

CHAPTER 10   EXAMPLES: ALL OP. 14 NO. 6
('GESANG EINER GEFANGENEN AMSEL')

Ex. 10.15. (*a*) C.d. sketch (PSS, film 101:0592); (*b*) final version, mm. 19–20.

Ex. 11.1. 'Nachts', Op. 14/5, c.d. sketch, p. 1, vocal line, mm. 2–5 (PSS, film 101:0585).

Ex. 11.2. (*a*) 'Die Sonne' (1918), mm. 1–5 (PSS, film 104:0423); (*b*) final version, Op. 14/1, vocal line, mm. 2–7.

Ex. 11.3. 'Die Sonne', opening vocal phrase. Comparison of vocal lines in four versions.

Ex. 11.4. (*a*) 'Die Sonne', c.d. sketch, mm. 1–2 (PSS, film 101:0554); (*b*) 'Die Sonne', Op. 14/1, final version, mm. 1–2; (*c*) 'Verklärung' No. 6, mm. 1–2 (PSS, film 101:0557); (*d*) Berg, *Four Pieces* for clarinet and piano, Op. 5/1, m. 1.

Abbreviations

GENERAL

c.d.   continuity draft
DTV   Georg Trakl, *Das Dichterische Werk* (Munich: Deutscher Taschenbuch Verlag, 1987)
M.   Moldenhauer number
pc   pitch-class
PSS   Paul Sacher Stiftung, Basel

INSTRUMENTS

b. cl.	bass clarinet	hp.	harp
b. dr.	bass drum	mand.	mandolin
bn.	bassoon	ob.	oboe
c.a.	cor anglais	pf.	piano
c.bn.	contrabassoon	picc.	piccolo
cel.	celesta	str.	strings
cl.	clarinet	tbn.	trombone
d.b.	double bass	timp.	timpani
E♭ cl.	E♭ clarinet	tpt.	trumpet
fl.	flute	va.	viola
glock.	glockenspiel	vc.	violoncello
gtr.	guitar	vn.	violin
hn.	horn	xyl.	xylophone

Part I
Webern and Trakl

1. Introduction: Webern and Lyric Expression

The music of Anton Webern (1883–1945) has been justly celebrated for its sparseness, severity, and control. Indeed because of these qualities Webern's rarefied vision has never gained the place in the repertory or the popular consciousness accorded to Berg, Stravinsky, or even Schoenberg, and it is safe to suppose now that it never will. Though voices have been raised now and then in favour of a more humanist Webern—Theodor Wiesengrund Adorno and Luigi Rognoni were among the first to oppose the 'Darmstadt project'[1]— his association with a cerebral, detached aesthetic remains strangely unaffected.[2] Since the Second World War, Webern's music has served two causes: first, serial composition in Europe and America, and second, the closely related development of serial and atonal analysis in America. Held up as the model for the new serialism of the 1950s and 1960s, Webern's twelve-tone instrumental works were said to embody a complete break with what Henri Pousseur called 'sentimental nineteenth-century understanding' by building structures from sound itself.[3] American analysts of the 1960s and 1970s found Webern's aphorisms ideal for elucidating the synchronous structures believed to be at the heart of all atonal music. Stravinsky's metaphor in *Die Reihe* (the bible of post-war serialism) of Webern's 'dazzling diamonds' presciently anticipated the scientific analogies to come.[4]

Some pieces (all, not coincidentally, instrumental works) lent themselves more easily than others to the anti-Romantic agenda of the post-war serialists. The extreme sparseness and brevity, for example, epitomized by the *Five Movements for String Quartet*, Op. 5 No. 4 or *Five Pieces for Orchestra*, Op. 10, are not shared by other works from this period, such as the first movement of Op. 5 or the

---

[1] Theodor W. Adorno, 'Anton von Webern', in *Klangfiguren* (Berlin and Frankfurt am Main: Suhrkamp, 1959), 110–25, and Luigi Rognoni, *The Second Vienna School: The Rise of Expressionism in the Music of Arnold Schoenberg, Alban Berg, and Anton von Webern* [1966], trans. Robert Mann (London: John Calder, 1977), which devotes over half of its discussion of Webern to the middle-period vocal music, in a chapter entitled 'The Humanism of Anton Webern'.

[2] See for example Hans Oesch, 'Webern und das SATOR-Palindrom', in Hans Oesch (ed.), *Quellenstudien I* (Winterthur: Amadeus, 1991), 101–56.

[3] '. . . sentimentalen Auffassung des vorigen Jahrhunderts': Henri Pousseur, 'Strukturen des neuen Baustoffs', *Die Reihe*, 1 (1955), 42.

[4] Igor Stravinsky, preface to *Die Reihe*, 2 (1955), p. vii.

second of *Four Pieces for Violin and Piano*, Op. 7.[5] And although many of Webern's twelve-tone works display a high degree of control over their serial materials (most notably *Concerto*, Op. 24 No. 1; *Variations for Piano*, Op. 27; and the last works, from *String Quartet*, Op. 28 to *Second Cantata*, Op. 31), others such as *Two Songs* for chorus and instruments, Op. 19, and *Das Augenlicht*, Op. 26, seem to explore the possibilities of row *disorder* with equal vigour.[6] The 'atypical' pieces have simply been bracketed out of the Webern canon.[7] Webern's solo vocal music, which makes up nearly half of his output, forms the largest 'exception' of all, since it features neither brevity nor system.[8] These forgotten works—in particular the series of songs composed between 1915 and 1925 (Op. 12 to Op. 18)—show another side of the cerebral master of control: Webern as champion of the lyric genre.

Instead of portraying an intellectually driven genius who paves the way to a post-war avant-garde, Webern's songs, through their texts, can situate him in a quite different intellectual and cultural milieu that is only beginning to be understood in connection with his music. His settings of Hans Bethge's adaptations from the Chinese link him with Mahler and *Das Lied von der Erde*, whose sound-world echoes

[5] The English titles of Webern works follow those used by Hans Moldenhauer in his book (with Rosaleen Moldenhauer), *Anton von Webern: A Chronicle of His Life and Work* (New York: Knopf, 1979). The book has been translated into German: *Anton von Webern: Chronik seines Lebens und Werkes*, trans. Ken W. Bartlett (Zurich: Atlantis, 1980). This version is useful, since it preserves the original language for Webern letters and other material originally in German. (Hereafter, the short citation form designates the English version, unless qualified with 'Ger.')

[6] With respect to *Das Augenlicht*, Kathryn Bailey points out the 'undisciplined handling of the row and the almost complete separation of row content from musical structure', in *The Twelve-Note Music of Anton Webern: Old Forms in a New Language* (Cambridge University Press, 1991), 56. Even some of the most strictly controlled works have elements of ambiguity and disorder: see Arnold Whittall, 'Webern and Multiple Meaning', *Music Analysis*, 6 (1987), 333–53.

[7] Webern's most discussed pieces among the early works remain Opp. 5, 9, 10, and 11; and Opp. 21, 24, and 27 of the twelve-tone works. (Zoltan Roman's useful Webern bibliography lists more studies of any *one* of Opp. 5, 9, 21, and 27 than of the five works Opp. 12 to 16 put together; see *Anton von Webern: An Annotated Bibliography* (Detroit: Information Co-ordinators, 1983).) Paul Griffiths's article on Webern in the *New Grove* succumbs to the same tendency; the section on the middle period describes Webern's entire output for fourteen years as transitional: 'Towards Serialism 1914–27', *The New Grove Second Viennese School: Schoenberg, Webern, Berg* (New York: Norton, 1983), 87–134.

[8] There have been a few attempts to systematize this music, usually by treating the vocal line (if at all) as an instrument: see Heinz-Klaus Metzger, 'Analyse des Geistlichen Liedes op. 15 nr. 4', *Die Reihe*, 2 (1955), 80–4. This approach was vividly brought home to me in seminars on Schoenberg with Rudolf Kolisch at the New England Conservatory (Boston) in 1977–8. As we studied *Pierrot Lunaire*, we were not permitted to make any reference whatsoever to the poem or the *Sprechstimme* vocal line. Kolisch considered only the instrumental parts—or the voice in the few places where exact pitches are designated—relevant to analysis.

in many of Webern's works.[9] By setting Goethe, Webern placed himself in the company of Schubert, Schumann, Wolf, and others in the long line of composers who did so. Webern's three long fragments on poems of Karl Kraus and the one finished song, 'Wiese im Park' (Op. 13 No. 1), pay homage to a thinker whose ideas about the purity of art and language greatly influenced Schoenberg and his circle.

Yet it was with the works of his contemporary Georg Trakl (1887–1914) that Webern found a voice that most closely resembled his own. Though Webern and Trakl probably never met, Webern occupied himself intensively with Trakl's poems over a period of seven years, during which he sketched sixteen different settings, drafting several many times. These efforts yielded seven completed songs, six of which make up the *Six Songs on Poems of Georg Trakl*, Op. 14; another Trakl poem, 'Ein Winterabend', was placed as the fourth of *Four Songs for Voice and Orchestra*, Op. 13. Both miniaturists, both misfits, both mystics, Webern and Trakl struggled to create individual modernist languages out of the artistic revolutions that preceded them. Though Webern did not share Trakl's aesthetic of despair, the First World War made him aware of its relevance. One result of Webern's obsession with Trakl was his seven completed Lieder. But reading all of Trakl's poems and attempting musical translations of sixteen of them led to a much larger consequence: the development of his atonal language into a complex but fundamentally lyrical form of expression.

Though Adorno and Rognoni attempted to establish Webern's Op. 14 as a 'masterpiece',[10] it, like most works of Webern, resists this categorization. Webern's settings of Trakl are intensely private, almost hermetic works, and as such never achieved the landmark status of Schoenberg's *Pierrot Lunaire*, Op. 21, or *Das Buch der hängenden Gärten*, Op. 15. While the latter is a striking example of that typical Modernist trope of 'öffentliche Einsamkeit' (public loneliness),[11] Webern's Op. 14 eschews outward display and is better characterized by contrast as a work of 'innerliche Einsamkeit' (inward loneliness). This inwardness he shares with Trakl as well; the works

---

[9] Both Rudolph Stephan and Luigi Rognoni have discussed Webern's links to Mahler, in Stephen, 'Zu einigen Liedern Anton Weberns', in *Österreichische Gesellschaft für Musik, Beiträge '72–73: Webern-Kongress* (Kassel: Bärenreiter, 1973), 135–44, and Rognoni, *The Second Vienna School*, 337–8.

[10] See Theodor W. Adorno, 'Berg and Webern—Schönberg's Heirs', *Modern Music*, 8 (1931), 37, and Luigi Rognoni, *The Second Vienna School*, 351.

[11] As described in the title of Albrecht Dümling's book, *Die fremden Klänge der hängenden Gärten: Die öffentliche Einsamkeit der neuen Musik am Beispiel von Arnold Schönberg und Stefan George* (Munich: Kindler, 1981).

of both shun rhetoric by paring expression down to its barest essentials. Both Webern and Trakl believed, under the strong influence of Karl Kraus, that art should express only that which is absolutely necessary; art therefore becomes purified and freed from the mere aesthetic beauty that can lead to kitsch.[12] In setting texts, Webern similarly focused inward. In his sketches he leaves traces of intensive readings and rereadings of the poetry, seemingly less concerned with a final 'public' product than with the activity of composing itself. With Op. 14, Webern has taken the Lied off the stage. The narrative and dramatic aspects of the German Lieder tradition have been compressed to a vanishing point; the reflective moments that freeze the passage of time in *Winterreise* have now become the primary mode of discourse.

Webern's attraction to the lyric genre is shown on one level by the fact that he composed only vocal works for ten years, and that they make up slightly more than half of his published output. But it goes deeper than that. Rather than a tangent or transition, composing songs was for many years essential to Webern's compositional process and to the development of his technique. As he started writing a song, the opening line of text provided the first inspiration; he continued by projecting the long horizontal spans of a vocal line, deriving the other parts from this initial impetus. The lyric quality of Webern's middle-period songs is displayed by their compressed, non-narrative structure as well as by their melodic prominence. This compression, a quality shared by the lyric poem, heightens the direct, intense projection of emotion so characteristic of Webern's songs.

Throughout his creative life, Webern turned to vocal composition at every important juncture. His *Five Songs from Der siebente Ring by Stefan George*, Op. 3 and *Five Songs on Poems of Stefan George*, Op. 4 (1908–9) mark his first steps into atonality. In 1924, his first completed works using the twelve-tone method were solo songs, *Three Traditional Rhymes*, Op. 17 and *Three Songs*, Op. 18 (although he probably first drafted the twelve-tone piano piece, *Kinderstück*, M. 267). More significantly, Webern's very first essay in row composition, in some 1922 sketches for 'Mein Weg geht jetzt vorüber' (later Op. 15 No. 4), grew directly out of a vocal line.[13] Even later, while writing twelve-tone instrumental pieces, he would often turn to a vocal setting to give him enough melodic ideas to proceed, as he

---

[12] See Hermann Broch, *Hugo von Hofmannsthal and His Time: The European Imagination, 1860–1920*, trans. and ed. Michael P. Steinberg (Chicago and London: University of Chicago Press, 1984), 166–83.

[13] See my forthcoming essay, '"Mein Weg geht jetzt vorüber": The Vocal Origins of Webern's Twelve-Tone Composition', *Journal of the American Musicological Society*, 47 (1994), 275–338.

did by composing the Hildegard Jone songs Opp. 23 and 25 during work on the *Concerto*, Op. 24.[14] Near the end of his life, Webern finally achieved through composition of vocal works the long forms that had previously eluded him: the two cantatas Op. 29 and Op. 31, and *Das Augenlicht*, Op. 26.

Webern set texts not simply to produce pieces with voice, but rather to help his creative process: 'Please understand me correctly,' Webern wrote to Jone in 1941, 'I have *never* gone out looking (as it were) for a "text", with the intention—indeed *I could never have such an intention*—of writing something vocal (a song, a choral piece, etc.). It was never thus; *the text was always provided first*! Given a text, then of course "something vocal" should be the result.'[15]

THE VOCAL DECADE 1914–1924

Webern's intense cultivation of the intimate genre of Lied between 1915 and 1924 (see Table 1) contrasted with the larger-scale preoccupations of his colleagues Schoenberg and Berg. The latter spent most of these years (between 1917 and 1922) on his first opera, *Wozzeck*. Schoenberg was able to complete only the *Four Songs*, Op. 22 (1913–16) during this time (*Pierrot Lunaire* had been finished in 1912). In the first two war years, Schoenberg sketched a Symphony with choral movements, but did not complete it. The main product of the following years (1917–22) was the huge fragmentary oratorio *Die Jakobsleiter*, in which he struggled with the ideas of faith and redemption (he would take these themes up again in another giant fragment, the opera *Moses und Aron*, in 1930–2).

Webern's involvement with song composition was at first a response to the extreme miniaturization of his pre-war instrumental works, the minute *Six Bagatelles for String Quartet*, Op. 9, *Five Pieces for Orchestra*, Op. 10, and *Three Little Pieces for Violoncello and Piano*, Op. 11. That Webern fully realized how radical these pieces were—and how potentially unfruitful as a direction—is shown by his defensive tone in a letter to Schoenberg from July of 1914: 'I am sending you by the same mail a copy of what I last wrote [Op. 11]. . . . I beg you not to be indignant that it has again become something so short. I should like to tell you how this happened and thereby try to justify

---

[14] See Lauriejean Reinhardt, ' "Ich und Du und Alle": Hildegard Jone, Ferdinand Ebner, and Webern's Drei Gesänge Op. 23', paper read at the national meeting of the American Musicological Society, Chicago, 1989.

[15] *Anton Webern: Letters to Hildegard Jone and Josef Humplik*, ed. Josef Polnauer, trans. Cornelius Cardew (Bryn Mawr, Pa.: Theodore Presser, in association with Universal Edition, 1967), 43.

TABLE 1. Webern's Published Works, 1915–25

Op. No.	Title	Date	Poet	Instruments
12	*Four Songs*			piano
	'Der Tag ist vergangen'	1915	P. Rosegger	
	'Die geheimnisvolle Fl.'	1917	Li Tai Po (Bethge)	
	'Schien mir's'	1915	Strindberg	
	'Gleich und Gleich'	1917	Goethe	
13	*Four Songs*			small orch.
	'Wiese im Park'	1917	Karl Kraus	
	'Die Einsame'	1914	Wang Seng Yu (Bethge)	
	'In der Fremde'	1917	Li Tai Po (Bethge)	
	'Ein Winterabend'	1918	Georg Trakl	
14	*Six Songs*		Georg Trakl	cl. + E♭ cl.,
	'Die Sonne'	1921		b. cl., vn.,
	'Abendland I'	1919		vc.
	'Abendland II'	1919		
	'Abendland III'	1917		
	'Nachts'	1919		
	'Gesang einer gefangenen Amsel'	1919		
15	*Five Sacred Songs*			fl., cl. + b.
	'Das Kreuz'	1921	*P. Rosegger	cl., tpt.,
	'Morgenlied'	1922	*Des Knaben W.*	hp., vn. +
	'In Gottes Namen'	1921	*P. Rosegger	va.
	'Mein Weg geht jetzt vorüber'	1922	*Chorale text	
	'Fahr hin, o Seel''	1917	P. Rosegger	
16	*Five Canons on Latin Texts*			cl., b. cl.
	'Christus factus est'	1924	liturgical	
	'Dormi Jesu'	1923	*Des Knaben W.*	
	'Crux fidelis'	1923	liturgical	
	'Asperges me'	1923	liturgical	
	'Crucem tuam adoramus'	1924	liturgical	
17	*Three Traditional Rhymes*			cl., b. cl., vn. + va.
	'Armer Sünder, du'	1924	*P. Rosegger	
	'Liebste Jungfrau'	1925	*P. Rosegger	
	'Heiland, unsre Missetaten'	1925	(unknown)	
18	*Three Songs*			E♭ cl., gtr.
	'Schatzerl klein'	1925	*P. Rosegger	
	'Erlösung'	1925	*Des Knaben W.*	
	'Ave, Regina coelorum'	1925	liturgical	

* New attribution.

myself.'[16] We do not know Schoenberg's response, but it is quite possible that he proposed writing songs in order to get out of this impasse. Schoenberg later recalled that this is exactly what he did in his own compositions: 'A little later I discovered how to construct larger forms by following a text or a poem. The differences in size and shape of its parts and the change in character and mood were mirrored in the shape and size of the composition, in its dynamics and tempo, figuration and accentuation, instrumentation and orchestration.'[17]

Here Schoenberg makes the breathtaking claim that the mere presence of a text adequately substituted for 'the tonal and structural functions of harmony'. While using a text did enable Schoenberg and Berg to write longer pieces, this was true primarily for dramatic forms, not lyric ones, and it did not seem to make any appreciable difference in Webern's music. Webern never composed a work as long as *Wozzeck* or *Erwartung*; even the longest songs from his Opp. 13 and 14 are not as long as 'Seraphita', the first song of Schoenberg's Op. 22. There are extended atonal movements without texts as well, such as Berg's *String Quartet*, Op. 3, and Schoenberg's *Three Piano Pieces*, Op. 11, among others. Moreover, composing with a text did not in itself lengthen pieces in Webern's case; his songs written before the war—including 'Die Einsame' (Op. 13 No. 2) and the posthumously published 'Leise Düfte'—are just as short as the instrumental works of that time.

Webern's own later remarks about how they came to use texts are a little less confident than Schoenberg's:

All the works created between the disappearance of tonality and the formulation of the new twelve-note law were short, strikingly short. The longer works written at the time were linked with a text which 'carried' them (Schoenberg's 'Erwartung' and 'Die Glückliche Hand', Berg's 'Wozzeck'), that's to say, with something extra-musical. With the abandoning of tonality the most important means of building up longer pieces was lost. . . . As if the light had been put out!—that's how it seemed. (At least this is how it strikes us now). At the time everything was in a state of flux—uncertain, dark, very stimulating and exciting, so that there wasn't time to notice the loss.[18]

---

[16] Moldenhauer, *Anton von Webern*, 205.

[17] Arnold Schoenberg, 'Composition with Twelve Tones (I)', in *Style and Idea: Selected Writings of Arnold Schoenberg*, ed. Leonard Stein, trans. Leo Black (Berkeley and Los Angeles: University of California Press, 1984), 217–18. The original lecture was written in 1934, and was given on many occasions until its publication in the first edition of *Style and Idea*, 1950.

[18] Anton Webern, *The Path to the New Music*, ed. Willi Reich, trans. Leo Black (London and Vienna: Universal Edition, 1975), 53–4. The last sentence in the original German reads: 'Damals war alles in unsicherem, dunklem Flusse—sehr an- und aufregend, so daß die Zeit

Though Webern dutifully recounts Schoenberg's version of events, he names as examples three works of music theatre which are indeed the longest atonal pieces, and does not mention lyric forms at all. In this passage he also struggles to reconcile his current (1932) sense that atonality must have been a time of chaos with his actual memories of the earlier period, which are much more positive: 'very stimulating and exciting, so that there wasn't time to notice the loss'. With disarming honesty he admits that the instability of pre-twelve-tone music is apparent only in retrospect: 'As if the light had been put out! . . . (At least this is how it strikes us now).'

The idea that setting texts temporarily solved the structural problems of atonal music has become a truism, but it cannot be taken literally. What does it mean for a text to 'carry' the music, as Webern described? How can a verbal text *replace* musical functions such as harmony and form? What is then the relationship of the new 'music-carrying' text with earlier vocal music that possessed texts as well as traditional harmonies and forms? How is this use of text different from the overwhelmingly large proportion of text-based pieces in the works of Schoenberg, Berg, and Webern before 1914? The explanations of Webern and Schoenberg do not really consider these issues, because that was not their goal.

Both Webern's and Schoenberg's versions of their musical history in the excerpts quoted above were articulated in the early 1930s, that is, after the twelve-tone method had been firmly established. Their remarks must be seen in the light of the fact that Schoenberg and his disciples viewed the development of twelve-tone music as inevitable, and all earlier stages of music as somehow preliminary. (Schoenberg began the essay quoted above by saying, 'The method of composing with twelve tones grew out of a necessity.') The adoption of the twelve-tone method eventually caused Schoenberg to see text-setting as a weakness. He spoke of the twelve-tone method as a way to 'liberate' music from the confines of an 'extramusical' structuring such as a text.[19] Schoenberg's desire to get away from needing a text, and to achieve 'pure' instrumental music that would stand on its own, has strong echoes of the nineteenth-century debate over absolute music versus programme music. Along with the urge to solve the problems of musical structure presented by the abandonment of

fehlte, den Verlust zu merken.' *Der Weg zur neuen Musik*, ed. Willi Reich (Vienna: Universal Edition, 1960), 58.

[19] As Schoenberg wrote in 'Analyse der 4 Orchesterlieder op. 22', 'wenn auch erst durch die Komposition mit 12 Tönen die formalen Möglichkeiten einer absoluten Musik befreit zum Durchbruch kamen, befreit von aller Mitwirkung außermusikalischer Elemente.' *Stil und Gedanke: Aufsätze zur Musik*, ed. Ivan Vojtech ([Frankfurt am Main]: S. Fischer, 1976), 287.

tonality, Schoenberg had an equally strong desire to ensure his place in music history. The place he wanted was that of successor to the great abstract contrapuntalist Bach and the absolute musician Brahms. In order truly to make his mark, then, Schoenberg believed he had to write extended contrapuntal pieces for instruments alone. The archetype of twelve-tone music is in fact instrumental; the concept of a Basic Shape, a preformed idea, is inimical to a vocal piece, whose musical ideas must respond to the content, sound, and form of the poem.

For Webern, the real break came not with the onset of the twelve-tone method, but with the crisis of the instrumental miniatures.[20] Setting texts, as he began to do again with Op. 12 in 1915, did change Webern's music, but not simply by substituting wholesale for other musical functions. The process of finding musical counterparts to the words and verse-structures of Goethe, Kraus, Trakl, and the translations from the Chinese by Hans Bethge caused Webern to expand his musical vocabulary. This was necessary—paradoxically—because he held to assumptions about text-setting that were traditional in the late nineteenth century: a through-composed setting, a prominent vocal line, a largely syllabic delivery for greater comprehension of the words.[21] Other constraints he brought over from his own previous vocal works, particularly the Stefan George songs Op. 3 and Op. 4. Like these, Webern's middle-period songs are all faithful to the poem's structure and (in different ways) to its spoken metres and rhythms. Whereas brief melodic figures of three or four notes worked well in the pointillistic textures of the instrumental miniatures, Webern had to invent and use longer ones in order to set a continuous vocal line syllabically. The floating, metreless character of the pre-war pieces was likewise not adequate to create a vocal line for a strongly metrical poem. Contrasts or stanza breaks in the poem required the articulation of contrasting sections. As the decade proceeded, Webern's text-setting changed from a descriptive, almost mimetic approach based on individual words, to a more abstract approach that 'instrumentalizes' the vocal line.

Between 1915 and 1925 alone Webern completed thirty songs on texts by half a dozen poets. The motivically based atonality of Opp. 12, 13, 14, 15, and 16 provided a rich and flexible vocabulary that proved quite responsive to the demands of the poetry he chose.

---

[20] Here I agree with Adorno's description of Webern's development; see 'Anton von Webern', 119.

[21] These features were not however typical of the handful of songs that Webern wrote during his aphoristic phase. 'Leise Düfte', 'O sanftes Glühn der Berge', and 'Schmerz immer blick nach oben' took on the characteristics of the instrumental miniatures, including extreme brevity, short broken phrases, and non-pitch elements (in some cases *Sprechstimme*).

When recounting that they had used a text to 'carry' the music during this period, Webern used a shorthand phrase to describe a complicated matter. Rather than being a simple expedient, his intensive preoccupation with poetry changed the way he wrote music. Most notably, it resulted in a new linear emphasis that was to continue prominently throughout the later twelve-tone works as well.

ROLE OF THE MANUSCRIPT SOURCES

In this study of Webern's Trakl settings, I shall draw heavily upon the plentiful source material for these works, most of which is found in the Paul Sacher Foundation in Basel.[22] The value of document studies has been debated in recent years.[23] The controversy has centred on the usefulness of sketches in understanding a composer's 'compositional thinking', and by extension, in formulating an analysis of a work (since their importance in 'historical and biographical documentation' is unquestioned).[24] Exactly what, and how much, can sketches actually tell us about the composer's compositional process? The marks on the page are after all mere vestiges of a train of thought that can never be reconstructed again, even by their author. The point is not just that such a reconstruction is impossible from our vantage-point outside the composer's head; more pertinently, it is the wrong goal. Source studies will not provide a secret key to unlock the mysteries of the music at hand; their value lies instead in their power to change our perception of that music. The issue becomes one of work reception rather than elucidation of an autonomous object.[25]

---

[22] The Paul Sacher Foundation (hereafter PSS) also contains the manuscripts and papers of Stravinsky, Boulez, Maderna, Berio, and Carter, among others. The Webern manuscripts in the PSS represent mainly the early stages of Webern's composition (sketches and fragments); there are relatively few fair copies. A catalogue is available: Felix Meyer and Sabine Stampfli (comps.), *Anton Webern Musikmanuskripte* (Inventare der Paul Sacher Stiftung, 4; Winterthur: Amadeus, 1988). For an account of the convoluted but fascinating history of the Webern *Nachlass*, from its rediscovery in the 1960s by Hans Moldenhauer to its acquisition by the PSS, see Hans Moldenhauer, 'Excelsior! Die Genese des Webern-Archivs', in Hans Jörg Jans (ed.), *Komponisten des 20. Jahrhunderts in der Paul Sacher Stiftung* (Basel: Paul Sacher Stiftung, 1986), 131–5. Most of the ink fair copies of scores that Webern prepared for publication are in the Pierpont Morgan Library, New York (Robert Owen Lehman Collection). Other Webern manuscripts can be found in Washington, London, Vienna, Berlin, and Cambridge, Mass.

[23] For a summary of the debate, which began with Douglas Johnson's article 'Beethoven Sketches and Beethoven Scholars' (*Nineteenth-Century Music*, 2 (1978–9), 3–17), see Joseph Kerman, 'Sketch Studies', in D. Kern Holoman and Claude V. Palisca (eds.), *Musicology in the 1980s: Methods, Goals, Opportunities* (New York: Da Capo, 1982), 53–65.

[24] See Lewis Lockwood, '*The Beethoven Sketchbooks* and the General State of Sketch Research', in William Kinderman (ed.), *Beethoven's Compositional Process* (Lincoln, Nebr. and London: University of Nebraska Press, 1991), 6.

[25] Particularly valuable in this respect is Philip Gossett's *Anna Bolena and the Artistic Maturity of Gaetano Donizetti* (Oxford: Clarendon Press, 1985) in this series.

On this account I have tried to avoid the pitfall of the 'master narrative' in which sketches progress from incomplete to more fully realized, culminating in an aesthetically and structurally perfect work. A logical problem of this approach is that results are of necessity determined retroactively; in a circular process, first the artwork is deemed great, then the sketches are analysed to show just how that greatness came about.[26] Rather than serving a circular argument of validation, though, sketch studies can open up a work, reducing our perception of its autonomy by making audible the different voices present at various stages of its becoming. If sketches are not forced teleologically into steps towards the finished work, but instead are considered as points along a continuum (a path that could even have taken different directions), then sketch and work can inform each other in interesting and fruitful ways.[27] Instead of treating the sketch material as leading to a single culminating work, I hope to allow Webern's Trakl settings, both complete and incomplete, to draw us outwards, illuminating other Webern works as well as altering the conventional view of his aesthetic.

The special nature of the Webern sources was first brought to light by the works list in Hans and Rosaleen Moldenhauer's 1979 biography of Webern.[28] While there are thirty-one opus-numbered works (plus another dozen or so published posthumously in the 1960s), the Moldenhauers list 347. Though this number resulted in part from the Moldenhauers' extremely generous definition of a 'work'—they counted student harmony exercises as well as brief fragments—it does suggest that a view of Webern's music based only on the published works is incomplete.

The sheer amount of material available for the years 1915–22 is surprising in view of the relatively few published compositions from the same time (Opp. 12, 13, 14, and 15). Yet Webern sketched some pieces many times, as well as attempting many other settings which he did not finish; the result is eighty-four distinct manuscript drafts, covering about 130 pages.[29] Of these, Trakl settings comprise thirty-

---

[26] Clearly, sketch studies lend themselves most readily to composer- and work-centred approaches, which have themselves become problematized. See for example Rose Subotnik, *Developing Variations: Style and Ideology in Western Music* (Minneapolis and Oxford: University of Minnesota Press, 1991), 144–5, and Janet Wolf, 'The Ideology of Autonomous Art', in Richard Leppert and Susan McClary (eds.), *Music and Society: The Politics of Composition, Performance, and Reception* (Cambridge University Press, 1987).

[27] The use of sketches to validate analytical points would seem to be denied only if one approaches a musical work as an autonomous object that defines a self-contained universe (as Douglas Johnson appears to do in 'Beethoven Scholars and Beethoven's Sketches').

[28] Moldenhauer, *Anton von Webern*, 697–750.

[29] Including fair copies, piano/vocal scores, and songs written in 1914, the page count is over 300.

four drafts (about fifty-three pages). Others are sketches and fragments on poems of Kraus, Goethe, and adaptations from the Chinese
by Hans Bethge. Webern's sketches and fragmentary attempts on
Trakl's poems document the stages of development of *Six Songs*, Op.
14, but they also illuminate Webern's attitudes to the relationships
between the pre-existing text, the vocal part that 'carries' it, and the
interactive instrumental parts. The sketches also show that he often
considered orchestration, contour, and register as crucial as pitch,
interval, and motive; awareness of his concerns could help us to
develop analytical techniques that take them into account.[30] We also
learn from the manuscripts that Webern was capable of composing
very quickly. The image of the cerebral, calculated worker who took
great pains over every expression mark needs to be modified for the
whole middle-period output; Webern's composing began to take on
these characteristics only later.

Most of the work on Webern's sketches has of necessity focused on
twelve-tone compositions, since the only published sketch material
pertains to later works.[31] While work on Webern's twelve-tone
sketches proceeds apace,[32] the middle-period sketches and fragments
are unpublished and almost completely unknown. Table 2 displays
the Trakl poems that Webern set and the number of drafts for each.
For the sixteen poems listed in Table 2, Webern composed thirty-
four musically distinct drafts. Of those, seven were completed (these

[30] Some work in these areas has begun: see Paul Andrew Kabbash, 'Form and Rhythm
in Webern's Atonal Works' (Ph.D. diss., Yale University, 1983); Edward Murray, 'New
Approaches to the Analysis of Webern' (Ph.D. diss., Yale University, 1979); Gregory Woodward, 'Non-Pitch Aspects as Structural Determinants in the Atonal Works of Anton Webern'
(Ph.D. diss., Cornell University, 1986); and Christopher Hasty, 'Composition and Context in
Twelve-Tone Music of Anton Webern', *Music Analysis*, 7/3 (Oct. 1988), 281–312, in which he
writes about his analytical methods: 'In return we may hope to gain a better understanding of
Webern's profound lyricism, a quality too often ignored in analysis' (p. 285).
[31] Hans Moldenhauer (ed.), *Anton von Webern: Sketches (1926–1945)* (New York: Carl
Fischer, 1968). See also studies by George Perle, 'Webern's Twelve-Tone Sketches', *Musical
Quarterly*, 57 (1971), 1–25; Roger Smalley, 'Webern's Sketches', *Tempo*, 112 (1975), 1–12, 113
(1975), 29–40, and 114 (1975), 14–22; R. Larry Todd, 'The Genesis of Webern's Op. 32',
Musical Quarterly, 66 (1980), 581–91. Sketches for earlier works, or indeed for most of the
twelve-tone works, have been largely unavailable until 1984. See however the valuable early
study by Elmar Budde, *Anton Weberns Lieder Op. 3 (Untersuchungen zur frühen Atonalität bei
Webern)* (Wiesbaden: Franz Steiner, 1971). Other important source studies of the pre-serial
repertoire include Reinhold Brinkmann, 'Die George-Lieder 1908/9 und 1919/23—ein Kapitel
Webern-Philologie', in *Webern-Kongress 1973*, 40–50; Reinhard Gerlach, 'Die Handschriften
der Dehmel-Lieder von Anton Webern: Textkritische Studien', *Archiv für Musikwissenschaft*,
29 (1972), 93–114; Peter Westergaard, 'On the Problems of Reconstruction from a Sketch:
Webern's *Kunfttag III* and *Leise Düfte*', *Perspectives of New Music*, 11 (1973), 104–21.
[32] See Bailey, *The Twelve-Note Music*; Catherine Nolan, 'Hierarchic Linear Structures in
Webern's Twelve-Tone Music' (Ph.D. diss., Yale University, 1989); and Donna Lynn, 'Genesis,
Process, and Reception of Anton Webern's Twelve-Tone Music: A Study of the Sketches for
Opp. 17–19, 21, and 22/2 (1924–1930)' (Ph.D. diss., Duke University, 1992).

TABLE 2. Webern's Trakl Settings

Op. or M. No.	Title of Poem	Portion Set	Instrumentation	Designated Date
214	'In der Heimat'	vv. 1–7	piano	Wien 1915 Auhofstr.
215	'In den Nachmittag geflüstert'	1st stanza	cl., c.a., vn., hp., [others]	Wien, Auhofstr, Winter 1915
218	'Mit silbernen Sohlen'	(1) 1st sentence	b. cl., tpt., tbn., hp., str., cel., timp., tam, xyl.	Hietzing 1917]
		(2) 1st 3 words	vc. [others]	[1917]
(14/6)	'Gesang einer gefangenen Amsel'	(1) vv. 1–5	fl., cl., b. cl., 2 tpt., 3 tbn., va., vc., 3 d.b., hp., cel., mand., (glock).	1917
225	'Verklärung'	(2) vv. 1	solo d.b., str.	1917 [before July 4]
		(1) vv. 1–5	2 cl., b. cl., tpt., tbn., vn., va., vc., hp.	1917 Klagenfurt
247	'Nachtergebung'	(2) v. 1–3	piano	1917
		(3) vv. 1–3	vn. [others]	[1917]
		(1) vv. 1–2	c.a., b.cl., tbn., va., 2vc., d.b.	[1917]
		(2) 1st word	b. cl., tbn., vc.	[1917]
227	'Siebengesang des Todes'	vv. 1–4	fl., cl., b. cl., bn., tpt., tbn., hn., tutti str., hp., cel., bells	1917 Klagenfurt
14/4	**'Abendland III'**	entire	E♭ cl., b. cl., vc.	23.6.1917
13/4	**'Ein Winterabend'**	entire	fl., cl., b. cl., c.a., tpt., tbn., str., cel., hp.	10.7.1918
(14/1)	'Die Sonne'	1st 2 stanzas	fl., ob., cl., b. cl., tpt., vn., vc., d.b., cel.	Mödling 1918
—	'Klage'	vv. 1–2	fl., b. cl., tbn., c.bn., vn. vc., d.b., hp.	[before autumn 1918]

TABLE 2. (cont.)

Op. or M. No.	Title of Poem	Portion Set	Instrumentation	Designated Date
(14/6)	'Gesang einer gefangenen Amsel'	(3) vv. 1–4	fl., cl., tpt., va., vc., d.b.	Mödling (Herbst) 1918
(14/6)	'Gesang einer gefangenen Amsel'	(4) vv. 1–4	cl., b. cl., tpt., vn., va., vc., d.b., hp., cel., glock., b. dr.	Mödling (Herbst) 1918
		(5) v. 1	picc., cl., tpt., vn., vc., hp.	1918
		(6) v. 1	cl., tpt., hn., vn., vc., hp.	[1918–19]
		(7) vv. 1–3	fl., b. cl., vc., d.b.	1918
14/3	**'Abendland II'**	entire	cl., vn., vc.	7.7.1919
(14/6)	'Gesang einer gefangenen Amsel'	(8) vv. 1–4	fl., b. cl., va.	[1919]
14/6	**'Gesang einer gefangenen Amsel'**	entire	cl., b. cl., vn., vc.	11.7.1919 Mürzzuschlag
14/5	**'Nachts'**	entire	E♭ cl., b. cl., vn.	18.7.1919
225	'Verklärung'	(4) 1st 2 stanzas	b. cl., vc.	[1919–21]
		(5) 1st 2 stanzas	ob., cl., b. cl., vn., vc., hp., tbn., cel., glock.	[1919–21]
14/2	**'Abendland I'**	entire	b. cl., vn., vc.	28.7.1919 Mürzzuschlag
248	'Die Heimkehr'	(1) vv. 1–3	fl., b. cl., tbn.	[1920]
		(2) v. 1	cl., vn., vc., d.b., hp., glock., cel.	[1920]
247	'Nachtergebung'	(3) 1st stanza	piano	1920
254	'Jahr'	v. 1	b. cl., va., vc.	1921
225	'Verklärung'	(6) v. 1	cl., tpt., va., vc., hp.	[1921]
14/1	**'Die Sonne'**	entire	cl., vn., vc.	12.8.1921

are shown in bold type), and some twenty-seven drafts remained fragments.

Webern left many more pieces incomplete than he finished; during the 1910s, fragments make up the bulk of his compositional efforts. Some of the drafts are as long as, or longer than, his completed pieces; many are quite thoroughly worked out, with instrumentation, articulation marks, dynamics, and even tempo marks designated. At least three could be completed and performed. These fragments are not juvenilia, but match the completed works of this time in style and complexity. What can Webern's failures tell us? Rather than as evidence of a lack of fluency caused by a kind of impotence of language, the fragments can be seen as remnants of an over-abundance of ideas.

This is shown by one of the most unusual aspects of Webern's compositional process during these years: the almost complete absence of reworkings of the same music. Instead each sketch begins with a new musical conception. Rather than perfecting a given musical idea for a line of verse, Webern preferred to abandon it and start again with another (in marked contrast to his later practice). The paper remnants of this process are crucial for understanding how he approached the texts. They show Webern's dialogue with the poetry as it is happening; in the finished work, this interaction is obscured as the composer's voice predominates.[33]

Studying the manuscript sources for Webern's middle-period vocal works also helps to modify the view that his music progressed steadily in the direction of the twelve-tone technique. Instead many of his sketches and fragments show directions that he tried but did not pursue. Some seem incompatible with twelve-tone technique and even with Webern's own completed works before 1924. Some of these deadends include use of large ensembles with percussion, long melodic motives that recur untransposed, ostinatos that imply a tonal context, and elaborate musical analogies to rhyming lines of poetry. The primary message of the sources, however, is that this music was generated horizontally. The opening line of text provided the first inspiration; he composed by projecting the long lines of a vocal part, deriving the other parts from this initial impetus.

Knowing the essential role that poetic texts played in all of Webern's music between 1915 and 1924 can alter our reception of his later twelve-tone music. Let us recall for a moment some of the features of that music. After some experimentation with vertical

---

[33] For the concept 'composer's voice' I am of course indebted to Edward T. Cone, *The Composer's Voice* (Berkeley: University of California Press, 1974).

disposition of twelve-tone rows (resulting in the *String Trio*, Op. 20), Webern began to explore the implications of horizontal row presentation. In a series of works from the *Symphony*, Op. 21, until his last work, the *Second Cantata*, Op. 31, he invented a staggering variety of ways to write with horizontally disposed rows, many of which involved canon. Unlike Schoenberg, Webern did not pay much attention to the vertical organizing force of combinatoriality. Writing rows melodically and accompanying them with similarly linear figures presents a situation very similar to that of writing songs. Webern's experience in composing vocal music predisposed him to writing this way, and set up habits he was to continue all his life.

In a letter to his publisher Emil Hertzka, Webern apologizes for the predominantly lyrical character of his work: 'I know very well that my work means very little from the commercial point of view. But that is probably due to its almost exclusively lyrical nature until now. Poems [Gedichte] are certainly not very profitable, but after all they must be written.'[34]

Though Webern says simply that songs do not sell as well as instrumental music, his statement can be interpreted in a wider context. He refers to his songs as *Gedichte*, analogizing—even identifying—music with poetry. Poems must be written, however unprofitable they may be, and likewise music must be composed for them. But the 'lyrische Natur' that Webern acknowledges to be the basis for his songs also lies at the heart of all his music.

In the following chapters I start by examining how Webern got to know Trakl's poetry in the context of their shared Austrian culture and intellectual climate, pointing out the many aesthetic points of contact as well as differences between them. Part II focuses on how Webern composed, first describing the general procedures he used between 1915 and 1921, then the evolution of the Op. 14 songs, from the first sketches of 1917 to the work's performance and publication in 1924. In Part III, I concentrate on the Trakl fragments. Chapter 5 examines Webern's earliest Trakl fragments from 1915, showing how Webern tried to extend his motivic technique in order to write longer pieces. In Chapter 6, I shall focus on an unusual group of fragments from 1917, which feature ostinato and hints of tonality. Chapter 7

---

[34] 'Wohl weiß ich, daß mein Werk rein geschäftlich noch immer äußerst wenig bedeutet. Aber das liegt wohl auch in seiner bis heute fast ausschließlich lyrischen Natur begründet. Gedichte sind freilich wenig einträglich, aber schließlich müssen sie eben doch geschrieben werden.' To Emil Hertzka, 6 Dec. 1927. Photocopy in the PSS, original in the Stadt- und Landesbibliothek, Vienna.

treats the phenomenon, so characteristic of Webern, of sketching the same poem more than once with different music.

Part IV deals entirely with the completed works belonging to Op. 14; here I choose a salient feature of each song (and often its sketches) that illuminates a particular aspect of its text-setting. Because the six songs of Op. 14 are so different from one another, each suggested different points of departure for analysis. The particular approach chosen for one piece might work equally well for the others; ideally one might combine all the techniques used here and focus them on a single piece. In order best to describe the intimate and continual interaction of poem and music, I discuss them together, rather than in separate sections.

First, I treat the three 'Abendland' songs in the order in which Webern composed them (Op. 14 Nos. 4, 3, and 2). The heart of the group, treated in Chapter 8, is 'Abendland III', the first Trakl poem Webern completed (1917). The analysis will focus on what I have called *multiple reference*; this describes how a motive may refer simultaneously to more than one previous motive, or even to one in the future. In 'Abendland II' (Op. 14 No. 3) (Chapter 9), I shall look at how a network of fixed-pitch motives creates a complex variant of strophic form in which the text of one strophe becomes the 'subtext' of another. The analysis of 'Abendland I' (Op. 14 No. 2) traces two figures that function as dramatic gestures, and whose contrasting characters are exaggerated, not reconciled.

In Chapter 10, 'Gesang einer gefangenen Amsel' (Op. 14 No. 6) will be examined in relation to the eight fragments on this text that preceded it. The final version represents Webern's avoidance of the tone-painting he had explored earlier and his increasing emphasis on musical analogues to the poem's structure. In 'Nachts' (Op. 14 No. 5) (Chapter 11), Webern draws the parallels between musical and poetic structure even more closely, resulting in a kind of stylized, artificial Expressionism. The discussion of 'Die Sonne' (Op. 14 No. 1), the last of Webern's Trakl songs to be composed, centres on its relationship to a sketch that shows the work's roots in an earlier language. Finally, situating 'Die Sonne' firmly in Webern's free atonal style challenges the view that the piece is a proto-twelve-tone work. I conclude in the Afterword with an evaluation of Webern's Op. 14 as a quintessentially modernist work.

2. Webern and Trakl: Historical and Aesthetic Connections

That Webern encountered the poet Trakl should be taken symbolically. Both, in common, are at home in a realm where there is neither common interest nor home any more. The works of both grow out of detached, submerged inwardness; both cry out the need of the soul, bound by itself in suffering. Both bear pure witness to God's abandonment of living creatures. Their [Webern's and Trakl's] discourse, whose echo has vanished, is intended for Him.[1]

With these words the philosopher and critic Adorno linked Webern closely with Trakl's pessimistic vision. Here Adorno describes Webern not as a composer who 'interprets' Trakl's poems, but as a soul mate of the poet's. He and Trakl share a rarefied spiritual realm, a space that no longer has 'Gemeinsamkeit' or 'Heimat'. They met symbolically if not in real life; their common condition arises not from influence but from a shared response to the world. Both drawn into themselves, their works grow out of a 'detached, submerged inwardness'; this individuality paradoxically brings them kinship.

Yet Adorno's beautiful—if characteristically obscure—comment paints Webern in distinctly dark Trakl-like colours. His description of their works as 'cry[ing] out the need of the soul, bound by itself in suffering' bears stronger witness to Trakl's apocalyptic message—and his short tormented life—than to Webern's almost pantheistic optimism. Adorno's view of Trakl also influences his judgements about Webern's music. For Adorno, Webern's instrumental miniatures represented the end of musical discourse; 'their continuation would be only a sigh', he wrote about Opp. 9, 10, and 11.[2] Schoenberg heard Webern's aphorisms quite differently; their brevity resulted not from an attenuation of material but rather from a compression of

---

[1] 'Daß Webern dem Dichter Trakl begegnete, darf symbolisch genommen werden. Beide gemeinsam sind heimisch in einem Bereich, wo es keine Gemeinsamkeit und Heimat mehr gibt. Beider Werk entwächst der abgelösten, sinkenden Innerlichkeit, beider Werk tönt von der Not der bei sich selbst gefangenen Seele in Schwermut. Sie beide bezeugen rein die Verlassenheit der Kreatur von Gott. Ihm gilt ihre Rede, der das Echo schwand.' Theodor W. Adorno, 'Zur Aufführung der fünf Orchesterstücke in Zürich', in Heinz-Klaus Metzger and Rainer Riehn (eds.), *Musik-Konzepte Sonderband: Anton Webern I* (Munich: edition text + kritik, 1983), 271.

[2] 'ihre Fortsetzung wäre der Seufzer allein': Adorno, 'Zur Aufführung der fünf Orchesterstücke', 271.

many potential sounds: 'You can stretch every glance out into a poem, every sigh into a novel. But to express a novel in a single gesture, a joy in a breath—such concentration can only be present in proportion to the absence of self-pity.'[3] Whereas Webern and Schoenberg viewed their radical departures from traditional musical vocabularies optimistically, as brave explorations of unknown territory, Trakl's disjunct verses on the other hand articulated an aesthetic of despair. The clarity—even purity—of Webern's music seems at odds with Trakl's poems, with their emphasis on decay and decline.

Yet if they had such disparate visions, why did Webern choose Trakl, especially when none of his peers or predecessors had done so? How did Webern understand the poems? In this chapter, I shall investigate Webern's reception of Trakl from both historical and aesthetic viewpoints. First, I shall outline the historical context for both, in particular the specific connections between them, suggesting that Webern's experience in the First World War made him more receptive to Trakl than he might have been otherwise. Then I explore the disjunct syntax and ambiguous imagery characteristic of Trakl's poetry and suggest that these features resonated especially strongly for Webern. Rather than 'deciphering' the meanings of Trakl's poems or 'translating' them into music, he fashioned an analogously complex music, which like Trakl's verse operates on multiple levels of meaning. The connection between them was not primarily a matter of technique, however. In the poetry of Georg Trakl, Webern found a fellow modernist whose poetic ideals sprang from many of the same sources as his own musical ones. They shared in addition an almost fanatic distrust of beauty for its own sake and a concomitant distaste for display. The 'absence of self-pity' to which Schoenberg referred could have served as a creed for them both.

HISTORICAL CONTEXT

Webern and Trakl, both Austrians, were near-contemporaries. Webern was born in 1883 (Dec. 3) in Vienna; Trakl, a little over three years later in Salzburg (3 Feb. 1887). Though Trakl lived in Vienna for a time while Webern was there, and they had many acquaintances in common, they probably never met. One point of

[3] 'Jeder Blick läßt sich zu einem Gedicht, jeder Seufzer zu einem Roman ausdehnen. Aber: einen Roman durch eine einzige Geste, ein Glück durch ein einziges Aufatmen auszudrücken: solche Konzentration findet sich nur, wo Wehleidigkeit in entsprechendem Maße fehlt.' Arnold Schoenberg, preface to score of Webern's *Six Bagatelles for String Quartet*, Op. 9 (Vienna: Universal Edition, 1924).

intersection, however, was the Akademischer Verband für Literatur und Musik in Wien, a group of intellectuals interested in promoting— or more accurately, fighting for—the cause of modern art.[4] This group's many activities included the publication of the magazine *Der Ruf*, and sponsoring concerts and festivals, such as the 'counter-festival' to the Vienna Festival Weeks in the summer of 1912.[5] Trakl joined this group during his stay in Vienna in 1910. Webern and Schoenberg were also members of the Akademischer Verband; the first of Webern's *Four Pieces for Violin and Piano*, Op. 7, was first published in *Der Ruf*, as were several of Schoenberg's musical and prose works. The Akademischer Verband also sponsored the in-famous evening of 31 March 1913, which became known as the *Skandalkonzert*. The audience broke out into fist-fights, and the concert, which included works of Berg and Webern, had to be stopped. Trakl's friend Erhard Buschbeck, as the president of the association, tried unsuccessfully to calm the crowd. Two days after the concert, Trakl wrote to Buschbeck of his outrage at the reception Schoenberg and his pupils had received and his sympathy for their cause.[6] Through the Akademischer Verband, Webern and Trakl must have known of each other's existence at least from 1912 on— when Webern's first piece came out in *Der Ruf*—if not earlier. By 1913, Trakl had become acquainted with Karl Kraus, Adolf Loos, and Peter Altenberg, all of whom were well known to the Schoenberg circle.

Kraus was one of the first, and most vocal, supporters of Trakl. He promoted the poet through *Die Fackel*, the magazine he edited, published, and mostly wrote, as well as in his celebrated public readings. Shortly after Trakl and Kraus met, Trakl dedicated a new poem to Kraus, 'Psalm'.[7] In response Kraus wrote an aphorism ('Siebenmonatskinder'), prefaced by the note 'Georg Trakl zum Dank für den Psalm', for the next issue of *Fackel*.[8] Among Kraus's aphorisms was a poem called 'Verwandlung', which is regarded as an

[4] Herbert Lindenberger, *Georg Trakl* (New York: Twayne, 1971), 21. O. Basil, in *Georg Trakl in Selbstzeugnissen und Bilddokumenten*, describes the group as a 'Kampfgemeinschaft musischer Hochschulstudenten' who put on exhibits, readings, and 'zumeist turbulente Konzerte' (Reinbek bei Hamburg: Rowohlt Taschenbuch Verlag, 1965), 87.

[5] Moldenhauer, *Anton von Webern*, 131, 158.

[6] H. H. Stuckenschmidt, *Arnold Schoenberg: His Life, World and Work*, trans. Humphrey Searle (New York: Schirmer, 1977), 187.

[7] Georg Trakl, *Das Dichterische Werk* (Munich: Deutscher Taschenbuch Verlag, 1987), 200 (1st version) and 32 (2nd version) (hereafter cited as DTV). These texts are taken from the standard critical edition: *Georg Trakl: Dichtungen und Briefe. Historisch-Kritische Ausgabe*, ed. Walther Killy and Hans Szklenar (2 vols.; Salzburg: Otto Müller, 1969).

[8] *Die Fackel*, 360–2 (Nov. 1912), 24.

admiring imitation of Trakl.[9] Issues of *Die Fackel* from the winter
and spring of 1914 contain advertisements for Trakl's first collection
of poems, *Gedichte* (1913).[10] Trakl's admiration of Kraus as prophet
and protector of Art is encapsulated in his aphorism—itself a Krausian
genre—entitled 'Karl Kraus':

> Weißer Hohepriester der Wahrheit,
> Kristallne Stimme, in der Gottes eisiger Odem wohnt,
> Zürnender Magier,
> Dem unter flammendem Mantel der blaue Panzer des Kriegers klirrt.[11]

In terms that evoke both Old-Testament prophet and modern warrior,
Trakl paid homage to the man who had become his patron. Webern,
like Schoenberg, Berg, and many others of the Viennese avant-garde,
read *Fackel* religiously from its earliest days.[12]

Though Kraus's journal may have brought Trakl's name to
Webern's attention, his first exposure to the poetry came through the
Innsbruck literary magazine *Der Brenner*.[13] In a letter to Schoenberg
from 1914 (shown in facsimile in Plate 1), Webern relates that though
he was now familiar with both of Trakl's books, he first encountered
the poems in *Der Brenner*.

> Last autumn for the first time I read poems by him [Trakl] in *Der Brenner*.
> They made a big impression on me. Since then I have read a book of his
> poems [*Gedichte* (1913)]. Ever since then I have thought of him with great
> sympathy. Now I have read the book again. I think these poems are
> wonderful. Trakl was from Salzburg. He only lived to the age of 27. A
> second book of poems has just come out [*Sebastian im Traum*].[14]

---

[9] Gerald Stieg, *Der Brenner und die Fackel: Ein Beitrag zur Wirkungsgeschichte von Karl
Kraus* (Salzburg: Otto Müller, 1976), 265. Stieg also reports that Trakl began to be considered
such a special protégé of Kraus that when Trakl asked one of his friends for money, he was
refused and told to go and ask the *Fackel* instead (p. 263).

[10] See *Die Fackel*, 11 Jan. 1914 and 21 Apr. 1914, among others.

[11] Although I use English translations of prose quotations, all quotations from poetry will be
given in the original language, with translations in footnotes. 'White high priest of truth, |
Crystalline voice, wherein dwells the icy breath of God, | Angry magician, | Beneath whose
flaming robe clashes the blue armour of the warrior.' *Brenner*, III/18 (15 June 1913), 840.
Reprinted in DTV 68.

[12] See Alexander Goehr, 'Schoenberg and Karl Kraus', *Music Analysis*, 4 (1985), 59–72; and
Susanne Rode, *Alban Berg und Karl Kraus* (Frankfurt: Peter Lang, 1988). Rode lists several
Berg–Webern exchanges about Kraus in 1911 and 1912. Webern also set several poems of
Kraus that had originally appeared in *Die Fackel*, including 'Wiese im Park' (Op. 13 No. 1).

[13] Ludwig von Ficker (ed.), *Der Brenner* (Innsbruck: Brenner-Verlag, 1910–54).

[14] 'Ich habe vorigen Herbst von ihm im "Brenner" zum erstenmale Gedichte gelesen. Die
haben mir tiefen Eindruck gemacht. Seither las ich einen Band Gedichte von ihm. Seitdem
habe ich immer mit großer Sympathie an ihn gedacht. Jetzt habe ich wieder den Gedichtband
gelesen. Ich finde diese Gedichte ganz wunderbar. Trakl war Salzburger. Er ist nur 27 Jahre alt
geworden. Ein zweiter Gedichtband ist nun erschienen.' Letter from Webern to Schoenberg, 11

The brain-child of Ludwig von Ficker, its editor and guiding light, *Der Brenner* advocated a 'kind of Christian existentialism', as the Trakl scholar Lindenberger put it. Of the *Brenner* group, he writes, 'From their isolated Alpine bastion, Ficker and his circle stood for earnestness and integrity against what they took to be the decadence and triviality of the fashionable views emanating from Vienna.'[15] Contributors to the journal eschewed brief witty *feuilletons* like those in the Viennese daily newspapers. Essayists, including Carl Dallago and Karl Borromäus Heinrich, instead produced long tracts about the ideal unity of man and nature, the alienating force of urban industrialism, and relations between the sexes, among other topics. They reprinted and commented upon writings of Kierkegaard, Dostoevsky, and Otto Weininger. There were close ties between *Brenner* and *Fackel*, as well as between their two editors Ficker and Kraus, before and during the First World War, although they—both the journals and their editors—drifted apart during the 1920s. *Die Fackel* commanded the greater respect because of the greater stature of Kraus, and also because of its position in the capital city; *Der Brenner* has even been described as the '*Fackel* of the provinces'.[16] Yet *Brenner* was critically important for the early dissemination of Trakl's poetry, just as Ficker's friendship and financial help nurtured Trakl in his personal life.[17]

Webern read *Der Brenner* until the end of his life; his connection with the later Brenner circle in the 1920s and 1930s, through his friends Hildegard Jone and Josef Humplik, is well known. The above letter to Schoenberg indicates that Webern had begun reading the magazine at least by the autumn of 1913. It is likely that he had also read issues from the spring of that year. These contained the much talked about 'Rundfrage über Karl Kraus', in which various artists, intellectuals, and writers, including Schoenberg, Peter Altenberg,

---

Nov. 1914; Washington, Library of Congress, Schoenberg Collection. The second Trakl volume to which Webern refers, *Sebastian im Traum*, is in his *Nachlass* (PSS), initialled 'W' and dated 1916 (Leipzig: Kurt Wolff Verlag, 1915). Webern's copy of *Gedichte* (1913) did not survive.

[15] Lindenberger, *Georg Trakl*, 23. See also Sieglinde Klettenhammer and Erika Wimmer-Webhofer (eds.), *Aufbruch in die Moderne: Die Zeitschrift 'Der Brenner' 1910–1915* (Innsbruck: Haymon Verlag, 1990).

[16] 'Provinzfackel': Stieg, *Der Brenner und die Fackel*, chapter heading (p. 273). Kraus also recorded favourable reviews of *Der Brenner*; quotations from these were reprinted in various issues of *Brenner*. Gerald Stieg points out that such exchanges of announcements were made purely out of goodwill, since neither journal accepted paid advertisements (*Der Brenner und die Fackel*, 15).

[17] Alfred Doppler discusses the Brenner circle's influence on Trakl in '"Der Brenner" als Kontext zur Lyrik Georg Trakls', in *Die andere Welt, Festschrift für Hellmuth Himmel zum 60. Geb.*, ed. Kurt Bartsch (Berne and Munich: Francke, 1979), 249–59.

and Adolf Loos, were asked to contribute evaluations of the controversial author.[18] Berg was strongly urged by one of his friends to purchase these issues, and he (or Schoenberg) might in turn have told Webern about them.[19] Webern must have also read the 1915 *Brenner-Jahrbuch*, which was a memorial issue to Trakl, since it included several poems Webern set that had not appeared in either of the two published Trakl volumes.[20]

Although Trakl was practically unknown to the general public of Vienna, he was an extremely important and well-regarded figure in exactly the circles in which Webern moved. In 1914, Webern was well enough acquainted with people who knew Trakl to be able to relate to Schoenberg some of the tragic circumstances surrounding Trakl's death only a few days after it happened:

I believe you know of the poet Georg Trakl. He had died. He was an army pharmacist in the war against the Russians. In a field hospital he tried to kill himself after seeing terrible horrors. He was prevented from doing so and was brought to Cracow for observation. There he recently died; we don't know any more about it.[21]

Given Webern's sympathy with the poetry and the admiration of Trakl by so many of the people Webern respected, one wonders why they did not meet. The answer may be simply that Webern discovered Trakl too late. He only began to read the poems a year before Trakl's premature death in November 1914, and by December of 1913 Trakl had left Vienna for good. The event of Trakl's death itself, and its subsequent commemoration in a special issue of *Der Brenner*, may well have been the catalyst that spurred Webern to reread the poems.

Effect of First World War

That Webern was drawn to themes such as decay and decline during the years he was occupied with Trakl's poetry (1915–21) was surely due to his experiences of the First World War. The war caused tremendous disruptions in the lives of Schoenberg, Berg, and Webern.

---

[18] *Brenner*, III/18, 19, 20 (1913). See also Stieg, *Der Brenner und die Fackel*, 37–48.

[19] Letter from Paul Hohenberg to Berg, postmarked 16 July 1913, cited in Rode, *Alban Berg und Karl Kraus*, 393.

[20] These poems are 'Die Heimkehr', 'Klage', 'Nachtergebung', and 'Mit silbernen Sohlen' (from 'Offenbarung und Untergang').

[21] 'ich glaube, du weisst von dem Dichter Georg Trakl. Er ist gestorben. Er war Feldapotheker im Krieg gegen die Russen. In einem Feldlazarett wollte er im Anblick furchtbarer Schauer sich selbst vernichten. Er wurde daran behindert und kam zur Beobachtung nach Krakau. Dort ist er vor kurzem gestorben; man weiss noch nicht Näheres.' Webern to Schoenberg, 11 Nov. 1914, Library of Congress, Schoenberg Collection.

All did some military service, and all suffered the material deprivation that affected everyone in Europe during and after the war, when the catastrophic inflation destroyed so many family fortunes, including Webern's. They were all cut off from the outside world, with the usual avenues for performance abroad blocked. Webern could not even get his works published with Universal Edition in Vienna; the initial agreement was supposed to start in 1914 but had to be delayed for six years. Their music too bore the traces of the devastation of war, Germany's subsequent defeat, and the breakup of the Austro-Hungarian Empire. Schoenberg later described these years as a time of musical crisis, but at the time his concerns seemed to be more spiritual and philosophical rather than technical (as shown in the texts to the choral symphony and the oratorio, *Die Jakobsleiter*, that he worked on during these years). The musical outcome of his crisis of faith was the formulation of the system of 'twelve tones related only to one another', which he first articulated publicly in 1923. Berg's war experiences enabled him to empathize even more with Büchner's character Woyzeck because, as he wrote to Webern in August 1918, 'I have been spending these war years just as dependent on people I hate [as Wozzeck], have been in chains, sick, captive, resigned, in fact humiliated.'[22] Webern's initial enthusiasm for the war—like that of many others—had faded after being confronted with its realities.[23] Having served almost two years in the Austrian army—though never at the front—he was well aware of the unprecedented extreme destructive powers of this, the first modern war.

Webern distilled his reactions into expressions of the utmost lyric intensity, often choosing for his song texts poems that reflect upon themes of destruction. These include Rosegger's folk-poem 'Der Tag ist vergangen' (Op. 12 No. 1), Kraus's 'Wiese im Park' (Op. 13 No. 1), and Trakl's three-part poem 'Abendland' (Op. 14 Nos. 2, 3, and 4), all set between 1917 and 1919. Though Trakl wrote 'Abendland' in 1914, before the war started, the poem anticipates not only the destruction of war but the decline of the empire. In 1918, Webern attempted, but did not finish, another of Trakl's war poems: 'Klage'. This poem—along with its companion piece 'Grodek'—would establish Trakl's reputation as a major poet of the First World War.[24] The

[22] Cited in George Perle, *The Operas of Alban Berg*, i: *Wozzeck* (Berkeley: University of California Press, 1980), 20.

[23] Moldenhauer, *Anton von Webern*, 209–22. From his father's house in Klagenfurt, where Webern lived during the summer of 1917, he reported that he could occasionally hear the rumble of the cannons at the front (p. 219).

[24] This fragment was previously unidentified in any list of Webern's works: see A. Shreffler, 'A New Trakl Fragment by Webern: Some Notes on "Klage"', in *Mitteilungen der Paul Sacher Stiftung*, 4 (Jan. 1991), 21–6.

poem describes the horrors of the war in a very personal, interior language. Trakl wrote 'Klage' in 1914 while serving on the Eastern front in Galicia; what he experienced there precipitated his subsequent insanity and suicide. 'Abendland' and 'Klage' therefore foreshadow other apocalyptic themes of the time, for example Spengler's book, *Der Untergang des Abendlands* (*The Decline of the West*, 1918–22), and Kraus's play, *Die letzten Tage der Menschheit* (*The Last Days of Mankind*, begun in 1915). Trakl, like Kraus and other Austrian artists of the time, had prophesied the impending catastrophe before the war broke out. To Webern writing in 1917–19, these were no longer premonitions but stark realities.

POEMS WEBERN CHOSE

From Trakl's Gedichte *(1913)*

Of the sixteen Trakl poems Webern chose, only two came from Trakl's first published collection: 'In der Heimat' and 'In den Nachmittag geflüstert' (see Table 3).[25] Unlike Trakl's mature poetry, most of the poems in *Gedichte* (1913) are cast in strict metres and rhyme-schemes. Many, including 'Nachmittag', conform to a traditional three- or four-stanza shape, each stanza made up of four lines of four pulses each, with a rhyme-scheme of ABBA. In a few poems Trakl essays five- or six-pulse lines. There are even a couple of sonnets; 'In der Heimat' is one of these.[26]

During the time Trakl wrote 'In der Heimat' and 'Nachmittag' (between the second half of 1912 and early 1913), he began to break out of strict forms into free verse, and to develop the characteristic vocabulary of images that is so prominent in his later poems.[27] A transition to freer verse seems inevitable after these strict early poems. The disconnected, often brutal images in them seem to break the bonds of the regular metrical settings. The images in the two Trakl poems from *Gedichte* are frankly morbid, as in these lines from 'In den Nachmittag geflüstert': 'Schatten drehen sich am Hügel | von Verwesung schwarz umsäumt'.[28] The second stanza of 'In den Nachmittag geflüstert' joins images which fit into the four-beat pattern and rhyme-scheme, but none refers directly to any of the others;

[25] *Gedichte* (1913) would have been Webern's only source for 'In der Heimat', while 'In den Nachmittag geflüstert' was published first in *Brenner* in 1912. Webern probably chose both poems from *Gedichte*, where they appear together.

[26] Also in this volume is 'Die Junge Magd', later set by Hindemith as his Op. 23.

[27] Lindenberger, *Georg Trakl*, 58.

[28] 'Shadows swirl on the hill | Rimmed blackly with decay.' DTV 32.

TABLE 3. Trakl Poems Set by Webern

Text (Op. or M. No.)	Place and date of poem's first publication	Subsequent publication	Critical Edition
1. 'In den Nachmittag geflüstert' (M. 215)	Der Brenner, III/3 (1 Nov. 1912), 110	Gedichte (1913)	54
2. 'In der Heimat' (M. 214)	Gedichte (1913)		60
3. 'Nachts' (14/5)	Der Brenner, III/16 (15 May 1913), 721	Sebastian (1915)	96
4. 'Gesang einer gefangenen Amsel' (14/6)	Der Brenner, IV/7 (1 Jan. 1914), 306	Sebastian (1915)	135
5. 'Die Sonne' (14/1)	Der Brenner, IV/7 (1 Jan. 1914), 306	Sebastian (1915)	134
6. 'Siebengesang des Todes' (M. 227)	Der Brenner, IV/11 (1 Mar. 1914), 479	Sebastian (1915)	69–70
7. 'Abendland' (14/2, 3, 4)	Der Brenner, IV/14–15 (1 May 1914), 636–41 (early version)	Sebastian (1915) (4th version)	139–40
8. 'Jahr' (M. 254)	Der Brenner, IV (16) (15 May 1914), 715	Sebastian (1915)	138
9. 'Verklärung' (M. 225)	Sebastian im Traum, 1915		120
10. 'Ein Winterabend' (13/4)	Sebastian im Traum, 1915		102
11. 'Die Heimkehr' (M. 248)	Der Brenner, V (1915), 10		162
12. 'Klage' (no number)	Der Brenner, V (1915), 13		166
13. 'Mit silbernen Sohlen' (M. 218) ('Offenbarung und Untergang')	Der Brenner, V (1915), 56–9		170
14. 'Nachtergebung' (M. 247)	Der Brenner, V (1915), 12		93

there is no intrinsic reason why they should belong in the same stanza:

> 5 Sterbeklänge von Metall;
> 6 Und ein weisses Tier bricht nieder.
> 7 Brauner Mädchen rauhe Lieder
> 8 Sind verweht im Blätterfall.[29]

The fact that one poem encompasses so many diverse images within a strict verse-structure may have caused Webern problems not presented by the relatively simpler texts he had used in his vocal miniatures of 1913–14. Trakl's complex verse demanded a more extended musical treatment, which may be why Webern's first efforts were not successful.

After 1915, Webern did not return to *Gedichte* (1913), instead choosing the rest of his Trakl texts from his second published volume, *Sebastian im Traum* (published posthumously in 1915), and from *Brenner*. Thus the poems Webern set after 1915 represent examples of Trakl's mature style; the *Brenner* poems in particular are among the poet's last and most extreme poetic utterances.

Trakl's Later Poems: Discontinuity and Recurrence

Compared with Trakl's earlier poems, his work in *Sebastian im Traum* and after is characterized by a disjunct, almost non-syntactical structure. By distorting traditional images and dissociating them from one another, Trakl produces something very much like atonality in music. He removed the unifying force of a single voice, an 'ich', resulting in a fragmentation of perspective. In this he was not alone, but was responding to an intellectual crisis experienced similarly by many artists in the early years of the century; this loss of personal identity, and therefore language itself, was described in terrifying detail in 1902 by Hofmannsthal's fictional Lord Chandos.[30]

In Trakl's poem 'Verklärung', for example, we can see this kind of dissociation of image and structure.

Verklärung (Transfiguration)[31]

Wenn es Abend wird,	When dusk falls,
Verläßt dich leise ein blaues	A blue face softly leaves you.
Antlitz.	

---

[29] 'Metallic sounds of dying; | And a white beast breaks down. | Brown girls' coarse songs | are scattered among the leaves.' DTV 31. Lindenberger points out, 'even Trakl's rhymed quatrains provide only a semblance of unity for the lines of any particular stanza' (*Georg Trakl*, 50).

[30] Hugo von Hofmannsthal, 'Der Brief des Lord Chandos', in *Gesammelte Werke in zehn Einzelbänden*, vii (Fischer Taschenbuch Verlag, 1979), 461–72.

[31] Trakl, DTV 67, trans. after Georg Trakl, *Poems*, trans. Lucia Getsi, 121.

Ein kleiner Vogel singt im Tamarindenbaum.	A small bird sings in the tamarind tree.
Ein sanfter Mönch Faltet die erstorbenen Hände. Ein weißer Engel sucht Marien heim.	A gentle monk Folds dead hands. A white angel appears to Mary.
Ein nächtiger Kranz Von Veilchen, Korn und purpurnen Trauben Ist das Jahr des Schauenden.	A nocturnal wreath Of violets, grain, and purple grapes It is the year of the one who watches.
Zu deinen Füßen Öffnen sich die Gräber der Toten, Wenn du die Stirne in die silbernen Hände legst.	At your feet The graves of the dead open, When you lay your brow in your silver hands.
Stille wohnt An deinem Mund der herbstliche Mond, Trunken von Mohnsaft dunkler Gesang;	Quietly the autumnal moon Lives upon your mouth, Drunk from the dark song of poppy wine;
Blaue Blume, Die leise tönt in vergilbtem Gestein.	Blue flower, That softly sounds in yellowed stone.

Line 3 speaks of 'a small bird singing in a tamarind tree', yet this image does not recur. Instead, it is preceded by the seemingly unrelated ones of 'becoming dusk' and 'a blue face softly leaves you'. Perhaps there is a connection between the 'blue face' in line 2 and the 'blue flower' in line 16, but here again, a representational image is presented in an unreal context. Flowers don't 'ring' as bells do (Blaue Blume, | Die leise tönt), nor do they sound in stone; the voices of inanimate things resonate here in the Symbolist language of Baudelaire, whom Trakl greatly admired.

We might look for a central event in the poem, such as a religious transfiguration, to which the others lead, but instead we find the religious scenes baldly juxtaposed with images of nature: birds, stones, and trees. How does the 'nächtiger Kranz' ('night-like wreath') of violets, corn, and purple grapes in stanza 3 relate to the following image of graves opening at the feet of the unnamed object of address? As in so many of Trakl's poems, the order of the stanzas could even be changed without altering the poem's effect.[32] The 'structure' that

---

[32] Herbert Lindenberger admits that, 'indeed, after years of reading Trakl I must confess that I still have trouble remembering what line belongs to what poem' (*Georg Trakl*, 50). See

results is not one of linear continuity; if one imagines the poem as theatre, then its images would be scenes or events that take place simultaneously in different corners of the stage. The discontinuity of Trakl's images recalls, and perhaps owes something to, the theatre pieces of Kokoschka.[33] The reader takes in the various aspects and must put together his own composite picture. The almost complete lack of linking narrative material in Trakl's poems is unusual even in the genre of the lyric poem; asyntactical language to this degree had been approached earlier only by Rimbaud, Mallarmé, and Hölderlin.

Trakl's poetry is full of references to other poets, some of which are near-quotations. In 'Verklärung', the 'blue flowers' certainly allude to Novalis. In addition to speech-patterns from Hölderlin and Rimbaud, Trakl relies heavily on the stock images of German romantic poetry: flowers, night, monasteries. His portrayal of these traditional images owes an especially great debt to the *Hainbund* poets of the eighteenth century.[34] Many typical images turn up in poem after poem, giving Trakl's verse a repetitive quality. In fact, a central controversy in Trakl criticism is whether these recurring images constitute a unified 'mythology', or whether each one is given meaning only by its context in the poem. One critic, somewhat tongue in cheek, characterized this dissonance between traditional images and modern form as 'Moderne Lyrik im Dirndlkleid'.[35]

For images do recur. Open a book of Trakl's poems anywhere, and the same words and images jump out over and over again. Especially prevalent are nature images, such as trees—*Baum, Wald*, or more specific types such as *Hollunder* or *Eiche*—birds—*Amsel, Taube*, and *Drossel*—or animals—*Tier, Wild*. People seldom appear in Trakl's poems, and when they do, they are either ghostly strangers—a *Wanderer, Fremdling*, or even an *Engel*—or they are nameless 'types', such as *Jäger* (hunter) or *Hirt* (shepherd). Adding to the sense of alienation, the human artifacts most often encountered are walls (*Mauer*), which may be stony, icy, white, fading, or crumbling, and boats (*Kähne*), which are usually described only with a single colour word, such as black or gold. While the former is immobile and sets up boundaries, the latter allows fluid motion from place to place, even between the earthly and spiritual realms. Perhaps the most

---

also Trakl's revisions of his poetry, in which whole lines are often substituted with entirely different images (cf. the two versions of 'Ein Winterabend', DTV 58 and 210).

[33] Trakl knew Kokoschka personally, and in fact gave the title to one of Kokoschka's most famous paintings: 'Die Windsbraut' (1913–14), Kunstmuseum Basel.

[34] Wolfgang Preisendanz, 'Auflösung und Verdinglichung in den Gedichten Georg Trakls', in W. Iser (ed.), *Immanente Ästhetik/Ästhetische Reflexion: Lyrik als Paradigma der Moderne* (Munich: Fink Verlag, 1966), 255.

[35] Preisendanz, 'Auflösung und Verdinglichung', 486.

ubiquitous words in Trakl's poetry are those that evoke night or darkness: *Abend, Nacht, Schatten, Dunkel, schwarz*. Poems may present endless variations on a basic image, such as that of the thorn-bush associated with dew or bleeding:

> So leise blutet Demut
> Tau, der langsam tropft vom blühenden Dorn
>   (from 'Gesang einer gefangenen Amsel', 6–7)
>
> Ein Dornenbusch tönt
> Wo deine mondenen Augen sind.
>   (from 'An den Knaben Elis', 10–11)
>
> Ein blaues Wild
> Blutet leise im Dornengestrüpp.
>   (from 'Elis', 19–20)

or the favourite image of wings rapidly fluttering upwards:

> Aufflattert mit trunkenem Flügel die Nacht
>   (from 'Gesang einer gefangenen Amsel', 5)
>
> Aufflattert mit schwarzen Flügeln die Fäulnis
>   (from 'Am Moor', 6)

Because of the way Trakl juxtaposes the lines, it is difficult to understand these images as descriptions of real, natural scenes. How can one connect, for example, the images of the figure Elis and the deer in the following lines from 'Elis' (16–20)?

> Ein sanftes Glockenspiel tönt in Elis' Brust
> Am Abend,
> Da sein Haupt ins schwarze Kissen sinkt.
>
> Ein blaues Wild
> Blutet leise im Dornengestrüpp.[36]

One can readily visualize each separate image, but not a single world that would include them all. The lack of a common background or narrative structure within a poem distances the reader from the poem. Rainer Maria Rilke described just this feeling of alienation with respect to Trakl's poetry in the following beautiful lines: 'I imagine that even one who stands close experiences these images and insights as an outsider, as if looking through a glass. For Trakl's experience unfolds as images in a mirror; its whole world is unreachable, like the world in the mirror.'[37] Therefore Trakl's recurring

---

[36] 'A gentle glockenspiel rings in Elis' breast | In the evening, | As his head sinks into black pillows. | A blue deer | Bleeds quietly in the thorn-bushes.' DTV 51.

[37] 'Ich denke mir, daß selbst der Nahstehende immer noch wie an Scheiben gepreßt diese Aussichten und Einblicke erfährt, als ein Ausgeschlossener: denn Trakls Erleben geht wie in Spiegelbildern und füllt seinen ganzen Raum, der unbetretbar ist, wie der Raum im Spiegel.' Rainer Maria Rilke, in *Erinnerung an Georg Trakl* (Innsbruck: Brenner-Verlag, 1926), 11.

images of trees, birds, or animals refer primarily to themselves; when a poem presents a series of such self-referential images, their often contradictory implications prevent total identification with any one meaning. As Wolfgang Preisendanz put it, the word emphasizes its 'thingness' (*Verdinglichung*), valued and perceived as much by its sonic characteristics as by its potential meaning.[38] Further, one cannot even speak of enigmas, puzzles, or paradoxes, because the juxtaposed images are so unrelated that they scarcely create tension by rubbing against each other.[39] There is nothing to decipher or decode, no key to the mysteries.

To try to integrate Trakl's disparate images into a common context would reduce their force. According to Walther Killy, the author of the first comprehensive study of Trakl, recurring words and phrases— such as 'Mauer' and 'Vogel'—do not form part of a coherent mythology, but are *Zeichen* (signs).[40] More recently, Francis Sharp used Killy's conclusions as his starting-point: 'for the reader either to ignore or to make absolute any of its multiple perspectives was to limit the poem's polyvalence, its capability of simultaneously radiating various meanings'.[41] By tearing apart the traditional connections between images, Trakl brought his poetry to a crisis point. Much in the same fashion that Schoenberg loosened the traditional tonal connections between pitches, Trakl dislocated the structural functioning of classical poetic rhetoric.

How Webern Understood the Poems

It is easy to see how certain aspects of Trakl's poetry appealed to Webern. The outdoor scenes from the Austrian countryside would have struck a resonance, given Webern's almost mystical reverence for nature. Similar images imbue other poems he set, such as Bethge's translations from the Chinese, and later, poems of Hildegard Jone. Certainly the 'Dirndlkleid' aspect of Trakl was part of what attracted Webern; his orchestra pieces, with their cowbells 'aus der Ferne', evoke the Austrian countryside in the same distant yet potent way that Trakl's poems do.

---

[38] See Preisendanz, 'Auflösung und Verdinglichung', 241.

[39] '. . . daß hier von Verschlüsselung, Verrätselung, Verweisung oder gar Verfremdung schlecht die Rede sein kann, weil ja kein Spannungsverhältnis zwischen Zeichen und Bezeichnetem, Präsentiertem und Repräsentiertem vorliegt.' Preisendanz, 'Auflösung und Verdinglichung', 254.

[40] Walther Killy, *Über Georg Trakl* (Göttingen: Vandenhoeck & Ruprecht, 1960), 28.

[41] Francis Michael Sharp, *The Poet's Madness: A Reading of Georg Trakl* (Ithaca, NY: Cornell University Press, 1981), 161. Richard Detsch has tried, I believe unsuccessfully, to contradict this point of view by proposing that the disparate images in a Trakl poem can be reconciled into a 'union of opposites'; see *Georg Trakl's Poetry: Toward a Union of Opposites* (University Park and London: Pennsylvania State University Press, 1983).

Another feature of Trakl's poetry that stands out to any musician is its beauty of sound. Lines such as these from 'Jahr' (1–2) have their own music in the gentle dactylic metre and the alternation of opposed vowels, such as *u* and *o* on one side, and *i* and *e* on the other (as well as the not-so-subtle allusion to Wagner's *Stabreim* in 'bläulichen Blickes').

> Dunkle Stille der Kindheit. Unter grünenden Eschen
> Weidet die Sanftmut bläulichen Blickes; goldene Ruh.[42]

It was probably the beautiful sonorities of this line that induced Webern to try to set the poem, even though with twelve long lines, it would have been manifestly unsuitable (he only got as far as the first sentence). Sound and image are inextricably linked in Trakl's poems; ambiguous images, whose meaning is often indeterminate, can be better understood as part of an overall sound-pattern.[43]

But was it just their shared Austrian heritage and the mellifluous quality of the poems that attracted Webern? How can we know what else Webern valued about Trakl? Unlike Berg or Schoenberg, Webern was not very communicative about how he worked. His letters often relate only the bare facts, as for example a letter to Berg in 1919, in which he states simply that he has composed four songs on poems of Trakl.[44] In his telegraphic style, he also may wax enthusiastic about a writer or painter, as he did on separate occasions about Strindberg, Trakl, Klimt, and sacred texts. Of Trakl, as we have seen, he wrote to Schoenberg, 'They [poems in *Brenner*] made a big impression on me. Since then I have read a book of his poems. Ever since then I have thought of him with great sympathy. I think these poems are wonderful.'[45] Four years later he confided to Jalowetz, 'I want to write a couple more songs on Trakl poems. They touch me so very closely.'[46] These comments tell us only what one could already surmise from the number of attempted settings: that Webern was entranced with Trakl's poetry. Though Webern was personally introspective, he was not verbally expressive.

---

[42] 'Dark stillness of childhood. Under budding ash-trees | feasts the gentleness of blue gazes, golden peace.' DTV 75.

[43] See Heinz Wetzel, *Klang und Bild in den Dichtungen Georg Trakls* (Göttingen: Vandenhoeck & Ruprecht, 1972), 15.

[44] In *Anton Webern: Briefe der Freundschaft*, ed. Heinrich Lindlar (Rodenkirchen: P. J. Tonger Musikverlag, 1958), 128.

[45] See n. 14 above.

[46] 'Ich will auch noch ein pa[a]r Lieder nach Trakl-Gedichten schreiben. Diese gehn mir so sehr nahe.' Letter from Webern to Jalowetz, 25 July 1918, PSS. (I am grateful for the special permission from the PSS to quote this letter, as the Jalowetz collection is not yet generally available.)

Yet we can understand something about Webern's thinking from the very lack of analytical comments. First, Webern's prose is not incompetent; it is like his music in that only the most important things are said.[47] In his elliptical style he skips from one idea to another, often leaving out 'non-thematic' filler. The complete absence of small talk in his letters means that every line that he writes is charged with either informational or emotional significance (his generous use of underlining supports this). When he writes to Schoenberg of Trakl's death at the age of 27 (only three years younger than Webern is at the time), he does not need to say explicitly that he is shaken by it. And when he writes that the poems from *Brenner* made a deep impression on him, the level of his engagement is made clear by the fact that he reports this at all. Second, Webern's letters (or anyone's letters) do not need to communicate what the other party already knows. When Webern writes of completing a work, this is essential and new information. He does not explain to Berg or Schoenberg why he likes Hans Bethge's translations of Chinese poems, whose spare, understated depiction of scenes from nature in an unemotional yet moving way attracted many composers who wanted an alternative to more effusive types of nineteenth-century German poetry. In Webern's Trakl letter, the phrases 'tiefen Eindruck gemacht' and 'mit großer Sympathie' serve as shorthand for a wide range of powerful emotions. His other comments indicate Webern's acknowledgement that Trakl is one of the group; not only as a young Austrian, but also as a member of the branch of the avant-garde led by Kraus and Schoenberg.

Webern's most communicative utterances about aesthetic matters are found not in discussion of art but in his descriptions of nature. In a letter to Berg from the summer of 1919, Webern describes a mountain excursion during which he saw stunning rock formations and an interesting variety of plants. Then he explains that he feels close to them, 'But not because they are "beautiful". It is not the beautiful landscape, the beautiful flowers in the usual romantic sense that move me. My motivation: the deep, unfathomable, inextinguishable meaning in all of these, especially these manifestations of nature.'[48] This letter points to one of Webern's and Schoenberg's

---

[47] Regina Busch discusses the private nature of Webern's writings and his writing style in 'On the Horizontal and Vertical Presentation of Musical Ideas and on Musical Space (I)', *Tempo*, 154 (1985), 2–4.

[48] 'Aber nicht weil sie so "schön" sind. Nicht die schöne Landschaft, die schönen Blumen im üblichen romantischen Sinne bewegen mich. Mein Motiv: der tiefe, unergründliche, unausschöpfbare Sinn in allen diesen, besonders diesen Äußerungen der Natur.' *Anton Webern: Briefe der Freundschaft*, 128.

primary aesthetic beliefs: that mere surface beauty of an artwork, or
its 'style', was superfluous to the inner truth, or 'idea', that lies
within.[49] They were strongly influenced here by the ideas of Adolph
Loos and Karl Kraus. Loos aimed to design buildings in which every
physical feature had a function; he despised decoration and ornament
for their own sakes.[50] Kraus believed that he had a moral duty as a
writer to eschew rhetoric and flowery phrases in order to tell the
truth in the strongest and most direct language possible. Even Ludwig
Wittgenstein's great philosophical work, the *Tractatus Logico-
Philosophicus*, has been characterized as 'an ethical deed' that grew
directly from this particular Viennese intellectual environment.[51]
These thinkers described and enacted art as a necessity, even a moral
imperative, and directly opposed the pseudo-art of *feuilleton* and
fashionable salon.

Trakl's personal demons also did not allow him to indulge in
'beautiful' poetry for its own sake; for him a poem's ethical and religious ideas possessed an urgency not shared by the purely aesthetic.
In a conversation with his *Brenner* colleagues Carl Dallago and
Ludwig von Ficker, Trakl reportedly described the poetry of Walt
Whitman as 'verderblich' (pernicious, destructive). Ficker interjected
that Whitman, as one who celebrates all aspects of life, has the
opposite point of view from Trakl, who is a pessimist through and
through. Dallago then asked Trakl if he didn't have any joy in life,
then 'Don't you get any enjoyment from your work?' 'Sure,' answered
Trakl, 'but one must be mistrustful of this enjoyment.'[52] This mistrust
of contentment, of accomplishment for its own sake, is evident in
Webern's work too, most of all in his highly self-critical attitude that
resulted in the very small number of completed works. Webern's
suspicion of enjoyment in a context similar to Trakl's above is
demonstrated in his letter to Berg; here Webern goes to great lengths
to prevent the impression that his response to nature is a Whitman-
like celebration of beauty: he feels close to the natural objects, 'but
not because they are so beautiful'.

Trakl's use of the word 'verderblich' to attack Whitman's poetry
points to another significant aspect of his thinking, one shared by
Webern and others of their circle: the notion of art as moral and

---

[49] See Schoenberg's essay 'New Music, Outmoded Music, Style and Idea', in *Style and Idea*,
113–24.

[50] Allan Janik and Stephen Toulmin, *Wittgenstein's Vienna* (New York: Simon & Schuster,
1973), 92–101.

[51] Janik and Toulmin, *Wittgenstein's Vienna*, heading for ch. 6, p. 167.

[52] 'ob ihm denn z.B. sein Schaffen gar keine Befriedigung verleihe? Doch, aber man muß
gegen diese Befriedigung mißtrauisch sein.' Reported by Hans Limbach, 'Begegnung mit Georg
Trakl', in *Erinnerung an Georg Trakl*, 116.

ethical responsibility. For Trakl, who is completely blind to the Anglo-American traditions of thought that influenced Whitman's work, Whitman's optimism is not simply an alternative way of seeing nature; it is a pernicious and destructive one. Groundless optimism is a dangerous illusion that prevents the artist from seeing things 'as they really are', as Hofmannsthal's Lord Chandos discovered in his painful coming of age. Art should instead strip away all extraneous layers to uncover the Truth, however painful and ugly it might be.[53] Even responding to artworks carries with it a moral responsibility. After hearing the first performance of Mahler's *Das Lied von der Erde*, Webern wrote to Berg of his enthusiasm for the work, but then asked whether they were even entitled to hear it at all. The only solution was for them 'to strive in such a way that we merit it'.[54] In a similar vein, Trakl wrote to Buschbeck that: 'I always have to check myself again and again in order to give to the truth what belongs to the truth.'[55]

In this context we can begin to understand the sense of art as a moral and even religious obligation that was so self-evident to the Viennese avant-garde. The creation of the artwork itself was the sacred act, the artist the priest; Trakl alludes to this when he described Kraus as a 'Weißer Hohepriester der Wahrheit' ('Karl Kraus', line 1). Schoenberg's remarks about Webern's cryptic aphorisms strike a similar note: 'If faith can move mountains, disbelief can deny their existence. And faith is impotent against such impotence.'[56] For Schoenberg and Webern the artwork itself is a necessity, not a luxury. It does not define itself in the framework of bourgeois requirements for adornment and beauty, but as part of a larger ethical imperative. One manifestation of this can be seen in the Schoenberg-led Verein für Musikalische Privataufführungen (Society for Private Musical Performances), in which the 'rites' of performance carried out before invited members placed music at the centre of the ritual, in a conscious rejection of the normal concert event.

This shared belief in the sacrosanct nature of artistic creation formed the largest common ground between poet and composer, even

---

[53] In a letter to Schoenberg from 1914, Webern writes: 'All that you told me is of immeasurable value to me. How you have unveiled everything for me. Through you I came to know "how things really are".' Moldenhauer, *Anton von Webern*, 101.

[54] Letter from Webern to Berg, 23 Nov. 1911, excerpts in Moldenhauer, *Anton von Webern*, 151.

[55] '...ich werde mich immer und immer wieder berichtigen müssen, um der Wahrheit zu geben, was der Wahrheit ist.' *Erinnerung an Georg Trakl*, 140.

[56] 'Kann der Glaube Berge versetzen, so kann dafür der Unglaube sie nicht vorhanden sein lassen. Gegen solche Ohnmacht ist der Glaube ohnmächtig.' Schoenberg, preface to Webern's Op. 9.

though Trakl, the pessimist, differed from Webern, the visionary, on the role that the created work could play in the world. Though the meeting of Webern and Trakl was artistic, not personal, they shared a sense of aesthetic necessity, and a common mission to create art that could not lie.

Part II
Webern's Compositional Process

3. Compositional Process

Though the physical evidence of Webern's sketching process during the decade between 1915 and 1924 remained remarkably consistent, the musical content of the sketches and fragments contradicts the appearance of routine. Most of Webern's efforts during this time were devoted to composing vocal music, for which he had developed a fairly regular procedure of working. Each surviving sketch can be easily recognized as belonging to a certain stage in the compositional process, and for most pieces the whole sequence of events can be reconstructed. Yet the most common feature of the sketches, paradoxically, is their diversity; most drafts of the same piece explore radically different musical ideas. Instead of hammering out and refining a certain musical response to a poem, Webern's imagination suggested a wide variety of realizations. The sketches are the remnants of a kind of musical diary; some are no more than isolated musings on a poem while others represent long-term preoccupations.

Going through Webern's manuscripts of vocal music, one gets a real sense of the urgency with which he composed songs. Sheet after sheet reveals hasty jottings of vocal lines, often trailing off into text and rhythms only. For Webern, the text was the driving force behind the composition. 'These texts will not let me go', he wrote to Berg about the 'alte geistliche Gesänge' that became Op. 15. 'And I believe very strongly [that] I won't compose anything else for the time being, until I have composed them all.'[1] This rare admission from the usually reticent Webern could well describe how he composed songs all his life. For him, a poem had its own imperatives, and elicited musical ideas almost involuntarily. These ideas find expression in the vocal line, which for Webern was the leading voice; after the instrumental introduction, he composed the vocal line first, only later filling in the instrumental parts.

Webern's habits in writing free atonal vocal music were significantly different from his later practice with twelve-tone music. While some characteristics of the middle-period sketches do hold true for the

[1] 'Ich komponiere wieder Lieder. . . . Mich lassen diese Texte nicht aus. Und ich glaube schon fest, ich werde vorläufig nichts anderes schreiben, bevor ich sie nicht alle komponiert habe.' Letter from Webern to Berg, 27 Aug. 1921, in Ernst Hilmar (ed.), *Anton Webern 1883–1983* (Vienna: Universal Edition, 1983), 72.

later music—for example the tendency to make repeated drafts of the beginnings of pieces—in the twelve-tone music the process had slowed considerably.[2] In the 1910s Webern composed fairly rapidly; he was often able to complete a work in one or two sittings. After about 1925, however, his sketches show that he painstakingly wrote and rewrote the same passage dozens of times, making the smallest imaginable alterations.[3] Since this careful attention to detail evident in the twelve-tone sketches appears equally often in vocal and instrumental music alike, it is unlikely that Webern had to spend more time sketching the twelve-tone works simply because most do not have a text. Rather the technical nature of the twelve-tone method evidently required more time. What we usually think of as Webern's working habits contrast markedly with the fluent compositional process of the middle-period vocal works.[4] Here Webern almost never altered his first idea for the beginning of a piece, though he did rework internal transitions and, especially, endings. Webern apparently devoted most of his energy to finding a good idea; once that was in place, the rest of the piece followed in a very short time.

This chapter will focus on Webern's compositional process as shown in manuscripts of his vocal music between 1915 and 1924 (when the first twelve-tone composition was written). I start with the mechanics: types of manuscripts, dating, habits of writing, and conventions of notation. Then, I shall outline how Webern composed during this period, tracing the process from preliminary sketches to the published score.

TYPES OF MANUSCRIPTS

Pencil Sketch

Webern wrote down his first musical ideas in pencil. These sketches range in length from the briefest notation to a draft of an entire piece; the idea can be musical notation, words, or a combination of the two.[5] Webern's pencil sketches look very different from his fair

---

[2] Roger Smalley points out examples of all of these features in 'Webern's Sketches', 1–12.

[3] In 'Twelve-Tone Symmetry: Webern's Thematic Sketches for the Sinfonie, Op. 21, 2nd Movement', Donna Lynn describes how Webern sketched the opening of the theme more than twenty times (*Musical Times*, 131 (1990), 644).

[4] Whether these compositional habits were established in works before 1915 is still impossible to say, since very little is known about how Webern composed his early works. See however Gareth Cox, *Anton Weberns Studienzeit: Seine Entwicklung im Lichte der Sätze und Fragmente für Klavier* (Frankfurt am Main: Peter Lang, 1992).

[5] There is, for example, a sketch of 'O sanftes Glühn der Berge' that consists largely of verbal descriptions: PSS, 'Drei Orchesterlieder', No. 3, film 103:0059–0060.

copies. When he sketched, he tried to squeeze every detail into the smallest possible space. Most of the paper he used was small as well, usually half or quarter sheets, and on a given scrap may be found sketches for several compositions. In spite of the crowding, most of the sketches still look clean and relatively uncluttered, because of Webern's diminutive handwriting and its clear appearance due to the sharp pencil with which he normally wrote. When he wanted to delete a chord, note, or instrument, he neatly crossed it out or circled it. To delete a whole measure he encircled it, or crossed it out with a single diagonal stroke. A sketch usually looks clean at the beginning, and becomes progressively messier with the increasing number of changes and deletions.

Within the category 'pencil sketch' I define two subgroups based on musical function: *fragment* and *continuity draft*.[6] 'Fragment' means a sketch of a piece that was never completed.[7] While there may be many preliminary sketches for a completed piece, the sketch that represents the last stage before the fair copy deserves a separate status, which I call the 'continuity draft' (adopting a useful term from Beethoven scholarship).[8] In the Webernian continuity draft, the piece is written out from beginning to end in condensed score, with instrumentation, dynamics, and articulation marks at least partially designated. Though it represents by definition the last stage of sketching, it may also be the first stage of composition, and may bear signs of considerable reworking. The determining criterion here is that the sketch reaches what Webern considered to be the end of the piece.

Fair Copy

After completing the pencil continuity draft, it was Webern's habit to write out an ink full score of a piece immediately. Though sketching often continued on the ink scores, others are true fair copies. These handsome scores were written in a calligraphic hand and often used coloured pencil for the braces at the beginning of the score and red ink for the song text. Since Webern grouped the pieces into opus-

---

[6] These subdivisions of the category 'pencil sketch' represent a refinement of the classification used in the catalogue of Webern manuscripts published by the PSS, which labels all of the above *Skizzen* (sketches).

[7] I use the word 'fragment' differently from the PSS catalogue as well: there *Fragment* means that the manuscript itself is incomplete in some way, for example, missing a page. My definition means that the piece, not the manuscript, is incomplete.

[8] According to Lewis Lockwood, who was the first to use this term in sketch studies, the phrase 'continuity draft' was coined by Joshua Rifkin. See Lockwood, 'On Beethoven's Sketches and Autographs: Some Problems of Definition and Interpretation', *Acta Musicologica*, 42 (1970), 42.

numbered groupings only later, each song may have its own title-page and its own list of required instruments. It may use a different kind of script for the text or different styles of clefs from its neighbours. Since Webern invariably revised pieces before publication, there is often more than one fair copy for a piece. The earliest ink scores, although they may have been clean to start with, are almost always heavily marked with layers of corrections, often in different colours: these I shall call *revision copies* (almost all the ink scores of Op. 13 and Op. 14 at the PSS fall into this category).[9] Later ink scores may preserve intermediate stages. Some fair copies were intended as gifts; these have no corrections at all and are essentially presentation copies. Such a copy may preserve a reading of a piece different from the final one. I call a fair copy that was used as an exemplar for publication a *printer's copy* (most of these scores, prepared for Universal Edition, are now in the Pierpont Morgan Library).

A Webern fair copy immediately communicates something of his conceptions of texture, intensity, and time spans in music. The generous use of space on the page lends the shortest gestures length and weight. Because of the blank stave-lines and the lack of crowding, one can see the lyric intensity of each melodic gesture. The numerous dynamic and expression markings have so much room around them that they do not give the impression of fussiness and over-precision one often notes in the closely printed published scores. There are very few measures per page, so that a brief song such as 'Die Einsame' (Op. 13 No. 2) takes six pages of score, whereas it fits on two in the published version.[10] Reading the widely spaced scores reinforces the sense of the paradoxically compressed but extended time spans that one gets listening to the music; in this context one can understand Webern's common overestimations of the lengths of his compositions by 100 per cent or more.

Piano/Vocal Score

A third category of autograph manuscripts is that of piano/vocal reductions of orchestral and chamber songs, which Webern made for all of his completed vocal works for rehearsal purposes. Some of these ink fair copies preserve interesting variants or early versions of pieces. While most have been published, Webern's piano/vocal reduction of his Op. 14 has not.[11]

[9] The terms 'fair copy' and 'revision copy' correspond to the PSS Webern Catalogue's *Reinschrift* and *Reinschrift mit Korrekturen*.
[10] Fair copy, 'Two Songs Op. 7', in the Pierpont Morgan Library.
[11] This score is now in Washington, DC, Library of Congress (Moldenhauer Collection).

HABITS OF WRITING

Webern used both German and Latin script in his music manuscripts. Though Latin script becomes more common as the decade progresses, Webern was not consistent about which script he used, and there is no hard and fast date when a change occurred. In general, Webern used German script (*Fraktur*) for informal and personal documents and Latin script for formal and public ones. German cursive was Webern's intimate script, which he used when writing letters or sketching music; it was more natural to him, as it was to other native German speakers of Webern's generation, including Trakl.[12] Latin script was obviously less comfortable for Webern to write. He commonly used this for non-German words in his letters and music manuscripts, and for fair copies of song texts. Correspondingly, Webern used German script for the German words for performance and instrumental indications ('langsam', 'etwas mäßiger', 'Geige', etc.). Exceptions to both conventions abound, however. In the fair copy of Op. 14 in the Paul Sacher Foundation, for example, all the song texts are written in Latin script, except that of No. 4, which is written in German script (see Plate 2).[13] Since No. 4 was the earliest composed, one might suppose that the use of German script reflects the 1917 date of composition. But there are several instances of manuscripts earlier than 1917 that use Latin script for their song texts, among them the fair copy of 'Die Einsame' (early version), written in 1914.[14]

A related issue of orthography concerns Webern's use of 'von' in his name. When the use of noble titles was forbidden in 1918 by the new Austrian government, Webern apparently complied. We see a corresponding shift in formal documents bearing his name, as in the case of his works published by Universal Edition. There is also a change on his music manuscripts. In the fair copy of Op. 14, written out between 1917 and 1921, Webern usually signed his name 'Anton Webern'. As one would expect, the one song of Op. 14 composed before 1918, 'Abendland III' (No. 4), is signed 'von Webern', but unpredictably, so is No. 3, composed in 1919. Each of the four songs in Op. 13 on the other hand, composed in 1918 or earlier, is signed 'von Webern'.[15] Because of these inconsistencies, the form of Webern's name is at best a partial aid to dating manuscripts. One can

[12] A good example of Trakl's greater familiarity with German script can be seen on the cover of a paperback reprint of Trakl's poems, which pictures the fair copy of 'Grodek'. Trakl wrote the first six lines in Latin script, then reverted to German for the rest (DTV, cover).

[13] PSS, Op. 14 full score, film 101:0529–0531.

[14] New York, Pierpont Morgan Library, Lehman Collection, Two Songs 'Op. 7' (with 'Leise Düfte').

[15] PSS, Op. 13 full score, film 101:0407–0441. Op. 14 full score, film 101:0515–0537.

state conclusively only that the signature 'Anton Webern' occurs only after 1918, while 'von Webern' is still found a few years after that date.[16]

Some of Webern's habits of musical notation also changed over the years; these can be helpful in pointing to earlier or later dates. One is the formation of C clefs. In all early fair copies, the tenor clef used is elaborate and curvy.[17] (One may see this type of clef in Plate 2.) In most manuscripts written after 1914 or thereabouts, Webern uses the standard C clef. However, one finds the elaborate C clef in the fair copy of 'Ein Winterabend' (Op. 13 No. 4),[18] written in 1918, as well as in the continuity draft of 'Abendland III' (Op. 14 No. 4) from 1917.[19] There was evidently a transition period of some years, between 1914 and about 1918, when Webern used both styles.

Another aspect of Webern's notation is the connection of note-stems by beams. Reinhold Brinkmann has pointed out how, in some manuscripts of the *George-Lieder* from 1908–9, Webern notated each syllable of the voice part with a separate stem and flag.[20] While this is conventional practice for the notation of vocal lines in much nineteenth- and twentieth-century music, in these songs, Webern notated the piano part in the same way, with small note-values tied together. Later, Webern began to beam notes together, in the vocal as well as instrumental parts. The continuity draft of 'Der Tag ist vergangen' (Op. 12 No. 1), composed in 1915, mixes the 'separated' notational style with occasional beamed notes in the vocal line.[21] A sketch for 'Gesang einer gefangenen Amsel' (Op. 14 No. 6) from 1917, on the other hand, uses separate beams for the vocal part (see Plate 3). By 1919, most vocal-line notes in sketches are beamed together, like the instrumental parts. In a 1921 sketch of 'Die Sonne' (Op. 14 No. 1), the notation of vocal and instrumental lines is practically indistinguishable.[22] In all but one of the editions of Webern's vocal music by Universal Edition, vocal lines are notated with connected beams, though the stem direction and beaming do not

[16] I resist Moldenhauer's attempt to restore the 'von' in Webern's name, a tendency which is unfortunately gaining wider circulation. We should retain 'Anton Webern', the name Webern himself used for the last 27 years of his life, and under which he published all his music with Universal Edition.

[17] I refer to fair copies of 'Die Einsame' (Op. 13 No. 2) and the *Three Little Pieces* (Op. 11) from 1914 in the Pierpont Morgan Library, Lehman Collection.

[18] PSS, Op. 13 full score, film 101:0435–0441.

[19] PSS, Op. 14 sketches, film 101:0575–0577.

[20] Brinkmann, 'Die George-Lieder 1908/9 und 1919/23', 42.

[21] PSS, Op. 12 sketches, film 101:0383–0385. The continuity draft of 'Abendland III' (Op. 14 No. 4) composed two years later shows the same practice; some notes in the vocal line are beamed and some are separated (PSS, Op. 14 sketches, film 101:0575–0577).

[22] PSS, Op. 14 sketches, film 101:0554–0560.

follow Webern's autographs but instead what was apparently a house policy.[23]

A change in notation can tell about things other than chronology; in this case, it reflects Webern's evolving views on the roles of voice and instruments. In early works, the voice has a function distinct from the instruments; usually its range is narrower and its melodic contour smoother. In later songs, the vocal line becomes more 'instrumental' in character, its wide leaps and extreme range resembling a clarinet part more than a traditional vocal one. As Webern's vocal lines became more instrumental, so did his notation.

Paper

Webern made his fair copies on large bifolios. These large sheets of 48 or 24 staves, cut into halves or fourths, provided the stock for his small sketching pages. Often sketches and the fair copy of a piece are written on the same type of paper. Webern also used rejected pages of an ink copy for further sketching; since we usually know when the ink copy was made, this habit can help to provide a *terminus post quem* for some undated sketches.[24] Most sketches are on sheets 5 by 8 inches or smaller; even those belonging to the same draft are often of different sizes. The sequence of pages can often only be determined by musical context; moreover, when there are drafts of several compositions on a sheet, each continuing onto a different sheet, the order can be hard to determine. This must have been occasionally confusing even for Webern, since after about 1924 he began to write in bound sketchbooks.

DATING OF SKETCHES AND FAIR COPIES

Fortunately for musicologists, Webern dated his manuscripts quite systematically. Unfortunately, the picture is sometimes clouded by

---

[23] Universal Edition's edition of the Op. 3 songs, published in 1921, uses separated stems for the vocal line, but Op. 4, published two years later, does not. Fair copies of Op. 3 and Op. 4 that I have seen in the PSS, in New York, Pierpont Morgan Library, and in Washington, Library of Congress do use separate stems for the vocal lines. This is also found in other MSS of early songs, such as Op. 8 (1910), and 'Die Einsame' and 'Leise Düfte' (1914) (both in the PSS). Brinkmann postulates that Webern changed his notation around 1922 ('Die George-Lieder 1908/9 und 1919/23', 46). But as we have seen, Webern began using connected beams as early as 1915, and by 1919 this was his habit. Perhaps Universal Edition's notation of Op. 3 and Op. 4 is inconsistent because Webern gave them scores that he had copied at different times, or it could also reflect a change in Universal Edition's printing policies between 1921 and 1923. (Elmar Budde, in *Anton Weberns Lieder Op. 3*, shows Webern's original notation for Op. 3, as does the Carl Fischer edition of the *Four Stefan George Songs*.)

[24] A study of paper types, like those done successfully for Bach and Mozart, would be less fruitful with Webern. The main reason is that Webern, like most of the musicians in Vienna, bought machine-made paper from the same company (Josef Eberle & Co.) all his life.

idiosyncrasies of those same systematic habits. There are two ways in which Webern dated a sketch. The first way is found only in the continuity drafts, in which he wrote the exact day, month, and year (and sometimes place) of completion after the double bar at the end of the sketch (this can be observed in Plate 4). A complication arises if the piece is later revised, since Webern often wrote the same date—the date of completion of the continuity draft—on every copy of that piece, regardless of when he actually copied the manuscript or the extent of the changes made.[25] He also apparently provided Universal Edition with only the earliest date. Webern's adoption of this dating system suggests that he considered the process of composition finished with the completion of the continuity draft. All subsequent changes, even substantial ones, seldom warranted recording a new date on the manuscript. Even when a revision is dated, the title-pages and published versions show only the original date.[26]

The second way Webern dated a manuscript was by writing the year, and sometimes the month or season, at the top of the page. This is usually found on miscellaneous sketches and fragments. Whereas Webern dated the continuity drafts immediately upon completion, he did not do so with the fragments until some later time. We know this because of the tentativeness and indecision shown in some of the dates. For example, on the fragment 'In der Heimat', Webern wrote 'Wien, Herbst 1915, Auhofstr.', and the word 'Herbst' is crossed out.[27] He could not have made this note at the time of composition because he did not live on Auhofstrasse in the autumn of 1915. Realizing this later, he crossed it out. Another example is the fragment 'Mit silbernen Sohlen', which is dated both 'Mödling 1918' and 'Hietzing 1917'; the former date is crossed out.[28] The presence of both dates shows that Webern initially could not remember whether he had composed 'Mit silbernen Sohlen' in 1917 or 1918. These inconsistencies are infrequent, however. Most of the time the dates and places noted are consistent with each other and with the probable time of composition. Moreover, since we know when Webern lived where (and he moved a lot in these years!), observing the place-names, such as 'Hietzing' or 'Klagenfurt', can narrow down the date of origin to within a month or so.

As Webern grew older, he became increasingly conscious of his

[25] This can be observed in the 1914 date that Webern applied to all versions of 'Die Einsame' (Op. 13 No. 2), which was composed in 1914 and much revised before its publication twelve years later.

[26] As in the song 'Ein Winterabend' (Op. 13 No. 4), which was composed in 1918; a revision copy is marked '1922 umgearbeitet'.

[27] PSS, vocal compositions, sketches, film 103:0736.

[28] PSS, vocal compositions, sketches, film 103:0741.

historical importance, and correspondingly considerate of his bio-graphers. In the five sketchbooks he kept from 1925 to the end of his life, he recorded much more information than he could possibly have needed for himself. Each book is accompanied by a reasonably complete table of contents, each text is identified, and each draft is dated to the day. He obviously meant to preserve these sketchbooks for posterity. As we have seen, Webern was more casual about his earlier sketches, sometimes not dating them at all.

When did Webern go back and date the fragments? There were two times in his life when he seems to have been especially occupied with reviewing or taking stock. The first is in the mid-1920s, after his music had begun to be published by Universal Edition. From 1920 to about 1925, Webern was involved in collecting earlier pieces into their opus-number groupings for the first time, as well as revising some of them extensively. It was also during these years that he became aware of the twelve-tone method and first attempted to compose with it. Perhaps conscious of the historical significance of the new method, he began keeping his sketches in bound books at around the same time. Because of his newly cultivated historical sense and the retrospective tasks he undertook at this time, the mid-1920s, specifically 1925, could well have been when Webern went back and dated the earlier fragments.

Another possible time is the early 1930s. There exists a work list in Webern's hand that includes works up to Op. 22.[29] The latest piece listed is his 1931 arrangement of Schubert dances. The list is written in a very personal hand, half in ink and half in pencil, with many crossings-out. It therefore seems to have been for Webern's use only. He tried to be very precise, noting dates and places of composition when possible, but the information is recorded in more detail with the later works. While he was making up the list and trying to remember the origins of each piece, it would also have been con-venient to assemble the fragmentary sketches and date them. What is important is not whether Webern dated the fragments in 1925 or after 1931, but the fact that he dated them long after composition, probably as he became aware that they would eventually be part of his *Nachlass*.

Can we trust Webern's dates? Whenever someone recalls something after a long time has elapsed, there may be inaccuracies. Memory can be notoriously unreliable. But Webern dated his manuscripts not just on the basis of memory; he also had available the detailed diaries he kept all his life. We know that Webern was neat and orderly in his

---

[29] PSS, uncatalogued.

personal life almost to the point of obsession. A man who would keep track of every event in his and his family's lives, make long lists of equipment for a mountain-climbing trip, and copy out railway timetables, can be relied upon, I believe, to remember accurately when he composed what pieces.[30]

SKETCHING PROCESS

The beginning of composition was almost certainly the selection of the poem. About this first stage we know very little. Even Webern's own copies of the books from which he drew his texts do not provide much information, since there are very few markings. For example, in Webern's own copy of Trakl's *Sebastian im Traum*, which he acquired in 1916, there are ticks in the table of contents next to some, but not all, of the poems he chose.[31] Some of the poems were marked by paper bookmarks, the book's string marker, or—in keeping with Webern's botany hobby—pressed flowers. These signs only show evidence of Webern choosing a poem; we cannot know how he read the poem and arrived at preliminary musical ideas. And unlike Berg, Webern was not given to writing long letters describing his intellectual life.

The first visible stage of composition is therefore the pencil sketch, which conforms in most cases to a remarkably uniform pattern. This 'typical' sketch starts with an opening instrumental gesture, continues with the first vocal phrase, and progresses line by line through the poem, in short score. There are no precompositional aids such as schemas, charts, plans, or diagrams. Composition is fluent and seemingly rapid; all details of the piece, including instrumentation, dynamic and articulation marks, seem to have been conceived at once. Hitches occur mainly at sectional divisions of the poem, like the beginning of a new stanza. When this happens, Webern does the revisions on the spot; he seldom returns to a section already sketched. The notational detail, quite plentiful at first, becomes steadily more sparse as the sketch progresses. The last part of a sketch is frequently

---

[30] In some personal notes made in 1940, Schoenberg accused Webern of 'many acts of infidelity with the intention of making himself the innovator' of the twelve-tone method (see Stuckenschmidt, *Arnold Schoenberg*, 443). This is not the place to go into the complex issue of priority (see my essay 'The Vocal Origins of Webern's Twelve-Tone Composition'), but there is in fact no evidence that Webern ever altered dates in order to establish himself as the inventor of the method. Since there are no twelve-tone sketches during the years in question, he would have had no motivation to do so.

[31] In the 'Inhalt' (at the end), the following poems are marked: 'Ein Winterabend', 'Verklärung', 'Siebengesang des Todes', 'Die Sonne', 'Gesang einer gefangenen Amsel', 'Jahr', and 'Abendland'. 'Nachts' (set as Op. 14/5) is not marked.

the vocal line alone, which by the end may deteriorate into rhythmic notation only. The closing gestures do not come as easily as the rest of the piece, and may require several drafts. This pattern holds true for the dozens of vocal sketches for over a decade. Let us examine each step of the process, looking at specific examples.

Instrumental Idea First

It is paradoxical that, while for Webern the vocal line was the leading voice of a sketch, he began almost all sketches with a purely instrumental section. This is a feature familiar to us from the published works as well. Five of the six songs of Op. 14 start with a gesture or longer passage for instruments alone. Because of the highly chromatic character of Webern's instrumental introductions, they do not seem to be designed for the practical goal of giving the singer her starting pitch. Usually they present a shape distinct from that of the voice, an arresting gesture that often defines itself as contrasting with the opening vocal phrase. Here Webern sets up a vocabulary of *figures* that may later be associated with specifically vocal or instrumental delivery. Yet even contrasting figures between voice and instruments usually share a common motivic basis. In this way an introduction can provide the material upon which the rest of the piece, vocal and instrumental parts alike, can draw.

Sometimes the sketch gets no further than the instrumental introduction. Unless there is a word or phrase of the text, these instrumental fragments are unidentifiable; there are dozens of such fragments scattered throughout the sketches. One 'Nachtergebung' fragment is identifiable only because of its single vocal note, the first syllable in the poem: 'Mön[chin]', which follows two measures of music for bass clarinet, trombone, and cello.[32] The second page of 'Siebengesang des Todes' also has several short instrumental incipits; one is a three-note vocal line which could fit a number of poems, including 'Ein Winterabend' and 'Verklärung'.[33]

Though the opening instrumental idea was often difficult for Webern to pin down, once he succeeded, the rest seems to have gone much faster. A page that contains two incipits for 'Verklärung' (No. 1), for example, begins with two separate instrumental introductions.[34] If they do represent sketches for the same poem, then Webern entertained quite different ideas about the opening gesture

---

[32] PSS, vocal compositions, sketches, film 103:0756.

[33] PSS, vocal compositions, sketches, film 103:0753.

[34] We know they were meant to be vocal, not instrumental pieces, because the top stave is blank with its own barline, as was Webern's habit in notating vocal pieces. PSS, vocal compositions, sketches, film 103:0750.

Ex. 3.1. 'Schien mir's . . .' (Strindberg), Op. 12/3, mm. 1–7.

of the piece more or less at the same time. His third try is different still, though it incorporates elements of both. When the introduction was completed in fairly detailed form (after yet another revision), he was able to continue the draft for 20 measures (to the end of the poem's second stanza). Evidently the introduction had to be 'right' before Webern could proceed even with the vocal line's leading role.

Webern lavished so much attention on the opening bars because, for him, they determined the content of the piece. The introduction does not simply 'play before' in the classical sense, but instead provides the raw material from which the voice then draws, moulding it into a clear—sometimes contrasting—motivic gesture. In 'Schien mir's . . .' (Op. 12 No. 3, shown in Ex. 3.1), the voice's opening fourth (D–A) seems to act upon a suggestion in the piano in m. 1 (E–A); moreover, it brings into close proximity two pitches which were widely separated in the opening measures. The D and A are invariant pitches of the same set (4–16), heard in the first four notes of the piano and in the first four of the voice.[35] The idea of 'fourth' is further suggested by the piano left hand in m. 2 (C♯–F♯). This relationship—a transformed variation—between the introduction and the voice is highly characteristic of Webern's songs.

Vocal Line as Leading Voice

Once the instrumental introduction was articulated, Webern's attention shifted immediately to the vocal line. We know this from various notational features, such as crowding, irregular number of staves, and empty spaces in the instrumental parts, as well as from the fact that so many sketches end with the vocal line alone. 'Verklärung' (No. 4) is a typical example (see Plate 5).[36] After the opening gesture

[35] These designations follow the terminology in Allen Forte, *The Structure of Atonal Music* (New Haven, Conn.: Yale University Press, 1973).

[36] PSS, vocal compositions, sketches, film 103:0746. A transcription of this fragment may be seen in Ch. 7, Ex. 7.3.

for bass clarinet, there follow three measures of music for voice, bass clarinet, and cello. The next words of the poem, 'ein blaues Antlitz', are presented with the vocal line alone. Then follow two more versions of these words. Underneath the last version are sparse instrumental gestures; these must have been written after the vocal line in order to coincide with it, because of the space between these gestures and the previous instrumental parts. The rest of the fragment consists of the vocal line alone, which continues through the second stanza of the poem. The fact that Webern would write up to nine bars for voice without accompaniment means that it is clearly the leading voice. He has to know how it will behave before he can write the instrumental parts. If Webern had finished this 'Verklärung' fragment, presumably he would then have gone back and filled in the instruments.

This fragment implies—as do so many others—that Webern composed his vocal music in layers; first the instrumental introduction, then the vocal line is composed for a phrase or two, then the instrumental parts are filled in. Webern's sketches show that he might write one strand of a piece from beginning to end, before starting on the rest.[37] This reveals a horizontal conception, where individual voices were composed separately, like a medieval motet. This raises questions about the degree to which Webern controlled the vertical sonorities that result from the counterpoint.[38]

Continuation and End of the Sketch

Within the long vocal line which provides the framework for a sketch, obstacles usually occur at the breaks between stanzas, or when the mood of the poem changes suddenly. In the continuity draft of 'Die Sonne' (Op. 14 No. 1), Webern makes several passes at the place where the poem shifts in tone and speed, at 'Langsam reift die Traube . . .'. Similarly in 'Abendland I' (Op. 14 No. 2), the smooth flow of composition stops at 'Nächtigen Schatten, Zackige Blitze . . .' (see Plate 6). In both of these sketches, Webern continues the vocal lines, but they soon dissolve into rhythmic notation. Sometimes the amorphous vocal lines are accompanied by equally cryptic notations

---

[37] There are several sketches that consist of a vocal line only, covering the entire text of a poem (Op. 15 No. 3, 'new sketches'). Schoenberg may have been speaking of Webern when he told how 'a friend' composed: 'He told me that, in several cases, he had written at first only the melody of quite a long section. Thereafter he would add a second line, an accompanying voice, without even looking at the first line. . . . The result was astonishing; nobody would discover that this had been produced in such an unusual manner. . . .' Schoenberg, 'Bach', in *Style and Idea*, 395–6.

[38] The same question has been raised by Kathryn Bailey with respect to Webern's twelve-tone music, which is also based primarily on counterpoint (see *The Twelve-Note Music*, 334).

for instruments. For these the rhythmic shape may be all that is visible; at other times instrumentation, articulation, and tempo may be indicated even in the absence of definite pitches. After this point, Webern then closes the piece with a firm double bar and his customary flourish. Even though the last bars may be incompletely notated, Webern considers that they had been composed. In several works the closing measures reach their final form only in the fair copy.

Instrumentation, Articulation, and Dynamics

For Webern, the musical idea originated simultaneously with an instrumental sound. Almost every note in the sketches is given a specific instrumental attribution. Sometimes there is great indecision about the matter, as in 'Ein Winterabend', where Webern's concern about exactly which instruments were to play each voice of the four-voice chords at 'dunklen Pfaden' results in near-illegibility. (Plate 7 shows these chords, with Webern's many instrumental indications.) Searching for the right instruments, therefore, was just as much a part of Webern's compositional process as getting the right notes or rhythms, and was apparently carried out at the same time. Webern moreover did not, apparently, start out with a particular fixed ensemble in mind, but simply sketched along in short score, indicating instruments as he needed them. He normally did not even try to see the total instrumental ensemble until he was ready to make up the fair copy (at which point he often made substantial changes in orchestration anyway).

Webern's sketches also display a surprising number of dynamic and articulation marks, though these are less detailed than the designation of instruments. The instrumental introductions in particular are worked out with great care; a sketch for 'Gesang einer gefangenen Amsel' (Op. 14 No. 6), for example, shows the violin's opening gesture with dynamics, crescendo–decrescendo, and staccato all marked as if in a fair copy (see Plate 8).[39] This level of detail is usually abandoned after the first few measures. The same is true with dynamics. In the three-page continuity draft of 'Abendland I' (Op. 14 No. 2), Webern indicated very few dynamic markings, but in the opening chord precisely notated a different dynamic for each instrument: *sff* for the violin, *sffp* for the bass clarinet, and *sfff* [*sic*] for the muted cello.[40] Evidently he had a very clear mental image of how the piece should begin, but had to struggle with its continuation.

[39] PSS, Op. 14 misc. sketches, film 101:0597.
[40] In the final version, the three different markings for m. 1 are all normalized to *sfpp*. PSS, Op. 14 sketches, film 101:0563.

Ex. 3.2. 'Die Sonne', Op. 14/1 (1918), mm. 11–12. Contrabass part (PSS, film 104:0423).

Ex. 3.3a and b. 'Verklärung' (No. 3). Two opening gestures (PSS, film 103:0745).

Conservation of Pitch

Another striking feature of Webern's sketches is the preservation of certain pitches across drafts, even among drafts of widely differing character. While Webern often revises orchestration, rhythm, or register, he seldom changes the original pitch-classes, particularly those of the vocal line.[41] A typical example of a revision that preserves most of the pitches is found in sketches for Trakl's 'Die Sonne', Op. 14 No. 1, from 1918. In the 'Die Sonne' sketch (shown in Ex. 3.2), the register and rhythm of the cello part are changed, but the revised version incorporates the same pitch-classes.[42] Sometimes pitch-classes are retained even when a figure is completely transformed. The instrumental introduction for 'Verklärung' (No. 3), for example, first presents the two thirds B–D and B♭–D♭ simultaneously, followed by another chord (see Ex. 3.3).[43] On the next system, the

---

[41] I use the term 'pitch-class', abbreviated as pc or (plural) pcs, to designate pitches that function globally, regardless of their registral placement. 'Pitch' on the other hand refers to a specific note in a specific context.

[42] PSS, Op. 14, film 104:0423.

[43] PSS, vocal compositions, sketches, film 103:0745.

first chord is transformed into a melodic gesture using the same pitches; the second chord stays the same. There are other examples where a figure is changed, but its pitches turn up elsewhere. For Webern apparently the total pitch content of a given passage mattered more than the pitches in a certain part.

FAIR COPIES AND REVISIONS

Webern did not stop composing with the last sketch, but continued to make changes when writing out the fair copy. Even though the continuity drafts contain most of the information needed to realize a piece, it was only in the fair copy that Webern finalized the rhythmic notation, instrumentation, dynamics, and articulation. As a result many of these manuscripts are heavily marked up and full of erasures (see for example Plate 2).

Only when he copied the piece out in score did he finalize exactly which and how many instruments were needed. The result was often impractical; the trombone might be called upon to play only one note, or there might be three trumpets used for a single three-voice chord occurring once in the piece. Webern regularized, and often reduced, the ensemble at this stage. For example, while he sketched 'Wiese im Park' (Op. 13 No. 1) for twenty-three instruments (including doubled strings), the full score written the same year uses solo strings among a total of fifteen instruments. 'In der Fremde' shows a similar reduction between the continuity draft and full score, from sixteen to nine instruments. Many of the large-scale fragments might likewise have been scaled down somewhat had they been completed.

In addition to realizing the continuity draft and completing the details it lacks, the fair copy may also change the musical reading. These changes may thin out the scoring or omit material, but most fair copies of Webern's vocal music in fact preserve a more detailed reading than do the published versions. There are numerous dynamic markings, and there may be one or more expression marks on practically every note. Webern covered his scores with verbal indications such as 'kaum zu hören' (barely audible), 'äußerst leise' (extremely quiet), and, especially ubiquitous, 'wie ein Hauch' (like a breath). He was quite liberal with tempo markings as well; some passages change tempo in practically every measure. Webern's fair copies also carry more precise designations for voices and instruments than do his published scores. He might specify the voice types 'Mezzosopran' or 'hoher Sopran', for example, instead of the simpler 'Gesang' that appears later (see Plate 2). He also states exactly what kinds of instruments are to be used, in particular the transposition of the clarinet. Moreover, some fair copies from Opp. 13, 14, 15, and 16 have indications for *Hauptstimme* (primary voice) and *Nebenstimme* (secondary voice) in the instruments. This level of precision is not found in the published scores.

Revision of Fair Copies

Webern signed a contract with the music publishers Universal Edition in Vienna in 1920, and the first publications of his music began to appear in 1921. In preparing pieces for publication, Webern revised them before copying out new scores. These revisions were often quite extensive.[44] While we know that Webern revised some of his early works, it is not as well known that he did the same for virtually every piece composed before 1921. In other words, the original versions of all works up to and including Op. 15 differ to some degree from the published ones. The most significant revisions have to do with reorchestration (though this applies much more to orchestral songs than it does to chamber settings such as Op. 14), reduction of notational detail, reduction of dynamics, and changes in articulation. The time span between composition and publication could be fifteen years or more; in general, the larger the gap, the more extensive the revisions.[45]

When Webern revised his scores for publication he also removed much of the detail, including performance indications, tempo markings, and dynamics. A comparison of tempo markings found in a 10-measure passage in the fair copy and in the published score of 'In der Fremde' (Op. 13 No. 3) shows the kinds of differences that are common.[46] In this fair copy, written in 1917, Webern has indicated a performance with a constant ebb and flow of tempo: in the space of ten measures, he indicates 'etwas zögernd', 'drängend', '! noch bewegter', 'Rit. . . . Tempo I', 'etwas zögernd', and 'ruhiger'. In the published version copied nine years later, the precisely notated rubato is reduced to a single 'Rit. . . . Tempo'. This is a typical example. In his autograph scores, Webern tried to specify every

---

[44] Brinkmann has shown that in the songs, Op. 3, Webern's revisions minimize tonal implications that were present in the original; see 'Die George-Lieder 1908/9 und 1919/23', 49.

[45] The changes in orchestration that Webern made in the 1920s reveal a significant shift not only in compositional style, but also in musical aesthetics. I described this shift in 'The Path from Expressionism: Webern's Transition from Instrumental to Vocal Works, 1913–24', paper read at the annual meeting of the American Musicological Society, Cleveland, 1986. See also Felix Meyer, 'Im Zeichen der Reduktion: Quellenkritische und analytische Bemerkungen zu Anton Weberns Rilke-Liedern op. 8', in Hans Oesch (ed.), *Quellenstudien I* (Winterthur: Amadeus, 1991), 53–100; and Felix Meyer and Anne Shreffler, 'Webern's Revisions: Some Analytical Implications', *Music Analysis*, 12 (1993), 355–79.

[46] PSS, Op. 13 full score, film 101:0430–34.

detail of performance, sometimes even including a personal reaction to a marking, as shown by the exclamation mark before 'noch bewegter' above.

Webern's original scores generally employ dynamics that are significantly louder throughout than the published versions. One can see the changes reducing the dynamic level written directly on the fair copies, often in red ink. In the printer's copies that Webern made for Universal Edition, he continued to revise the dynamic and articulation markings. The paper in these manuscripts is almost worn through in places because of constant erasing beneath or above the stave.[47] Virtually every time Webern wrote out a copy of a piece, he would alter small details, continually refining and changing his dynamic and articulation marks.[48]

Sometimes Webern revised a score after its performance, although this was rare because his music received very few performances before the 1920s. A manuscript of *Four Pieces for Violin and Piano*, Op. 7, is an unusual case. To make it easier to read, Webern wrote out the score with handwriting much larger than his customary minuscule hand on paper with widely spaced stave-lines. After the performance, he made revisions in red ink. There are significant differences from the final version in both the black- and red-ink layers.[49] This was not typical however. Normally the revisions were carried out years later in order to prepare the works for publication. The first fair copies therefore represent Webern's original ideas. They display more detailed tempo and dynamic markings, larger instrumental groups, and often different readings. Since they were written out immediately after composition, the first versions bear the freshness of Webern's initial impulse. Given that most were intended for publication, they represent valid early versions comparable to the later ones.

THE PROBLEM OF FRAGMENTS

A special problem with Webern's compositional process in this period is the large number of pieces that remained incomplete. Particularly from the period between the First World War and the beginning of the twelve-tone method, Webern left more fragments than finished

[47] All of the *Stichvorlagen* Webern made for Universal Edition are in the Pierpont Morgan Library, New York, Robert Owen Lehman Collection.

[48] Except in the cases of manuscript copies Webern made of pieces after publication; these are only dedication copies which were presented to a patron or performer.

[49] Allen Forte has examined aspects of the variants in this manuscript: 'A Major Webern Revision and its Implications for Analysis', *Perspectives of New Music*, 28/1 (1990), 224–55.

pieces. Some of these fragments are quite lengthy: 'Nächtliches Bild', 'Der Frühlingsregen' (both Chinese translations by Hans Bethge), 'Vallorbe', and 'Vision des Erblindeten' (both by Karl Kraus) exist in continuity drafts as complete as those of the published works.[50]

But more often the fragments are brief, breaking off soon after the sketch's beginning. One of Webern's most singular compositional habits was his practice of sketching the same poem more than once with different music. From about 1913 to 1924, he attempted multiple settings of over twenty poems. While most were never completed, some drafts reached completion and became part of published groups; among these are 'Wiese im Park', Op. 13 No. 1 (Kraus), 'In der Fremde', Op. 13 No. 3 (Bethge), and 'Gesang einer gefangenen Amsel', Op. 14 No. 6 (Trakl). These fragments are not preliminary studies in a conventional sense (they do not lead towards a final version), but instead approach the poem from different directions. They often do not even bear a family resemblance to their cousins with the same text.

Webern's failure to complete a sketch might at times have been a rejection of it, an acknowledgement of a defect or weakness. Sometimes it was a loss of confidence; the large number of fragments from 1918—some quite lengthy and fully developed—could be due to Webern's emotionally draining break with Schoenberg in the autumn of that year.[51] At other times, a sketch may have enabled him to work out musical problems in another context before adopting them for use in a finished piece. This is an unusual way of working, one not shared by any other composer of art songs that I know of. When a composer does make multiple settings of the same text, as Schubert did with Goethe's, they are completed works and represent fixed alternative readings.[52] Webern's resetting of a poem, on the other hand, is part of his compositional process. He often did not know what he would make of a given poem until he had tried several possibilities. By always starting to sketch at the beginning of a piece, he would encounter the poem anew, giving it the fresh impetus of a new idea.

Table 4 displays all the poems for which Webern made multiple settings between 1913 and 1924 (the titles in bold type were com-

---

[50] A score of 'Vision des Erblindeten' has been realized by Wallace McKenzie, but it is unpublished. The PSS has a photocopy of the McKenzie score.

[51] This is discussed in Moldenhauer, *Anton von Webern*, 223–4.

[52] The same circumstances obtain with Berg's two settings of 'Schliesse mir die Augen beide' (Storm), which he set once in 1907 in a chromatic tonal style, and once in 1925 in a twelve-tone style. These two completed settings are separated by many years and by different musical languages; they are not different settings that result from the sketching process.

Ex. 3.4. 'In der Fremde' (Bethge), 1915 sketch, mm. 1–2 (PSS, 'new sketches').

Ex. 3.5. 'Gegenwart' (Goethe), mm. 1–5 (PSS, film 103:0767).

pleted).[53] Some of these were composed years apart, and are so different from one another that one wonders if Webern consciously ignored the earlier draft (or did not have access to it) when writing the later. For example, he began a setting of Strindberg's 'Schien mir, als ich sah die Sonne . . .' for women's and boys' choruses with large orchestra in 1913, and composed a different setting of the same text for voice and piano in 1915; this became the third song of Op. 12. The poem 'In der Fremde' (Op. 13 No. 3)—an adaptation from the Chinese by Hans Bethge—underwent similarly disparate attempts. A fragmentary version from 1915 is scored for voice and piano, while the version completed two years later is an entirely different musical realization, scored for voice and chamber orchestra. The first fragment is notable for its piano harmonics; the player silently depresses keys in the right hand while striking other keys to produce sympathetic vibrations (shown in Ex. 3.4). At the time, this was quite new, having been first used by Schoenberg in his *Three Piano Pieces*, Op. 11 (1909).[54] Webern did not use this technique

---

[53] The information contained here augments Moldenhauer's works list (*Anton von Webern*, 706–50) by including earlier settings of texts used in published works. I have also added several new drafts which I found among sketches for other Webern pieces in the PSS, including fragments on 'Verklärung', 'In tiefster Schuld', and 'In Gottes Namen aufstehen'.

[54] Schoenberg also used this technique in the song 'Am Strande', composed in 1908 or 1909.

TABLE 4. Texts with More than One Musical Realization (works ultimately completed shown in bold type)

Poem	No. of different attempts	Date	Op. or M. number
'O sanftes Glühn der Berge' (Webern)	2	1913	184
'Schien mir's . . .' (Strindberg)	2	1913–15	198, Op. 12/3
'Die Einsame' (Wang Seng Yu–Bethge)	2	1914	Op. 13/2
'In der Fremde' (Li Tai Po–Bethge)	5	1915–17	Op. 13/3
'Wiese im Park' (Kraus)	4	1916–17	Op. 13/1
'Gesang einer gefangenen Amsel' (Trakl)	9	1917–19	Op. 14/6
'Fahr hin, o Seel'' (Rosegger)	4	1917	Op. 15/5
'Mit silbernen Sohlen' (Trakl)	2	1917	218
'Verklärung' (Trakl)	6	1917–21	225
'Nachtergebung' (Trakl)	3	[1917]–20	247
'Die Heimkehr' (Trakl)	2(+)	[1920]	248
'Die Sonne' (Trakl)	2	1918–21	Op. 14/1
'Cirrus' (Goethe)	4	1918	235
'Flieder' (Kraus)	4	1920	246
'Der Frühlingsregen' (Thu-Fu–Bethge)	3	1920	244
'In tiefster Schuld' (Kraus)	2	1920	210
'In Gottes Namen aufstehen' (Rosegger)	2	1920–1	Op. 15/3
'Morgenglanz der Ewigkeit' (chorale)	3	1924	265
'Mutig trägst du die Last' (Kraus)	3	[1924]	211

elsewhere in his output. In 1917, Webern finished the Op. 12 cycle for voice and piano, as well as drafting a lengthy version of Goethe's 'Gegenwart' for the same combination. The latter is quite conventionally 'pianistic', using techniques such as octaves in the left hand (the opening bars are shown in Ex. 3.5).

Another example of preliminary sketches that do not resemble the final version can be seen in 'Fahr hin, o Seel'' (Op. 15 No. 5). This piece, a double canon in inversion with the voice participating, is remarkable since it, with Webern's chorus 'Entflieht auf leichten Kähnen', Op. 2, is an early example of canon and foreshadows the prominent use of this technique in his twelve-tone music. But the canonic technique was not Webern's original idea for this piece; none of the three fragments on this text is canonic or even contrapuntal. One sketch, for voice and piano, is in duple rhythm, and the brief accompaniment is predominantly chordal; not only is the homophonic texture the opposite of canon, but the duple metre seems at odds with the strong triple-metre implications of the poem. The canonic technique appears only in the continuity draft; since no other sketches for the canon survive, it appears fully developed in its final state.[55]

Webern's fragments allow us to see a crucial early stage of composition, one which would not be visible from the sketches for the completed works alone. Each of the fragments embodies a musical idea, what Webern and Schoenberg called a *musikalischer Gedanke*. This phrase represents an integral part of Webern's and Schoenberg's thinking about organicism in music. The musical idea is the starting-point for a composition, representing its content and potential for development. Webern stated its importance with almost religious conviction: 'One had something to *say*.—What did one say?—Ideas [Gedanken].'[56] Many of Webern's fragments share technical features without sounding at all alike. A certain configuration of pitches, or an idea of symmetry, can spawn a wide variety of musical thoughts. The abstract, non-specific idea finds its expression in the particular.

The fact that Webern kept returning to the same poems suggests that the process of composing itself led to the formation of a musical idea. But as Schoenberg describes it, the act of composition consists of the *development* of a musical idea. For Schoenberg, a necessary condition for a musical idea was that it be continued: 'An idea is created; it must be moulded, shaped, developed, worked out, extended, and thought out all the way to the end.'[57] In order to do this, a composer must be able to see where a given musical idea will lead: 'The most important capacity of a composer is to cast a glance into the most remote future of his themes and motives. He has to be able to know beforehand the consequences which derive from the problems existing in his material, and to organize everything accordingly.'[58] Once Webern had a musical idea for a piece, he

---

[55] The continuity draft of 'Fahr hin, o Seel'' is incomplete; only the second page survives.
[56] '... man hatte etwas zu *sagen*. [Webern's emphasis]—Was sagte man?—Gedanken.' Webern, *Der Weg zur neuen Musik*, 18 (Engl., p. 17).
[57] 'Ein Gedanke entsteht; er muss gebildet, gestaltet, entwickelt, ausgearbeitet, durchgeführt und ganz zu Ende gedacht werden.' Schoenberg, 'Neue Musik, veraltete Musik, Stil und Gedanke', in *Stil und Gedanke*, 34.
[58] 'Es ist die wichtigste Fähigkeit eines Komponisten, einen Blick auf die entfernteste Zukunft seiner Themen und Motive zu werfen. Er muß imstande sein, die Folgen der in seinem Material existierenden Probleme im voraus zu kennen und alles dementsprechend zu

would have tried to imagine its consequences. If that projection were not satisfactory, then he would break off and start with a fresh idea. This could explain why he wrote successive drafts of the beginnings of pieces, and needed to spend comparatively little time on their working out. Webern's fragments are the fossil remains of what Schoenberg called the *Einfall* (first inspiration).

Webern's way of composing vocal music seems very close to Schoenberg's description: 'I had never done greater justice to the poet than when, guided by my first direct contact with the sound of the beginning, I divined everything that obviously had to follow this first sound with inevitability.'[59] As we have seen, the 'first direct contact' was both a timbral and a motivic idea, which Webern could then develop. When he composed songs, he began with the verbal *Gedanke* of the poem. He then 'translated' its essence into an instrumental gesture that opened the piece. The vocal composition of the poem's first line completes the *musikalischer Gedanke*, which can then follow the poem to the end. The following diagram illustrates the steps:

$$\text{Poem} \rightarrow \textit{Anfangsklang} \rightarrow \text{Poem}$$
$$\text{(thought)} \quad \text{(instruments)} \quad \text{(vocal line)}$$

Webern's conception of the *musikalischer Gedanke* therefore consisted of an interplay between the musical and verbal. When he composed, he circled around a text. Instead of honing and shaping one idea, the poems generate a series of different musical ideas. Webern's fragments are initial, visceral reactions to the poems, not attempts to impose one reading upon them. When they failed, their musical ideas often re-emerged in different guises.

Perhaps Trakl's poetry, with its multiple layers of meaning, is especially suited to this way of working (for there are more fragments for Trakl than for any other single poet); because of its complexity a Trakl poem does not lend itself to being pinned down to one specific realization. The texts ignited Webern's musical imagination, and enabled him to experiment with techniques he might not have tried otherwise. Just as the poetry of Hildegard Jone would later play a crucial role in the development of Webern's twelve-tone technique, Trakl's poetry allowed Webern to extend his atonal technique into a contrapuntal, highly motivic language.

---

organisieren.' Schoenberg, 'Brahms, der Fortschrittliche', in *Stil und Gedanke*, 56 (trans. in *Style and Idea*, 422).

[59] '. . . daß ich niemals dem Dichter voller gerecht worden bin, als wenn ich, geführt von der ersten unmittelbaren Berührung mit dem Anfangsklang, alles erriet, was diesem Anfangsklang eben offenbar mit Notwendigkeit folgen mußte.' Schoenberg, 'Das Verhältnis zum Text', in *Stil und Gedanke*, 5 (trans. in *Style and Idea*, 144).

4. Evolution of the Completed Trakl Songs (Op. 13 No. 4 and Six Songs, Op. 14)

This chapter will focus on how each of the six completed songs of Op. 14 and 'Ein Winterabend' from Op. 13 was composed, according to evidence in the manuscript sources, ending with some observations about the première of Op. 14 and its performance history and practice. The published version of each Op. 14 song is preceded by at least five manuscript stages: a continuity draft sketch, a fair copy (in score), a printer's copy, sketches for a piano/vocal reduction, and a piano/vocal reduction. For Nos. 1 and 6, as we have seen, Webern also made many preliminary sketches before the continuity draft. (The manuscript sources for Op. 14 are listed in Table 5.)

The Op. 14 set did not evolve from a specific plan to write a Trakl cycle, but came about as a result of Webern's setting various poems as they caught his attention. During the seven years between 1915 and 1922, Webern made dozens of sketches on texts by his favourite authors: Goethe, Strindberg, Kraus, Trakl, folk-texts from *Des Knaben Wunderhorn*, and translations from the Chinese by Hans Bethge (he also began what was later to become an intensive interest in folk- and religious poetry by setting Peter Rosegger and chorale texts). The completed works for compatible ensembles were gathered together into opus numbers only later. The result was several collections of miscellaneous songs: Op. 12, on poems by four different authors, unified only by the common instrumentation of voice and piano; Op. 13, with three different text sources and different chamber ensembles; Op. 15, on a variety of sacred texts, both Catholic and Protestant; and Op. 16, on liturgical Latin texts. Op. 14 is the only song-group from Webern's middle period in which all the texts are by the same author. Webern might also have intended to put together a group of orchestral Trakl settings at some point during these years. Of this set, only 'Ein Winterabend' was completed, and it was ultimately placed into Op. 13.

The story of Webern's Trakl settings properly begins with the fragments on 'In der Heimat' and 'In den Nachmittag geflüstert' from 1915, but since they will be treated in a chapter of their own, I will start with Webern's first completed Trakl setting, 'Abendland III'.

TABLE 5. Manuscript Sources of Webern's Trakl Settings, Op. 14

---

1. Sketches for Nos. 1–6, pencil (1917–21), 36 pp.
PSS, film 104 (No. 1 and No. 6), and film 101.

2. No. 4, fragment, 1 p.
Beginning of ink score page; rhythm of voice line incorrectly notated, then abandoned.
PSS, film 101:0581.

3. '5 [crossed out] 6 Lieder mit Begleitung von Solo-Instr. | Georg Trakl | A. Webern Juli (1919) | Die Sonne (1921) | Abendland III (1917) | op. 14' [plus other versions of ordering and content of set], two title-pages, 22 pp.
Fair copies in ink for 1–6, written at different times. Corrections in pencil and red ink. Upright format. Some *Hauptstimme* indications. Clarinets in A, B♭, and E♭.
PSS, film 101.

4. 'Anton Webern | Sechs Lieder | nach | Gedichten von Georg Trakl | für | eine Singstim[m]e, Klarinette, Baß-Klarinette, Geige und Violoncello | op. 14', 12 pp.
Ink *Stichvorlage*—with UE stamp, printer's markings. Full score in C. Oblong format. Twelve numbered pages, outer folio added later. (Probably copied from PSS MS.)
Pierpont Morgan Library, Lehman Collection.

5. Sketches for piano/vocal reduction: 'Klavierauszüge in Oktober–Nov 1923 angefertigt', 11 numbered pages, 2 missing.
MS not in good shape, pages missing. Pencil, mostly piano part only.
PSS, film 101.

6. 'Anton Webern | Sechs Lieder | nach | Gedichten von Georg Trakl | für | eine Singstim[m]e, Klarinette, Baß-Klarinette, | Geige u. Violoncello | op. 14 | —Klavierauszug—'. Verso of title-page: 'Seinem lieben Direktor | Hugo Winter | in herzlichster | Freundschaft | Anton Webern | Nov. 1938', pages numbered 1–13.
Ink fair copy of p/v score with corrections in pencil. Oblong format, home-made string binding, 15-stave paper (no brand visible). Rehearsal score for première in 1924.
Library of Congress, Moldenhauer collection.

7. 'Anton Webern | Sechs Lieder | nach | Gedichten von Georg Trakl | für | eine Singstimme, Klarinette, Bass-Klarinette | Geige und Violoncello | op. 14 | Partitur'. Inscribed 'Dr Werner Reinhart allerherzlichst überreicht, Wien, März 1932 von seinem Anton Webern'. 17 pp.
Ink fair copy of full score, in C. Upright format 22 × 35 cm. Marked throughout with red pencil, poss. Webern's hand. Performance score used at première at Donaueschingen in 1924 (conducted by Webern). Presented to Reinhart in 1932.
Stadtbibliothek Winterthur, Rychenberg-Stiftung, Dep. RS 72/3.

COMPOSITION SKETCHES

1915–17

Because of his service in the Austrian army during the war, Webern had been able to compose very little in 1915 and 1916. In January 1917, he returned to composition again after a break of almost two years. He began not with vocal works but with some string quartet sketches; his unproductive streak was finally broken with the completion of 'Gleich und Gleich' (Op. 12 No. 4) in March. The seven months he had available until he began work at the Deutsches Landestheater in Prague were immensely productive. The result of his work was six songs that would later belong to four opus-numbered groups: 'Die geheimnisvolle Flöte', Op. 12 No. 2; 'Gleich und Gleich', Op. 12 No. 4; 'Wiese im Park', Op. 13 No. 1; 'In der Fremde', Op. 13 No. 3; 'Abendland III', Op. 14 No. 4; and 'Fahr hin, o Seel'', Op. 15 No. 5.

On 24 June 1917 Webern wrote to Schoenberg: 'I am now hard at work. I think it is going well again. And I hope it will last. I have composed 2 orchestra songs. One on the poem "Wiese im Park" by Karl Kraus, one on a poem by Trakl. I am gradually gaining clarity again. For that I thank your "Pierrot"!'[1] He brought up these two songs again in a letter to Berg written a week later, and at the same time offered a judgement about his progress earlier that year: 'I am again deep in composition. At first I experimented a lot. Now I believe I have succeeded with two orchestra songs . . .'.[2] Although Webern speaks of having completed two 'Orchesterlieder', only one ('Wiese im Park') would normally be characterized this way; the other song Webern mentions is 'Abendland III', for voice and only three instruments.

Both 'Wiese im Park' and 'Abendland III' appear to have been written quickly. The three-page draft of 'Abendland III' was composed in one or two sittings (the continuity draft is dated June 23). After sketching the instrumental introduction and opening vocal gesture twice, Webern continued through the poem, producing a

---

[1] 'Ich bin jetzt gut im Arbeiten drin. Ich glaube, es ist mir wieder was gelungen. Und ich hoffe, es wird anhalten. Ich habe 2 Orchesterlieder geschrieben. Eines nach dem Gedicht "Wiese im Park" von Karl Kraus, eins nach einem Gedicht von Trakl. Ich gewinne allmählich wieder Klarheit. Das verdanke ich Deinem "Pierrot"!' In Ernst Hilmar (ed.), *Anton Webern 1883–1983*, 70–1.

[2] Webern to Berg, 1 July 1917: 'Ich bin wieder gut im Komponieren drin. Anfangs operierte ich noch viel herum. Jetzt sind mir zwei Orchesterlieder, glaube ich, gut gelungen . . .'. In Friedrich Wildgans, *Anton Webern: Eine Studie* (Tübingen: Rainer Wunderlich, 1967), 76. The two orchestra songs are Op. 13 No. 1 and Op. 14 No. 4.

reading that is not far from the final version. Only the last line, 'fallende Sterne', required several attempts. A stray indication on the first page of the sketch for 'Pos.[aune] m.[it] D.[ämpfer]', which Webern crossed out, suggests an initial plan to write for a larger ensemble.

1918/1919

During these two years, Webern's preoccupation with Trakl reached its most intense stage. He produced five of his seven completed Trakl songs in this time and sketched many other poems, including 'Klage' (which remained until recently unidentified; see Ch. 3). While composing the Trakl texts, Webern did not ignore other poets; he also wrote out complete pencil drafts of the Kraus poems 'Vallorbe' and 'Vision des Erblindeten', and Bethge's adaptation from the Chinese, 'Nächtliches Bild'.

In June 1918, Webern settled in the Viennese suburb of Mödling, where he was to remain for over thirteen years.[3] In the autumn of that year, he became actively involved in Schoenberg's Verein für musikalische Privataufführungen. Work in the Verein provided Webern many advantages, including performances of his music, contact with performers and colleagues, and—something especially important to Webern—proximity to Schoenberg. The main disadvantage was that the Verein schedule allowed Webern no opportunity to compose during the long concert season.

As one might expect, Webern did not produce much in 1918, since he could only compose in the summer. Though absorbed in vocal composition—he sketched 17 fragments on eight poems—he produced in the end only one piece that was later published, 'Ein Winterabend' (Op. 13 No. 4). Writing to Jalowetz that he had composed 'a Trakl song (with orchestra)', he re-emphasized his interest in Trakl: 'I want to write a couple more songs on Trakl poems. They touch me so very closely.'[4] On August 8 (two days after finishing a continuity draft of Kraus's 'Vallorbe'), Webern wrote to Berg that he was working: 'So far not too productively, but I feel that it will soon be different.'[5] The situation did not improve, as it turned out, since during the next month Webern did not finish a single piece. In September and October 1918 an event occurred that could well have damaged his productivity. In mid-September, Webern, apparently

[3] Moldenhauer, *Anton von Webern*, 222.
[4] Unpublished letter from Webern to Jalowetz, 25 July 1918 (PSS).
[5] 'Zunächst nicht sehr glücklich. Aber ich spüre, daß es bald anders werden wird.' Letter to Berg, 8 Aug. 1918. Moldenhauer, *Anton von Webern*, 223 (Ger., 202).

angered by Schoenberg's callous reaction to his financial worries, took the unheard-of step of breaking off their friendship.[6] They did not return to speaking terms until the first of November. Given Webern's emotional dependence on Schoenberg at the time, this could well have blocked his creative energies. By the time Webern and Schoenberg were reconciled, the first season of Verein performances was about to begin. Webern's time-consuming duties as *Vortragsmeister* prevented any further composition until the next summer.

The following year, the situation was much improved. Even though in 1919 Webern was still able to compose only in the summer (the Verein season had run to the end of June and was to start again in October), he accomplished a lot in that time. The month of July saw the composition of the remaining two parts of the 'Abendland' poem and 'Nachts', as well as the completion of 'Gesang einer gefangenen Amsel'. At the same time, Webern wrote out full scores of these pieces, and for the first time began to make plans for them as a group or cycle (which lacked at this point only 'Die Sonne' (Op. 14 No. 1)). Webern's productive streak was abruptly cut short, however, by the death of his father in August 1919.

The first piece Webern completed that year, 'Abendland II' (No. 3) on July 7, was another section from the 'Abendland' poem he had set two years earlier. Four days later he finally finished 'Gesang einer gefangenen Amsel' (No. 6, on July 11); though this was apparently drafted quickly, it was the ninth attempt on this text that Webern had made. The following week he completed a poem he had never tried before, 'Nachts' (No. 5, on July 18), in one or two sittings. Completing the last remaining section of the 'Abendland' poem was Webern's last compositional task of the year ('Abendland I' (No. 2), on July 28). This did not proceed as smoothly as the others; perhaps Webern had felt obliged to set the first section of the poem to avoid leaving it incomplete and not because he had been drawn to it from the start.

The emergence of four completed Trakl songs in a single month is striking, considering that four previous years of sketching Trakl's poetry had yielded only two works. Webern's many earlier attempts to come to terms with these difficult texts had finally broken the logjam, allowing him now to proceed at what for him was a rapid pace. One inspiration for finishing four songs in such a short time came from an unexpected source: Stravinsky. On 4 June 1919, Schoenberg had conducted Stravinsky's 'Berceuses du chat' and 'Pribaoutki' at a Verein concert. The 'Berceuses', scored for voice and three clarinets, made a particularly strong impression on Webern; he wrote to Berg

---

[6] Moldenhauer, *Anton von Webern*, 224.

five days later, 'Stravinsky was fantastic. These songs are wonderful. This music touches me unbelievably closely. . . . Something so indescribably moving like these cradle songs. How the three clarinets sound!'[7] A month later, Webern completed four of his Trakl songs very rapidly with an ensemble similar to Stravinsky's: clarinets in Eb, Bb, and A, bass clarinet, plus violin and cello.

Another reason for Webern's fluency this summer may have been that he could now project an image of how the whole poem might be treated at the outset, in contrast to the fragments where he seems intent on probing the sonic implications of a phrase or two. Before even beginning to sketch 'Abendland II', for example, Webern had some idea of its structure as a whole. In his copy of Trakl's *Sebastian im Traum*, he marked the time signature 3/8 at 'Wandern mit zögernden Schritten' (line 6), and 2/4 at 'Schatten nun im kühlen Schoß' (line 11); these correspond to the metrical changes that occur at these places in the finished piece. The 3/8 section (mm. 9–20), as in so many of Webern's songs, evokes the dance-rhythms of a ländler (hobbled with the occasional 2/8 measure). The transition to this section caused him the most ouble; he sketched the lines immediately preceding the 3/8 section twice (see Ex. 4.1). The first time, the music shifts from the prevailing 2/4 to a broader 3/4, but it trails off after the vocal line finishes the phrase 'und wir haben im Schlaf geweint' on the first beat; there is no transition to the new metre. Webern solved the problem of the transition by overlapping the ländler with the previous section (the 3/8 begins on the downbeat of m. 9, as it does in the final version). The transition back into the 2/4 (mm. 19–21) required several tries to restore the sense of a duple metre. Something of the ländler remained, however, especially in the vocal line, which from m. 23 to the end could be notated in 6/8 just as easily as in 2/4.

In sketching 'Nachts', Webern's initial idea carried him through most of the piece—he completed the entire vocal line and its accompanying instrumental parts relatively fluently—but he had problems ending the song. The first three attempts include a two-measure instrumental postlude (see Plate 4). This undergoes many changes, but in all its forms includes a melodic gesture and a cadential chord

---

[7] 'Strawinsky war herrlich. Wunderbar sind diese Lieder. Mir geht diese Musik ganz unglaublich nahe. . . . Etwas so unsäglich Rührendes wie diese Wiegenlieder. Wie diese 3 Klarinetten klingen!' In *Anton Webern 1883–1983*, 71. 'Berceuses du chat' is scored for various combinations of Eb clarinet, Bb and A clarinets, and bass clarinet. Stravinsky later said that he regretted that he did not know of this letter until long after Webern's death: see 'Introduction: A Decade Later', in Demar Irvine (ed.), Hans Moldenhauer (comp.), *Anton Webern Perspectives* (Seattle and London: University of Washington Press, 1966), p. xxiv.

Ex. 4.1a and b. 'Abendland II', Op. 14/3, c.d. sketch, two stages of mm. 7–9 (PSS, film 101:0569–0572).

on the down-beat of the last measure. On the fourth try (marked in the sketch with a crossed circle) Webern arrives at the solution: an abrupt ending in which the instruments break off and the piece concludes with the vocal gesture alone. The voice's last note starts out as a quarter-note, but is compressed to an eighth and finally to a sixteenth;[8] Webern denies even the vocal ending a cadential function, just as he had done with the instruments by cutting their postlude. The piece ends unsettled and unbalanced with a terrifyingly abrupt leap a minor ninth downwards into nothing, on the word 'Umnach-tung' (madness).

'Abendland I', the last Trakl poem completed this year, presented Webern with more difficulties than the others. His initial compositional idea carried him only about three-quarters of the way into the

---

[8] Webern undertook the last step only while copying out the piano/vocal score; this change was then entered on to the sketch and the earlier fair copy.

poem. After the line 'Nächtigen Schatten', the sketch trails off to the vocal line, which then further diminishes to rhythms jotted above the stave. The difficulty may well have stemmed from Webern's trying to accommodate the demands of vivid picturesque phrases like 'Nächtigen Schatten' and 'Zackige Blitze', while at the same time continuing the logical flow of musical ideas. On the third page of 'Abendland I', one can see two layers of composition: the rhythms of the vocal line to the end of the poem, and the more detailed working-out of the instruments. (The entire manuscript page can be seen in Plate 6.) Since the parts on the second system are not lined up properly, they seem to have been composed separately. After the vocal line's rhythms have been sketched out—incidentally in much longer note-values than in the final version—Webern provides a hint of a closing instrumental gesture for the last measure. Its pitches are not defined either, but its rhythmic shape is clear; its tone-colour and character are indicated by the *flageolet* marking and the fermata. Though Webern's initial idea has lost much of its original clarity, the inchoate rhythms continue its momentum.

After sketching the general shape of 'Abendland I' from beginning to end, Webern returned to the level of detail and notated the rapid bass clarinet figure that is later associated with the words 'Zackige Blitze'. Webern's musical realization of these words is an instrumental gesture that interrupts the prevailing texture; we shall see in the analysis of 'Abendland I' that such 'interruptions' then become a main idea of the piece. He then started a new sheet with the transition between 'Nächtigen Schatten' and 'Zackige Blitze', where he had first encountered difficulties. The sketch continues to the end again, this time specifying the pitches of the vocal line and most of the instruments. As is often the case, the last measure is still imprecisely notated. In the margins, all around the final double bar, we find sketches for the closing measure. These served as a reminder of what the general effect should be, but as in the closing measures of many other pieces, the final form appears only in the fair copy.

1920/1921

During the next two years Webern produced very little on account of his work with the Verein, whose 1920–1 season was to be its last in Vienna. He finished only three songs in the summer of 1921: 'Das Kreuz' (Op. 15 No. 1), 'Die Sonne' (Op. 14 No. 1), and 'In Gottes Namen aufstehen' (Op. 15 No. 3).

Though the last Trakl setting that Webern was to complete, 'Die Sonne', draws upon the same instrumental group that other Trakl

songs used—the same ensemble in fact as 'Abendland II'—the later
song is much more extreme than its predecessors. While the instrumental parts comment upon the voice with gestures in short
bursts of sound that often traverse most of the instrumental range,
the vocal part features that disjunct, jagged quality characteristic of
Webern's later songs. This is clearly shown in the sketch by the fact
that Webern is more incapable than usual of keeping each part on
one stave; the instrumental parts often take up five to six staves,
moving freely from one to the other as range and clef demand. A
good example of the new type of vocal and instrumental writing is
heard at the words 'unter dem runden Himmel fährt der Fischer leise'
(mm. 13–14), which is marked 'extatisch' in the sketch (but not in
the score). The voice swoops from a B♭ below middle C up to a high
C (on the word 'Himmel') within a single 2/8 measure. This extravagant gesture, which undoubtedly depicts 'Himmel' in Webern's
sign-system, is mirrored by an equally extravagant figure in the
clarinet: a two-and-a-half-octave swoop in the other direction, fortissimo, followed by string harmonics that produce the extreme high
ranges of the violin and cello. The next line, 'langsam reift die
Traube . . .', requires a contrasting sentiment, and accordingly required many attempts (the revisions of this passage will be discussed
further in the analysis of the piece). Here the instrumental parts of
the sketch break off, yet the vocal line—or a rhythmic reduction of
it—continues to the end of the text (see Ex. 4.2). The notated

Ex. 4.2. 'Die Sonne', Op. 14/1, c.d. sketch (PSS, film 101:0558).

rhythms match those of the final version very closely, though the contour and pitches do not. The last line, 'Sonne aus finsterer Schlucht bricht', is to be sung in sixteenth-note triplets, the fastest continuous note-values in the vocal line. Webern apparently planned from the outset that the piece should end with an a-metrical outburst; he even indicates the vaguest suggestion of the final sixteenth-note figure in the cello, although here it is marked *flgl* (flageolet) and would presumably be much softer than the accented fortissimo figure in the final version.

The vocal and instrumental writing of 'Die Sonne' is characterized by an intensification of rhythmic and gestural shape and a corresponding 'distancing' from the text. Perhaps not coincidentally, Webern did not even sketch any more Trakl poems after 1921, and turned instead to simpler, often religious poems that might be more malleable to extreme vocal display.

FAIR COPIES

Sometimes the pitches or rhythms of a passage will be defined only at the fair copy stage (Table 5, item 3). (Webern habitually wrote out a fair copy immediately after completing the continuity draft of a piece, as we have seen.) These manuscripts also bear traces of still later layers of revision. The pages of each manuscript are numbered separately, and none has an opus or sequence number, so that Webern could order and reorder the songs as he wanted. The main differences between the fair copies and the published version of Op. 14 are that the manuscript scores have *Hauptstimme* or *Nebenstimme* markings; specify the type of clarinet to be used; often have different dynamic, articulation, and expression marks; use different types of notation, including beaming; and use conventional transposing notation for the clarinet parts. The *Hauptstimme* markings are found only in the scores of 'Abendland I', 'Abendland II', and 'Nachts'. They are sometimes in surprising places; for example, in the 'Elis' section of 'Abendland I' (mm. 15–21), the *Hauptstimme* is the cello, a part that is usually inaudible on recordings. Webern's attention to detail is reflected in his designation of instruments. Op. 14 originally called for five clarinets to be played by two players: clarinets in E♭, B♭, A, and bass clarinets in B♭ and A.[9] For each song, Webern specified whether the clarinet part should be played on B♭ or A clarinet, a distinction that is dropped in the published scores (although

---

[9] The bass clarinet in A is rarely (if ever) encountered today; but according to Nicholas Shackleton, it was commonly used in the 19th century: 'Bass Clarinet', in *The New Grove Dictionary of Musical Instruments*, i (London: Macmillan, 1984), 170.

an A clarinet would be necessary in order to play the lowest note, $C\#^3$, in 'Die Sonne'). As with Webern's other scores, the dynamic and articulation marks are more detailed and plentiful in the fair copies than in the published version.

The peculiar treatment of 'Ein Winterabend', the only completed Trakl setting that was not included in Op. 14, and the number of Trakl fragments that employ large ensembles suggest that Webern might have had two Trakl cycles in mind, one for voice and three instruments and one for voice and chamber orchestra. The other orchestral settings would have been drawn from 'Mit silbernen Sohlen', 'Verklärung', 'Nachtergebung', 'Siebengesang des Todes', and 'Klage', had they been completed. Webern also made orchestral sketches for 'Gesang einer gefangenen Amsel' (Op. 14 No. 6) and 'Die Sonne' (Op. 14 No. 1) before deciding upon their final instrumentation.

Upon completing 'Abendland III' for two clarinets and cello in the summer of 1917, Webern was apparently in no hurry to finish composing the rest of his chamber cycle. The next summer, he instead completed a series of works and fragments calling for large ensembles, including a setting of 'Ein Winterabend' (Op. 13 No. 4) and sketches for 'Die Sonne' (Op. 14 No. 1), 'Klage', and 'Gesang einer gefangenen Amsel' (Op. 14 No. 6). The year before, in 1917, Webern had been similarly preoccupied with exploring the possibilities of instrumental colour, and had sketched the fragmentary 'Siebengesang des Todes', 'Verklärung', and 'Mit silbernen Sohlen'. Even after five of the six chamber settings had been completed in 1919, Webern did not immediately add to his Trakl songs with clarinets and strings. Instead in 1920 and 1921 he continued to make orchestral sketches, on the poems 'Die Heimkehr', 'Nachtergebung', and 'Jahr'. Even though most of these fragments are scored for smaller groups than was typical in 1917–19, none uses an ensemble that matches that of the Op. 14 group.

Webern may have kept trying to compose Trakl poems for orchestral combinations in order to create partners for 'Ein Winterabend'. As late as 1921, Webern did not include 'Ein Winterabend' with Op. 13 even though the other three songs that make up this opus had been completed. In an article on Webern's songs written in 1921, Egon Wellesz lists the four songs of Op. 13 as follows:[10]

---

[10] Egon Wellesz, 'Anton von Webern: Lieder opus 12, 13, 14', *Melos*, 2 (1921), 39.

1. Wiese im Park
2. Der Einsame [*sic*]
3. In der Fremde
4. Fahr' hin, o Seel'

The fourth song was originally the double canon 'Fahr hin, o Seel''
(later Op. 15 No. 5); this song, scored for only five players, seems an
unlikely partner for the three orchestral songs. By not including 'Ein
Winterabend'—a logical choice on the basis of instrumentation—
Webern may have been keeping it aside for another potential group.

By 1922, Webern probably realized that he would not complete the
Trakl fragments, and incorporated 'Ein Winterabend' into Op. 13 (of
course by now there were other songs on sacred texts with which to
group 'Fahr hin, o Seel''). Even though the Trakl poem does not
match the other poems of Op. 13, as an orchestral song there was no
other opus that would have been appropriate for 'Ein Winterabend'.
The other songs in Op. 13 were probably put there as 'next-best'
solutions as well; had Webern completed more of the fragments,
there could also have been Bethge and Kraus cycles.

Another reason for not completing an orchestral Trakl cycle could
have been Webern's gradual abandonment of orchestral writing in
general. While during 1917 and 1918 Webern had written for relatively large ensembles with percussion, by 1919 he had scaled down
his instrumental forces to groups of three to six instruments. His shift
to smaller ensembles may have been partly due to his involvement
with the Verein, since the group performed pieces most often in reductions. Webern himself had arranged his *Passacaglia for Orchestra*,
Op. 1, for two pianos, six hands, and his *Five Pieces for Orchestra*,
Op. 10, for violin, viola, cello, harmonium, and piano. In addition
Webern completed reductions of his *Six Pieces for Large Orchestra*,
Op. 6, for a chamber ensemble of ten instruments (the first of several
reorchestrations he would make of this piece), Schoenberg's *Four
Orchestral Songs*, Op. 22, and his opera *Die glückliche Hand*.[11]

In 1922 Webern extensively revised 'Ein Winterabend', reducing it
from seventeen (in the sketches) to ten instruments (in the final
version). The revised version is substantially different from the early
one (completed on 10 July 1918) in other ways as well, particularly
in the piece's structure, interpretation of the text, and the use of
instruments.[12]

[11] Webern also contributed to the 'Walzerabend' that the society put on to raise money in
May 1921 with his arrangements of the Johann Strauss 'Schatzwalzer'. Moldenhauer, *Anton von
Webern*, 236–7.

[12] The original version is preserved in a fair copy marked 'Nicht zur Veröffentlich. bestimmt.
| 1922 umgearbeitet.' (Not intended for publication | revised 1922.) PSS, Op. 13 full score, film
101:0435–0441, and PSS, Op. 13 sketches, film 101:0496–0498. For a more detailed analysis of

TABLE 6. Stages in the Compilation of Op. 14

1.	(1919)	'4 Lieder mit Instr. Op. 14' ['Abendland I, II, III', and either 'Amsel' or 'Nachts']
2.	(1919)	'Abendland von Georg Trakl . . . , Op. 14': 'Abendland I, II, III'
3.	(1919–21)	'5 Lieder mit Begleitung von Solo-Instr., Op. 14(15)': 'Nachts' 'Abendland I, II, III' 'Gesang einer gefangenen Amsel'
4.	(1921–3)	'5(6) Trakl-Lieder mit Instr. Begl., Op. 14(15)': 'Nachts' 'Abendland I, II, III' 'Die Sonne' 'Gesang einer gefangenen Amsel'
5.	(1923–4)	'Sechs Lieder . . . Op. 14': 'Die Sonne' 'Abendland I, II, III' 'Nachts' 'Gesang einer gefangenen Amsel'

COMPILATION OF THE OP. 14 COLLECTION

As we have seen, with all works composed before 1920, Webern usually decided which would go into an opus-numbered group only after composition (in some cases, long afterwards). The choice was often made more difficult by the presence of many pieces of the appropriate instrumentation from which to choose. Like other works, including the *Six Bagatelles for String Quartet*, Op. 9, and the *Five Pieces for Orchestra*, Op. 10, the Op. 14 group consisted of different configurations at different times. With the Trakl songs, there was not much choice, since the six in Op. 14 are the only works with that instrumental combination on Trakl's poems that Webern finished. The final selection of songs in Op. 14 was therefore not part of a grand design, but simply represents the state of the work in 1923, when Webern was ready to publish it. Op. 14 is therefore more accurately considered a *collection*, like Hugo Wolf's *Mörike Lieder*, rather than a song *cycle* like Schoenberg's *Das Buch der hängenden Gärten*, Op. 15.

Several distinct stages of the work's development between 1919 and 1924 are shown in Table 6.

some differences between the two versions, see Meyer and Shreffler, 'Webern's Revisions: Some Analytical Implications', *Music Analysis*, 12 (1993), 355–79.

Webern had already begun to think about how the songs ought to be grouped in 1919, two years after he wrote his first Trakl setting: 'I have written four songs on Trakl poems', he wrote to Berg, 'With accompaniment for E♭, B♭, and bass clarinets, violin, and cello, in varying combinations; except for one, all are with three instruments. Two years ago, I composed a Trakl song in this manner; I have picked it up again, and so I have completed a cycle of five Trakl songs, up to now, for this small combination.'[13] With an almost offhand tone, Webern says of 'Abendland III' that he 'picked it up again', therefore 'completing a cycle', which is none the less not closed yet ('up to now'). Nor does he mention why he started with the third part of 'Abendland', and continued to compose the poem 'backwards', Part I following Part II by about a month. Webern also gives no hint to Berg about the long process of composing 'Amsel' (which must be one of the songs he mentions); he had completed it only after eight previous unsuccessful attempts.

Around this time Webern also considered different configurations of three or four Trakl songs, as well as the group of five he described to Berg. In one of his own work lists, Webern made an entry (later crossed out) for 'op. 14 4 Lieder mit Instr.'[14] This is the last entry in ink; at some later time, Webern continued the list in pencil, entering works up to 1931. Judging from where the ink part of the list breaks off, this part must have been written by 1919. There is no indication as to which four songs Webern meant. Assuming that only songs on poems of Trakl would be included, then there are five possible 'songs with instruments'—that is, not 'orchestra songs' and not 'piano songs'—written by this time: Trakl's 'Abendland III' (1917), 'Abendland II', 'Amsel', 'Nachts', and 'Abendland I' (all 1919).

The existence of a separate, beautifully calligraphic ink title-page listing only the three 'Abendland' songs suggests that the '4 Lieder' to which Webern refers includes these three together, plus one of either 'Amsel' or 'Nachts' (Table 5, item 3).[15] Webern evidently considered at one time a group of three songs—'Abendland'—as Op. 14. He was undecided about this, however, since only four days after completing the last 'Abendland' setting, he wrote to Berg that

---

[13] 'Ich habe 4 Lieder nach Trakl-Gedichten geschrieben. Mit Begleitung von Es-Klar., B-Klar., Geige und Vcl. in verschiedenen Kombinationen; bis auf eines alle mit 3 Instrumenten. Vor 2 Jahren habe ich schon einen Trakl in dieser Art komponiert; das habe ich wieder aufgegriffen und so jetzt einen Cyklus von vorläufig 5 Trakl-Liedern mit dieser kleinen Besetzung fertig.' Webern to Berg, 1 Aug. 1919, in *Anton Webern: Briefe der Freundschaft*, 128. Trans. Moldenhauer, *Anton von Webern*, 268.

[14] PSS, list of works in Webern's hand, Opp. 1–22, uncatalogued.

[15] The title-page reads 'Abendland | von | Georg Trakl | für | eine Singstimme | und | Es-Klarinette, B-Klarinette (auch Baß-Klar.), | Geige u. Violoncello | von | Anton Webern | op. 14.' PSS, film 101:0521.

he now had a cycle of *five* songs. Perhaps the possibility of an Op. 14 consisting only of the 'Abendland' settings occurred to him some time later (between 1919 and 1921), but in any event, he never carried it out. Throughout all the cycle's transformations, however, the three 'Abendland' songs remained together and formed the central core of the Op. 14 collection.

Though Webern, in his letter to Berg, leaves open the possibility that he might someday add to the group, he evidently considered the five Trakl songs as a fixed unit at least for the next two years (see Stage 3 in Table 6). In a letter to Jalowetz from early 1921, Webern recommends his 'Op. 14 5 Lieder nach Trakl (1919)' for a possible performance at a concert Jalowetz was organizing in Prague. He reconsiders, however: 'But they are not really orchestra songs, only with single instruments (at most 4) . . . You also need extremely virtuosic instrumentalists and a high soprano (to 𝄞), (often high range around this C)[.]'[16] Wellesz likewise identifies five songs belonging to Op. 14: 'The songs Op. 15 [*sic*], composed in 1919, are written for voice accompanied by a few instruments.'[17] Though he does not name them, he does list the instrumental combinations for each song. From the instruments Wellesz indicates, we can deduce that the first song was 'Nachts', and the last, 'Amsel', with the three 'Abendland' songs in the middle.[18]

Violin, E♭ clarinet, bass clarinet	['Nachts']
Violin, bass clarinet, cello	['Abendland I']
Violin with mute, clarinet, cello with mute	['Abendland II']
E♭ clarinet, bass clarinet, cello	['Abendland III']
Violin, clarinet, bass clarinet, cello	['Gesang einer gefangenen Amsel']

This ordering was probably the same Webern had in mind in his letter to Jalowetz, and helps to explain Webern's warning about the extremely high vocal range required for the set. Four of the songs do

---

[16] 'Aber das sind nicht eigentlich Orchesterlieder, nur mit einzelnen Instrum. (höchstens 4) . . . Dazu nötig ganz virtuose Instrumentalisten u. ein hoher Sopran (bis C), (oft hohe Lage in der Nähe von diesem C)'. Unpublished letter from Webern to Jalowetz, 8 Feb. 1921. PSS, Jalowetz Collection (I am grateful for special permission to cite this letter).

[17] 'Die Lieder op. 15 [*sic*], 1919 komponiert, sind für Singstimme mit Begleitung einer weniger Instrumente geschrieben.' Wellesz, 'Anton von Webern: Lieder', 40.

[18] It is not clear where Wellesz got his information about Op. 14, but it was probably not from Webern's manuscripts, since Wellesz's list of instruments diverges in several details from the scores. For example, for 'Abendland I', he lists simply 'Geige, Baßklarinette, Violoncell', while the fair copy is more specific, noting the string parts 'm. Dämpfer'. Wellesz does indicate 'mit Dämpfer' for the strings in 'Abendland II', like the fair copy. The information probably came from Webern directly, perhaps in a letter similar to the one he had written to Jalowetz.

not in fact require a high soprano; all three of the 'Abendland' songs could be handled easily by a lyric mezzo. 'Nachts', however, calls for a much higher tessitura. Putting 'Nachts' first requires a singer willing to start cold on a high B; certainly only someone very confident of those notes could attempt it.

When Webern finished 'Die Sonne' in 1921, he placed it fifth in the group. On the title-page to the fair copy of the scores, 'Die Sonne' is listed this way, followed by 'Amsel' (Table 5, item 3; see Plate 9).[19] The songs are numbered 1 to 6, though in a differently coloured pencil; 1 and 5 ('Nachts' and 'Sonne') are reversed from their current order. Webern seems to have been undecided even at this point whether there would be five songs or six. At the top of the page, Webern first wrote: '5 Lieder mit Begleitung von Solo-Instr.', but the 5 is crossed out and replaced with a 6. Once all six songs were listed, he considered omitting one. The names 'Nachts', 'Abendland I', 'Sonne', and 'Amsel' are all circled—Webern's customary mark for deletion.

This title-page also shows that Webern could not decide whether the opus number was to be 14 or 15; both are crossed out, and ultimately replaced with another 14. There is similar confusion in Webern's work list—the part continued in pencil from the ink list mentioned above—which describes the work as 'Op. 15(14) 5(6) Trakl-Lieder mit Instr. Begl. (1919) eins 1917, eins 1921'.[20] Webern called the Trakl group alternately Op. 14 and Op. 15 until it was published; the discrepancy was due to the fact that at one time he had planned to publish '3 Lieder mit Orchester' as Op. 11, the *Three Little Pieces for Violoncello and Piano* (Op. 11) as Op. 12, and so on, adding a number to works through to Op. 14.[21]

Composed over the course of five years, Webern's Trakl songs reflect changes in the way he composed as well as differences between the poems on which they are based. Though several melodic figures recur in more than one song of Webern's Op. 14, these occur often in other Webern works as well, and are part of his language just as the triad is part of Schubert's.[22] Since Webern set poems as

---

[19] PSS, film 101:0515.   [20] PSS, list of works in Webern's hand.
[21] This also explains Wellesz's reference to 'Die Lieder, op. 15', in 'Anton von Webern: Lieder', 40. The three orchestra songs would have been 'Leise Düfte', 'O sanftes Glühn der Berge', and 'Kunfttag III', which were published in 1968 by Carl Fischer as 'Three Orchestral Songs (1913/14)'.
[22] Some of these figures include two descending minor thirds a semitone apart, as in 'Die Sonne' (at 'langsam reift die Traube') and elsewhere, and a descending fourth and semitone, as in 'Abendland III' (at 'Ihr grossen Städte') and elsewhere. The former occurs often in Webern's music, both in ascending and descending forms. The latter forms set-class 0,1,5, which is one of the most often used by Webern. (Richard Teitelbaum has pointed out that Webern's harmonic

they caught his attention and only grouped them together years later, the final ordering of Op. 14 (and even its very existence) was only one result of something that could have assumed several different forms. Webern's 'Trakl-Liederbuch' could have been much larger; we have seen how 'Ein Winterabend' could have been grouped with other orchestral Trakl settings, had they been finished. During the same years, Webern also sketched poems by Bethge (adaptations from the Chinese), Karl Kraus, and Goethe, though without the continuous efforts he applied to Trakl. These could also have resulted in collections based on one author, rather than being dispersed into various opus numbers as they ultimately were. The Trakl settings were rather more successful than the others; only they resulted in enough completed works with similar scoring to comprise an independent group.

PERFORMANCE AND PERFORMANCE PRACTICE

The next and final stage in the evolution of the Op. 14 cycle was its publication and performance, both of which took place in July 1924. For the publication, Webern prepared clean copies of the scores, making many revisions (mostly of dynamics and articulation) as he did so (Table 5, item 4).[23] These copies, by definition, resemble the published versions exactly, though one can see variants—particularly in dynamics and expression marks—through the erasures. Webern must have prepared the printer's copies long before the first performance, since the published score came out only days after the première.[24] The changes Webern made in the printer's copy therefore do not reflect practical changes due to a live performance.

The première, conducted by Webern, took place on July 20 at Donaueschingen; Clara Kwartin sang with an ensemble led by Rudolf Kolisch. The performers had to play from manuscript material, since the published score did not come out until afterwards.[25] The manuscript score bears Webern's conductor's markings in red pencil, such as enlarged metre changes notated above the stave, and numerals

vocabulary is much more restricted than Schoenberg's: see 'Intervallic Relations in Atonal Music', *Journal of Music Theory*, 9 (1965), 72–128.) Moreover the sketches for Op. 14 show that Webern originally wrote different pitches for several of these recurring passages.

[23] The printing copies that Webern prepared for Universal Edition are now in the Pierpont Morgan Library in New York (Robert Owen Lehman Collection).

[24] The *Stichvorlagen* were probably prepared in October and November 1923, when he made the piano/vocal reduction.

[25] The score Webern conducted from is now in the Stadtbibliothek Winterthur (Rychenberg-Stiftung, Dep. RS 72–3). Webern had inscribed a printed copy of Op. 14 to Schoenberg 'post festum'. Moldenhauer, *Anton von Webern*, 269.

Ex. 4.3. Voice parts as notated in piano/vocal score used in first performance (Library of Congress, Moldenhauer Collection): (*a*) 'Abendland I', Op. 14/2, mm. 4–5; (*b*) 'Nachts', Op. 14/5, mm. 2–3.

marking the beats or subdivisions in long measures (Table 5, item 7). Several years later, he presented this score to the Swiss patron Werner Reinhart, who had helped bring about the work's première.

A piano/vocal reduction of Op. 14, which Webern had prepared in 1923, was used to rehearse the singer (Table 5, item 6).[26] Some of the markings in the score are clearly aids to a more accurate performance, such as subdivisions of complex rhythms. Other markings can tell us something about vocal performance style, which must have been quite different from the dry, precise way this music is sung today. The most notable of these are the glissandos pencilled in between notes in the voice part. These glissandos always connect descending notes (and as such are the opposite of the Italianate 'slide' used to approach a pitch from beneath). In 'Abendland I', for example, Webern has notated slides between both descending leaps at the phrase 'und es fallen der Blüten' (see Ex. 4.3*a*); this type of performance, a clear response to the text, would minimize the effect of individual pitches and create a single connected falling gesture.

[26] Webern gave this score to Hugo Winter, the director of Universal Edition, just before Winter's emigration to the United States in 1938. Hans Moldenhauer acquired it in 1958; he attached sentimental value to it, since it was the first Webern manuscript he and his wife Rosaleen collected. It can now be seen in the Library of Congress, Moldenhauer Collection. The piano/vocal score of Op. 14, unlike that for Op. 13, has not been published. Though this version would be valuable for rehearsal purposes, it was surely not meant for performance, in spite of Moldenhauer's efforts to the contrary (the reduction was performed at the first International Webern Festival in 1962). The sketches for the p/v reduction are in the PSS, and bear Webern's indication: 'Klavierauszüge in Oktober–Nov 1923 angefertigt'.

Another striking glissando is marked between the syllables of 'Augen', in 'Nachts' (No. 5, m. 3, see Ex. 4.3*b*). This leap of a tritone plus an octave is the largest in the piece, plunging from the stratospheric opening into the prevailing low register of the next phrase. The presence of these markings does not mean that a singer is free to slide from note to note at will; the fact that they were marked at all shows that their use was restricted to specific situations. But we can conclude that a judicious glissando or two would not be out of keeping with an 'authentic' performing style. In the light of the freedom implied by these markings, Webern's advice for a performance of his *Five Songs from 'Der siebente Ring' by Stefan George*, Op. 3, may be relevant:

> The songs have metronome marks. I think they are good. But please: within these specifications one can and must have musical freedom. Let the melodic phrases live fully: but again pay attention to the line. Every song until the end should be sung very flowingly. . . . In Vienna *Frl. Mihascek* from the opera sang the songs; really superb. She didn't hit the notes carefully and painstakingly . . . rather [she] truly *shaped* [them]. [Webern's emphasis][27]

Webern's admonitions to Schulhoff, who was organizing a series of Verein concerts in Prague, make it clear that he wanted a rhythmically flexible performance in which the pieces 'become real songs', not a painfully accurate rendition with each note hit 'carefully and painstakingly'. Webern also expresses a rather naïve surprise that singing these intervals is difficult for singers 'even today'.

In any case, the performance of the songs was almost a fiasco on account of the reception of the *Six Bagatelles*, Op. 9, that preceded them. As Webern described the occasion to Berg, 'But the performance was very good all the same. After the first two movements [of the Bagatelles] there was laughter. I then considered not conducting my songs. Finally calm. The songs went excellently. Miss Kwartin performed brilliantly. She sang really beautifully, faultless in intonation, very convincingly, and had a very great success.'[28] The reviews

---

[27] 'Die Lieder sind metronomisiert. Ich glaube gut. Aber bitte: innerhalb dieser Angaben kann u. muss ganz frei musiziert werden. Lassen Sie die melodischen Phrasen ausleben: aber doch wieder auf den "Zug" schaun. Bis auf das Letzte sind die Lieder alle sehr fliessend zu singen. . . . In Wien sang die Lieder *Frl. Mihascek* [*sic*] von der Oper; wirklich ausgezeichnet. Da waren nicht mit Müh u. Not die Noten getroffen . . . sondern wirklich *gestaltet*.' Letter from Webern to Erwin Schulhoff, 19 Aug. 1919, in Ivan Vojtech (ed.), 'Arnold Schoenberg, Anton Webern, Alban Berg, Unbekannte Briefe an Erwin Schulhoff', *Miscellanea Musicologica* (Prague), 18 (1965), 40. The singer to whom Webern refers is Felicia Hüni-Mihacsek of the Vienna Staatsoper.

[28] 'Aufführung aber doch sehr gut. Nach den ersten zwei Stücken Gelächter. Dachte schon daran, meine Lieder nicht aufzuführen. Schließlich Beruhigung. Die Lieder gingen ausgezeichnet. Die Kwartin bewährte sich glänzend. Sang wirklich schön, tadellos rein und sehr

were mixed; one critic—using a highly Trakl-flavoured vocabulary himself—here originated the enduring misconception that Webern's music disregards the words: 'through their bizarre, jagged rhythms and melodies they do violence to the grave, broadly flowing, darkly glowing music of Trakl's verses. However, if one disregards Trakl, Webern's songs create, in a purely musical respect, a highly original impression.'[29] There were not many performances of the work after the première in Webern's lifetime, and it remains comparatively neglected.[30] This is—and was—partly due to the extreme difficulty of both vocal and instrumental parts, and perhaps also to the hermetic quality of the poetry, which does not lend itself to theatrical display. Although Webern's music is still not easy to play, its neglect is surprising, given the many highly competent performers today who have mastered the even more intricate scores of Carter, Berio, Boulez, and Ferneyhough.

überzeugend und hatte einen sehr großen Erfolg.' Moldenhauer, *Anton von Webern*, 260 (Ger., 235).

[29] '. . . [daß] sie durch ihre bizarren zackigen Rhythmen und Melodien in geradezu erstaunlicher Weise die schwerblütige, breit dahinströmende, dunkel strahlende Musik der Traklschen Verse vergewaltigen. Wenn man allerdings von Trakl absieht, so machen die Lieder Weberns in rein musikalischer Hinsicht einen höchst eigenartigen Eindruck.' *Deutsche Allgemeine Zeitung*, 26 July 1924, cited in Moldenhauer, *Anton von Webern*, 259 (Ger., 235).

[30] Moldenhauer notes that Op. 14 was performed in London in 1938 (*Anton von Webern*, 503). After Webern's death, Rudolf Kolisch coached many performances in Europe and in America until his own death in 1978.

Part III
The Trakl Fragments

5. *Proportion and Motive in Webern's Earliest Trakl Fragments*

Webern sketched his first Trakl poems in January 1915, after re-reading Trakl's first volume of poetry, *Gedichte* (1913), in response to news of the poet's untimely death two months earlier.[1] From this volume he chose two poems, 'In der Heimat' and 'In den Nachmittag geflüstert', but never completed them. Both fragments reveal much as interesting failures, but 'In der Heimat' is intriguing for several reasons. First, the two-page fragment seems self-consciously long, especially compared to Webern's previous aphoristic mode of expression. Second, as Webern's first Trakl setting, it bears the awkward traces of his first coming to terms with the ambiguities and challenges of Trakl's poetic language. As Webern experimented with various strategies to project the poems' metre, stanza structure, individual words, and moods, he began to develop a more conventionally motivic technique that would allow him to write longer pieces.

Whether Webern considered his early Trakl fragments and completed works from 1915 as mainly 'about' breaking away from aphorism we do not know. He was, however, quite plainly aware that his instrumental miniatures from 1911–14 had reached the point where no further compression was possible. As a remedy, he attempted an ambitious two-movement work for cello and piano, which he referred to as a 'major piece', continuing (in a letter to Schoenberg): 'My father asked me to do it. He likes cello music. For me, however, his wish becomes the occasion to find at last an approach to longer movements again—your idea.'[2] His embarrassment at producing the minute *Three Little Pieces* for cello and piano, Op. 11, instead is palpable in his next letter: 'I beg you not to be indignant that it has again become something so short.'[3]

Something similar happened with Webern's vocal compositions a year later; he first attempted to extend them, only to return to his customary—and seemingly unavoidable—brevity. While both Trakl fragments from 1915 clearly attempt a larger time-frame, the completed works from that year remain extremely concise utterances.

---

[1] Letter to Schoenberg, Nov. 1914, Library of Congress, Schoenberg Collection. *Gedichte* (1913) was Trakl's only published collection at the time Webern chose these poems.
[2] Moldenhauer, *Anton von Webern*, 205.
[3] Ibid.

'Der Tag ist vergangen' (Op. 12 No. 1) and 'Schien mir's' (Op. 12 No. 3) are at 23 and 41 measures not the briefest of Webern's works, but they last about as long as Nos. 1, 2, 3, and 5 of the *Five Pieces for Orchestra*, Op. 10, which are among Webern's most aphoristic works.

In order to be able to form longer pieces, Webern took two definitive steps; first, he chose texts that were longer and more complex than those he had attempted before, and second, he renounced the colouristic possibilities of the orchestra by returning to smaller combinations like voice and piano or groups of several instruments. The first step allowed him to experiment with the declamation of the vocal part, stretching the relationship between the poetic foot and musical metre to breaking-point. The second gave him the optimal conditions for composition based on connected and developing motives rather than the juxtaposition of tiny cells.

PROPORTION AND SCALE

In addition to Trakl's poems, Webern also occupied himself with other sources for song texts in 1915, including poetry by Kraus, translations from the Chinese by Bethge, a Peter Rosegger folk-song imitation, and a prose passage from Strindberg's *Gespenster-Sonate*. These diverse texts are longer than the poems that Webern had set in recent years, especially so compared with Webern's own aphoristic poems 'Schmerz, immer blick nach oben' and 'Leise Düfte'. The multi-stanza poems of Trakl, Kraus, and Bethge are moreover densely packed with images, and exhibit narrative qualities that would require a comparably extended musical development. Trakl's 'In der Heimat' and Bethge's 'In der Fremde' inspired the two most substantial fragments from 1915; they are composed on a larger scale than most of the completed songs from these years. Each of the two fragments is as long as either Op. 12 No. 1 or No. 3, yet in the fragments, half or less of the poem is set to music. A similar expansive length is found in other fragments for voice and piano, 'Wiese im Park' (Kraus, 1916) and 'Gegenwart' (Goethe, 1917).

Table 7 shows the relative lengths of the songs and fragments Webern composed between 1915 and 1917. The table shows the number of measures and the prevailing time signature, the number of beats, the note-value of a beat, and the tempo indication for each piece. For each fragment, I have extrapolated how many measures a completed version might have taken, based on the amount of time taken by the existing music and amount of remaining text.[4]

[4] A 'beat' is defined as the basic unit that subdivides the metre; counting beats is a more accurate way to describe the length of a piece than the number of measures. Tempo is also

[cont. on p. 90]

TABLE 7. Length and Proportion in Works and Fragments, 1915–17

Work or Fragment	No. of mm., metre	No. of beats	Metrical unit + MM
Op. 12/1, 'Der Tag ist vergangen' (UE score, 1915)	23, 2/4	50	quarter = c.60, sehr ruhig
Op. 12/3, 'Schien mir's . . .' (UE score, 1915)	41, 3/8	41	d. quarter = c.42, ruhig fließend
'In der Heimat' (frag.), 1915 (7 of 14 lines set)	27, 2/2	59 + [59 = **118**]	half, ruhige Bewegung
'Nachmittag' (frag.), 1915 (4 of 16 lines set)	12, 3/4	12 + [36 = **48**]	dotted half, sanft bewegt
'In der Fremde' (frag.), 1915 (5 of 7 lines set)	29, 2/2	58 + [23 = **81**]	half, Bewegt
Op. 13/3, 'In der Fremde' (PSS full score, 1917)	26, 2/4	54	quarter = 66, Allegretto, sehr frei
'Wiese im Park' (frag.), 1916 (8 of 12 lines set)	33, 3/4	99 + [50 = **149**]	quarter
Op. 13/1, 'Wiese im Park' (full score, 1918)	51, var	102	quarter = c.56, PSS Allegro moderato
'Gegenwart' (frag.), 1917 (7 of 18 lines set)	38, 2/4	38 + [60 = **98**]	half

From the standpoint of length, Op. 12 No. 1 and No. 3, at 50 and 41 beats respectively, can certainly be considered 'vocal miniatures'.[5] The fragment 'In der Heimat' has much larger proportions; it takes 59 beats even though only half of the poem (seven lines) is composed. If the remaining seven lines also took 59 beats, the entire song would last about 118 beats, or more than twice the length of either Op. 12 No. 1 or No. 3. Two other fragments are also on a larger scale than the two completed pieces: 'In der Fremde' and 'Wiese im Park' would take 81 and 149 beats respectively, if completed according to the dimensions established already. The 1915 fragmentary version of 'In der Fremde' is even longer than the later setting of the complete poem (Op. 13 No. 3, 1917), although the fragment only covers five out of seven lines. Similarly, the fragment 'Wiese im Park', which comprises only two-thirds of the poem, takes about the same amount of time as the completed setting of 1917 (Op. 13 No. 1). If completed according to the same proportions, each of these pieces would be substantially longer than the versions we know. The numerical measurements are not important in themselves; they are significant only because they show that in early 1915 Webern was trying to write on a much larger time-scale than before.

THE TRAKL FRAGMENTS OF 1915

Both early Trakl fragments, 'In der Heimat' and 'In den Nachmittag geflüstert', contain the first traces of motivic and declamatory techniques that Webern would later develop fully in the published songs. The declamation of the vocal lines begins to free itself from strict congruence with the musical metre, a seemingly paradoxical use of Trakl's formally conventional early poems. This represents a departure from the metrically faithful declamation of the earlier songs, which is epitomized in the metrically regular *Volkslied* quality of 'Der Tag ist vergangen' (Op. 12 No. 1).

The Trakl fragments from 1915 also feature a new technique of developing more extended motives. In 'In der Heimat', audible

---

taken into account; in 3/4 time, for example, the 'beat' can be either the quarter-note or the dotted half, depending on the tempo. Webern normally designated the basic pulse in his fair copies from these years, though usually without a metronome mark. When there is no tempo or beat indication in the earliest fair copy, I have used the markings in the published scores. In the case of unpublished works or fragments, I have deduced the basic pulse and tempo. When there is a change of beat within a composition, I have kept the unit of measurement constant by finding a note-value in the new metre which corresponds as closely as possible to the previous unit.

[5] By comparison, the aphoristic songs 'Leise Düfte' and 'O sanftes Glühn' (both from 1913) take 64 and 55 beats respectively.

melodic motives travel between voice and piano parts, an interchange
of function that seems to reach beyond the technique of the instrumental miniatures back to the imitative passages of 'Dies ist ein
Lied' (Op. 3 No. 1). In the fragment Webern achieves a tighter link
between music and text, as the motivic unfolding comes directly out
of the treatment of one word. Therefore the poetic text influenced
and perhaps even determined the musical technique used. A motive
associated with the first word of the poem recurs melodically in both
voice and piano, subverting the fragment's predominantly chordal
texture. The second Trakl fragment from 1915, 'In den Nachmittag
geflüstert', is quite brief at only twelve measures. But it is clear none
the less that Webern tried a different approach; instead of predominantly chordal textures, as in 'In der Heimat', one finds in
'Nachmittag' two- and three-voice counterpoint. Linear writing in all
parts, rare in his music up to this time, was to become fundamental
to Webern's technique in later years (and, as we have seen, to his
habit of sketching line by line). As in any time of transition, it is
difficult to point to unambiguous examples of the 'early phase' or the
'later' one. Webern's compositions from 1915 display a mixture of
early practices with later ones. This mixture sometimes causes clashes;
the fragments remained unfinished, one might argue, because of an
incompatibility between his intention to write longer pieces and the
technique he employed to achieve this.

'In der Heimat': Poem

Webern chose for his most radical experiments in vocal rhythm a text
in one of the strictest poetic forms: a classical German sonnet. The
fourteen lines of 'In der Heimat', with five iambic feet per line, are
divided into two quartets and a sestet, which exhibit the rhyme-
scheme ABBA ABBA CDD CEE. Webern's fragment covers exactly
half of the sonnet (seven lines, up to 'zerfliesst'). The longest rest
separates the two stanzas (between 'verwirrt' and 'Im Spülicht');
another break divides the first stanza in half.

In der Heimat (In the Homeland)[6]

Resedenduft durchs kranke Fenster irrt;
Ein alter Platz, Kastanien schwarz und wüst.
Das Dach durchbricht ein goldener Strahl und fließt
Auf die Geschwister traumhaft und verwirrt.

Im Spülicht treibt Verfallnes, leise girrt
Der Föhn im braunen Gärtchen; sehr still genießt

[6] DTV 35, trans. after Lucia Getsi, 62–5.

Ihr Gold die Sonnenblume und zerfließt.
Durch blaue Luft der Ruf der Wache klirrt.

Resedenduft. Die Mauern dämmern kahl.
Der Schwester Schlaf ist schwer. Der Nachtwind wühlt
In ihrem Haar, das mondner Glanz umspült.

Der Katze Schatten gleitet blau und schmal
Vom morschen Dach, das nahes Unheil säumt,
Die Kerzenflamme, die sich purpurn bäumt.

Fragrance of *Reseden* strays through the sick window;
An old square, chestnut trees black and wasted.
A ray of gold breaks through the roof and flows,
Dreamlike and bewildered, over brother and sister.

Decayed things float in the gutter, the wind
Coos softly in the small brown garden; so quietly
The sunflower enjoys its gold and expires.
The watchman's cry rings through the blue air.

Fragrance of *Reseden*. Bare walls grow dark.
The sister's sleep is troubled. The night wind stirs
Her hair, washed with moonlight.

Slender shadow of the cat glides blue and gaunt
From the mouldered roof, edged by approaching ruin,
Flames of candles leaping purple.

In the second stanza the pentameter is displaced. Though visually
arranged in five-stress lines as in the first stanza, the second stanza
sets up a cross-rhythm of 3, 5, and 7 stresses corresponding to the
syntactical units:

(5) Im **Spülicht treibt** Verfallnes,
leise girrt | (6) Der **Föhn** im **braunen Gärtchen**;
sehr **still genießt** | (7) **Ihr Gold** die **Sonnenblume** (und) zerfließt.

Webern's setting reflects this disruption of metre; the vocal line
follows the syntax, not the literal five-stress line. Even though he did
not complete the second stanza, he continued until the end of a
sentence.

In the poem's first line, we are directed to the smell of the *Resede*,
a green-flowering plant. Throughout the text, almost all the images
are non-solid, yet perceptible: smells, wind, sounds, and light from
the sun and moon. The *Resede* smell which wafts through the window
in the first stanza is more than just the fragrance of a flower. This
flower is of the *Mohn* (poppy) family, which for Trakl would have a
clear association with the drug opium, to which Trakl is known to

have been addicted.[7] In his poems, the drug is evoked by words such as 'Resede' or 'Mohn', and is also often associated with incestuous love, another recurring image in Trakl's poetry:

  1 Resedenduft durchs kranke Fenster irrt [. . .]
  3 Das Dach durchbricht ein goldner Strahl und fließt
  4 Auf die Geschwister traumhaft und verwirrt.

In other poems in *Gedichte* (1913), Trakl uses the image of the *Resede* in conjunction with eroticism. In Part 5 of 'Die Junge Magd', the woman wakes up in a bed filled with golden light, then smells the *Resede* flowers through the window:

          Schmächtig hingestreckt im Bette
50   Wacht sie auf voll süßem Bangen
          Und sie sieht ihr schmutzig Bette
          Ganz von goldnem Licht verhangen,
          Die Reseden dort am Fenster
          Und den bläulich hellen Himmel,
55   Manchmal trägt der Wind ans Fenster
          Einer Glocke zag Gebimmel.[8]

Here, as in 'In der Heimat', the *Resede* plant is near the window, while golden light flows over a bed. A more compressed version of the same image occurs in 'Verwandlung' (also in this volume):

10   Hollunderfrüchte, Flöte weich und trunken,
11   Resedenduft, der Weibliches umspült.[9]

In these poems the traditional Romantic image of the scent of flowers wafting over lovers has been grotesquely distorted by the implications of incest, and also by words such as 'schmutzig Bette', 'kranke Fenster', and even the noun-adjective 'Weibliches', which denatures the person involved and invokes a thing instead.

'In der Heimat' and Earlier Songs: Declamation

Webern's setting of 'In der Heimat' (shown in its entirety in Ex. 5.1) diverges from his earlier practices in several respects, particularly in

---

[7] According to the Brockhaus encyclopedia, this plant is found mainly in the Mediterranean area. One type is called the *Wohlriechende Resede* (sweet-smelling *Resede*) and is used to make fragrant oils. This type was also used in ancient Egypt for death wreaths. From the 18th century on, it was planted in botanical gardens all over Europe. On Trakl's addiction, see Lindenberger, *Georg Trakl*, 22.

[8] 'Stretched out slender on the bed | She awakens full of tender fears | And she sees her soiled bed | Curtained by a golden light, | The *Reseden* just outside the window | And the bright blue sky, | Sometimes the wind brings to the window | The faint sound of a bell.' DTV 11.

[9] 'Fruit of the elder tree, soft drunken flute, | Aroma of *Reseden*, that washes over something feminine.' DTV 24.

Ex. 5.1. 'In der Heimat', entire fragment (PSS, film 103:0736).

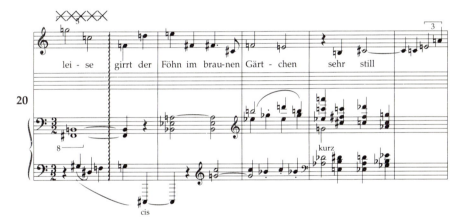

Ex. 5.2. 'In der Heimat'. Musical metre and poetic foot in 1st stanza.

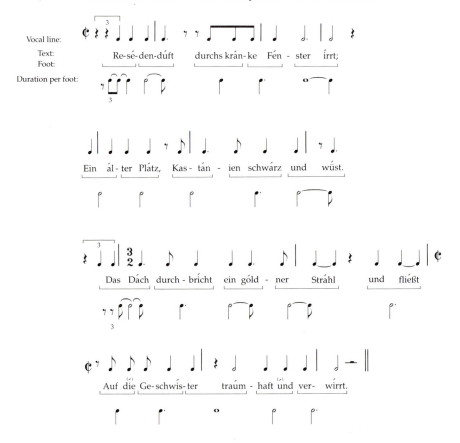

its unusually varied treatment of the vocal part's rhythm. In the first line alone, the length of a poetic foot varies from one quarter-note beat ('durchs krank-') to five ('-ster irrt') (these durations are displayed in Ex. 5.2). A similar compression and elongation occurs in the last line of the first stanza; the first foot takes one beat ('auf die') while the third is extended to four ('-ter traum-'). In the second line, by contrast, each foot receives a half-note. With the juxtaposition of regular and irregular metrical values, Webern's vocal line reflects a similar disjunction between poetic lines. The poem's first line, 'Resedenduft durchs kranke Fenster irrt', describes images both non-specific—the smell of the *Resede* flowers wafting in randomly, by accident—and strange—the surreal combination of the words 'kranke' and 'Fenster'. Webern's correspondingly free declamation distorts the metre by compressing and elongating the length of the poetic foot. The second line, by contrast, presents a consistent, specific visual image; one can easily picture the old town square and the black, wasted chestnut trees. Webern parallels the 'realness' of the image with a regular half-note pulse for each foot. In the last two lines of the stanza this relationship is reversed. From the straightforward visual image of the sunbeam breaking through the roof, the reader is led to a view of the brother and sister; though the adjectives 'traumhaft' and 'verwirrt' literally apply to the sunbeam, they seem to correspond to the mental states of the 'Geschwister' as well. Webern's vocal declamation of the third line continues with a regular metre, now with slightly longer note-value (dotted half-notes instead of half-notes for each foot). The fourth line, like the first, is again made up of unequal pulses; the words 'traumhaft' and 'verwirrt' are especially elongated.

These 'distortions' depart from Webern's earlier practice, in which the poetic foot corresponded closely to a metrical unit in the music.[10] His declamation in the early songs is quite traditional; such linkage between poetic and musical metre is more reminiscent of the songs of Schubert and Brahms than of Webern's nearer predecessor, Hugo Wolf. In Schoenberg's essay 'Brahms the Progressive', he pointed out a similar feature of Brahms's text-setting: 'It is well known that Brahms' aesthetic canon demanded that the melody of a song must reflect, in one way or another, the number of metrical feet in the poem.'[11] The vocal part of Webern's song 'Der Tag ist vergangen' (Op. 12 No. 1) preserves the almost complete identity between poetic foot and musical metre that obtained in Webern's earlier music. Throughout the first stanza, each dactylic foot receives exactly a half-note in value. In the second stanza, as Rudolf Stephan has pointed out, some feet receive more than a half-note and some less, but the average is always two beats.[12] When one unit is compressed, the next is extended to make up the difference. The only place this does not happen is in the last line, where the word 'ewige' (eternal) appropriately receives three times the normal value.

In Op. 13 No. 2 ('Die Einsame'), composed in 1914, Webern's highly flexible, expressive setting relies on the same principle. Here, Webern changes the pace of the foot/metre relationship by doubling

[10] With regard to Webern's songs Op. 3 and Op. 4, for example, Elmar Budde has pointed out the identity between poetic foot and metre, even though the surface rhythm may be quite free. See 'Metrisch-rhythmische Probleme im Vokalwerk Weberns', in Österreichische Gesellschaft für Musik, Beiträge '72–73: Webern-Kongress (Kassel: Bärenreiter, 1973), 57–8.

[11] Schoenberg, Style and Idea, 418.

[12] Rudolf Stephan, 'Zu einigen Liedern', 140–1.

Ex. 5.3. 'Die Einsame' (Bethge), Op. 13/2. Musical metre and poetic foot (2 lines).

or halving the note-values corresponding to a metrical unit. In the first line, 'An dunkelblauem Himmel steht der Mond', no one metrical foot of the poem has the same vocal rhythm, but each represents some variation of the half-note (the rhythms are displayed in Ex. 5.3). In the second line ('ich habe meine Lampe ausgelöscht'), the poem suddenly shifts its point of view from the distant, objective heaven to the earth-bound self.[13] Here Webern sets off the contrast between the two lines by speeding up the preceding pulse by half; each poetic foot now receives a quarter-note duration, rather than a half-note. The faster pulse, together with the low-register, almost monotone vocal part and the designation in the score *ohne Empfindung* ('without feeling'), captures the change of perspective and lends the line a furtive, whispered quality. Throughout the rest of the song, one of the two basic pulses—quarter- or half-note—reigns in each line, even when a particular word is extended for emphasis, such as 'ich weine' in line 4. When the duration of the foot is relatively fixed, a very flexible vocal line made up of many different note-values can be achieved (as Webern does in line 1). By using two different durations for the foot, Webern expands his possibilities enormously; yet already the regularity is beginning to break down.

In the fragments of 1915 Webern moves a step further, towards an almost prose-like freedom. His setting of the first line of the text, 'Resedenduft durchs kranke Fenster irrt', may seem wilfully contrary to the natural rhythms of the words, but it concretely illustrates their sense. The word 'Resedenduft' is separated metrically from the rest of the first line (see Ex. 5.1), its unaccented first syllable emphasized

---

[13] 'The moon stands in the deep blue heavens | I have put out my lamp'.

by its placement on the highest note of the line, F⁵. Here Webern sets this word apart just as Trakl does later, at the beginning of the sestet of the poem.

After the word 'Resedenduft' is given such a poignant, isolated setting, the rest of the line follows in a sudden burst of activity which finally slows to a standstill. The last word of the line, 'irrt', is delayed from what one would expect, due to the unusual emphasis on the second unaccented syllable of 'Fen*ster*'. Webern's original placement of the word 'irrt'—as a quarter-note falling on the last beat of m. 5—would have given it even less metrical emphasis. He moved the syllable to the down-beat of the next measure (adding a substantial leap as well), where it gains length but not metrical clarity, since the strong beat is not reinforced by the piano. Even in its final version the flexible vocal rhythm of the line literally evokes the sense of the word 'irren': to stray, rove, or wander.

'In der Heimat': Motivic Organization

Webern's special treatment of the word 'Resedenduft' has distinct consequences for the rest of his musical setting. The pitch-classes associated with the word 'Resedenduft' as it is first presented become the basis for motivic organization in the fragment. Though these pcs become separated from the word itself, they are often heard at their original pitch-level, evoking an audible reminiscence of their original text. The notes permeate the texture of the piece the same way the *Resede* smell is suffused through the world of the poem.

The first four pcs in the voice, sung on the word 'Resedenduft', are F–A–F♯–E; I will call these, in any order, the *Resedenduft* cell. Webern derives this motive from the piano introduction, in which four pitches stand out because of their registers: F♯–D in the top notes of the right-hand chords, and F–E from the left-hand part (this is shown in Ex. 5.4). Three of these pcs become the main notes in the

Ex. 5.4. 'In der Heimat'. Schema of opening bars.

mm.1-2

Re - se - den - duft

3

8

voice's opening gesture, as the piano's F–F♯–(D)–E turns into F–(A)–F♯–E (in terms of pitch-class sets, these are the closely related 0,1,2,4 (inverted) and 0,1,2,5, respectively). There is a voice exchange between vocal line and piano; the top F in the voice comes from the F three octaves below, while the vocal F♯ comes from the previous F♯⁵ an octave higher. Thus, the vocal line—a descending linear gesture—concretizes what was latent in the chordal piano introduction. The connection between voice and piano would be even more audible if, as Webern had originally written in this sketch, he had doubled the F and F♯ in the voice; these notes in the piano part in mm. 3 and 4 are crossed out (see Ex. 5.1).

In the second phrase of 'In der Heimat', the *Resedenduft* cell returns to the domain of the piano, though it is now influenced by the voice's statement. In m. 6, the piano sounds A, the only pc it lacked up to now, in octaves sforzando (this pc had also completed the total chromatic in the voice's opening gesture). In the right hand, F♯–D–F are sounded simultaneously; these equal the first two events in the piano (outer voices); they also recall the first three notes of the vocal *Resedenduft* cell, inverted. Here the disparate natures of the two parts, piano and voice, are brought together again in a different way. The piano sounds a note which 'belonged' formerly only to the voice (A), while at the same time it verticalizes a formerly vocal, linear, gesture. In the subsequent phrase, the material in both hands moves in returning-note patterns: the bass motion of a minor third (C♯–E–C♯) in mm. 6–8 expands upon the more concise minor third returning-note figure in the first measure. The right-hand chord in m. 6 moves up a semitone (m. 7) and then returns (m. 8), echoing the oscillation in the bass. The piano, after a veiled allusion to some vocal material in m. 6, continues solidly in 'its' world of chordal textures and returning-note figures. The second line of the poem ends with a cadential chord that is reminiscent—in terms of pitch-class, prominent intervals, and spacing—of the chords in m. 1.

Between lines two and three of the poem is a brief piano interlude (Ex. 5.1, mm. 9–10), which states a reordered version of the original *Resedenduft* cell (F–A–E–F♯). This is a spatial inversion of the opening vocal gesture; the four pcs ascend from an extremely low register, instead of descending as before. Though the register and contour have been changed, these pcs recall their first setting, at the word 'Resedenduft'. This interlude sums up not only the *Resedenduft* cell, but also the earlier material from which it was drawn. The first five pcs include the four outer-voice notes in the piano introduction, while the sixth (G♯) was also the partner of F in the opening measure. In fact, the low F of the gesture (F¹) is in the same register as the F in

m. 1; the entire interlude could be seen as a simultaneous reinterpretation of the first vocal and piano gestures:

mm. 9–10	F	A	E	F♯	D	G♯
m. 3 voice	F	A	F♯	E		
mm. 1–2 pf.	F♯				D	
	F				A♭ F	

In the third phrase (mm. 10–12), the *Resedenduft* cell returns—
again reordered—at '[gold]ner Strahl': F–F♯–A. In the piano part
immediately before that, the first two pcs of the motive are heard
exactly in the order and register in which they originally appeared in
the voice: F^5–A^4. The third phrase exhibits other parallels with the
first: the vocal line at 'auf die Ge[schwister]' is a transposition a tone
lower of 'durchs kranke . . .', in the same rhythm. Also, the piano
part in m. 13 is similar to that of mm. 4–5: the A♭–E♭ fifth recalls
the D♭–A♭ and D–A fifths.

The interlude between the first and second stanzas also recalls the
beginning of the piece. At m. 15, the left hand sounds F–A♭–F♭ in
the same register and rhythm in which the returning notes F–A♭–F
were heard in m. 1. The following low-register chord, marked
sff, reminiscent of the chord in m. 1, reinforces the impression of
starting over again. A hint of a strophic form remains in the open
fourths and fifths of mm. 17–19, paralleling mm. 4–5, although the
next stanza ('Im Spülicht treibt Verfallnes') begins with a contrasting
texture in response to the abrupt shift in tone. The only vestige of the
Resedenduft cell is the transformation heard in the voice in mm. 21–2
('Föhn im braunen Gärtchen'); after this it is not heard again.

Resedenduft cell:	E	F	F♯	A
mm. 21–2	C♯	E	F	F♯

The cell I have described is a 'fixed-pitch' motive: its register,
contour, and texture are varied, but some or all of its pcs are held
constant.[14] The occurrences of the motive in 'In der Heimat' mark
important structural points, such as the beginnings of sections. As a
melodic motive, it is a clearly audible surface feature that functions
as a sort of 'signpost'. Though related to (and possibly derived from)
the chordal material, the *Resedenduft* cell becomes associated with

---

[14] Fixed-pitch motives (motives with invariant pitches) are abundant in many other of
Webern's and Schoenberg's works. One example is discussed by Reinhold Brinkmann in
'Schoenberg und George: Interpretation eines Liedes', *Archiv für Musikwissenschaft*, 26 (1969),
17. Geoge Perle also shows examples of fixed-pitch motives in Webern's Op. 11 No. 3: *Serial
Composition and Atonality: An Introduction to the Music of Schoenberg, Berg, and Webern*, 3rd
edn. (Berkeley, Calif., 1972), 22–3.

the vocal line, especially with its first word. When it appears in the piano, it is still heard melodically and therefore contrasts with the predominantly chordal textures in that part; as such the melodic cell functions as a kind of quotation from the other part. Two layers of motivic activity result: one predominantly chordal, primarily in the piano, whose pitches undergo all kinds of transformations, and the other predominantly melodic, primarily in the voice, whose pitches remain for the most part fixed.

While the *Resedenduft* cell is part of a technique that enabled Webern to extend the length of a work, the static harmony in this fragment works against that. Many of the sonorities in the piano are constructed symmetrically. The first chord (m. 1) is made up of three minor thirds a tone apart (6–8: 3,5,6,7,8,10). The low-register chord at 'schwarz' (second half of m. 8) is also symmetrical, and shares three pitches—E♭, F♯, and B♭—with the chord in m. 1 (6–Z42: 3,6,9,10,11,0). The same three notes occur in another symmetrical sonority at 'und fließt' (6–Z28: 9,10,0,2,3,6). Symmetrical chords like these play a prominent role in Webern's earlier music; among many instances is the chord in the first measure of 'Dies ist ein Lied' (Op. 3 No. 1), but they are to become less frequent in the middle-period songs. In this 1915 fragment, Webern combined old and new techniques; he used symmetrical chords, while at the same time trying to extend the piece's length by motivic development. These two techniques, one controlling the vertical, the other the horizontal, were apparently difficult to reconcile, as this fragmentary effort shows.

The kind of motivic development that Webern tried in 'In der Heimat' was an important change from his earlier technique of using instrumental-derived motives, as in 'Die Einsame' (Op. 13 No. 2) from 1914. In this piece Webern uses a recurring figure that does not rely on specific pcs; its identity depends more on a characteristic melodic shape than upon its pcs or even its intervallic structure. Like the *Resedenduft* cell in the fragment, the opening figure of 'Die Einsame', played by the cello in m. 1, recurs several times in the piece. (Some of these recurrences are displayed in Ex. 5.5.) First, when a varied statement of this figure is heard in m. 11, it marks the beginning of a new section. The parallelism with the beginning is so strong that it seems that Webern's strategy is a kind of strophic form. The figure is next heard in the trumpet, transposed, immediately before the climax of the piece (mm. 26–7). As an 'aftershock', the clarinet sounds an intervallically expanded version of the cello figure in mm. 29–30, which is the only statement of the motive that starts on the original starting pitch, C♯, here two octaves higher.

The 'cello figure' in 'Die Einsame' is like the *Resedenduft* cell in

Ex. 5.5. 'Die Einsame' (Bethge), Op. 13/2. Development of 'cello figure'.

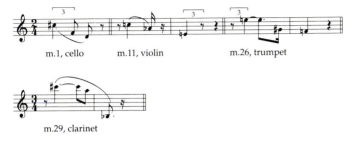

m.1, cello   m.11, violin   m.26, trumpet

m.29, clarinet

the sense that both are surface features which delineate the audible form of the piece. They differ however in that the 'cello figure' is not a fixed-pitch motive; the *Resedenduft* cell, by contrast, is identified solely by its pitch content; it is heard in different contours, rhythms, and registers. Therein lies its flexibility. Since the cell is freed from a specific melodic shape or order, it can permeate equally the voice and piano parts. The 'cello figure' of 'Die Einsame', on the other hand, is not heard in the vocal line at all.

Earlier Webern songs drew their vocal material from the instrument(s); the vocal part, though always the primary line in the texture, matched the instrumental parts more closely. To connect the vocal line with the instruments, yet assure their separate identities, becomes one of Webern's central compositional tasks in the years to come. The techniques he experimented with in his Trakl fragments from 1915 came to fruition in his later songs, especially Op. 14, in which he achieved a balance between vocal- and instrumental-derived motives. Fixed-pitch references remain to mark beginnings of sections and climaxes, but the primary means of development is through transposition and inversion of motives. In the fragment 'In der Heimat', the vocal line generates an idea of its own, an idea that originates in a specific word. Here Webern took a first step in the process of integrating instrumental techniques into vocal music.

'In den Nachmittag geflüstert'

This short fragment shows an approach very different from that which Webern took in 'In der Heimat'. Whereas the longer fragment is primarily chordal in texture, 'Nachmittag' takes counterpoint as a possible solution. The counterpoint used is not like that of the later songs, where there is a constant rotation of the twelve pitch-classes, but instead relies to an extraordinary degree on pitch repetitions. (The fragment 'Nachmittag' is shown in Ex. 5.6.)

Ex. 5.6. 'In den Nachmittag geflüstert', entire fragment (PSS, film 103:0739).

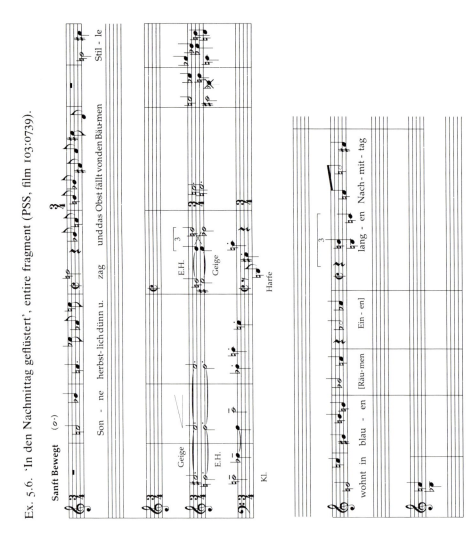

In den Nachmittag geflüstert (Whispered into the Afternoon)[15]

Sonne, herbstlich dünn und zag,	Autumn sun, rare and hesitant,
Und das Obst fällt von den Bäumen.	And fruit drops from the trees.
Stille wohnt in blauen Räumen	Silence dwells in blue spaces,
Einen langen Nachmittag.	A long afternoon.
Sterbeklänge von Metall;	Death bells of metal
Und ein weißes Tier bricht nieder.	And a white animal breaks down.
Brauner Mädchen rauhe Lieder	Brown girls' coarse songs
Sind verweht im Blätterfall.	Are scattered in falling leaves.
Stirne Gottes Farben träumt,	The forehead of God dreams colours,
Spürt des Wahnsinns sanfte Flügel.	Feels the gentle wing of madness.
Schatten drehen sich am Hügel	Shadows whirl upon the hill
Von Verwesung schwarz umsäumt.	Fringed black with decay.
Dämmerung voll Ruh und Wein;	Dusk full of sleep and wine;
Traurige Guitarren rinnen.	Mournful guitars flow.
Und zur milden Lampe drinnen	And as if in a dream
Kehrst du wie im Traume ein.	You turn toward the mellow lamp within.

The poem, like other poems in Trakl's *Gedichte* (1913), is in strict form; each of its four quatrains has the rhyme-scheme ABBA, and each line contains four trochaic stresses. As with 'In der Heimat', the recurring metres and rhymes seem inconsistent with the force of the images portrayed. After an almost pastoral first stanza that depicts an autumn afternoon outdoors, the second stanza introduces the violent urban sound of 'Sterbeklänge von Metall'. This outburst is not integrated into the scene or provided with its own context; the following three lines return to the outdoor scene, which now has a distinct aura of decay. In the third stanza the poet observes the nature scene through the fog of his personal madness; he imagines 'Stirne Gottes Farben träumt', and even remarks on his lack of clear perception: 'Spürt des Wahnsinns sanfte Flügel'. In the fourth stanza the afternoon has become a more comforting twilight ('Dämmerung voll Ruh und Wein'), while the narrator—who has shifted voice from an impersonal narration to addressing an unnamed 'du'—turns away both from the hallucinations and from the outdoors ('Und zur milden Lampe drinnen | Kehrst du wie im Traume ein').

Webern set only the first stanza, which does not yet feature the images of decay that saturate the rest of the poem. Each of the four lines contributes something to the picture, but they are syntactically

---

[15] DTV 31–2, trans. after Lucia Getsi, 56–7.

Ex. 5.7. 'In den Nachmittag'. Musical metre and poetic foot in 1st stanza.

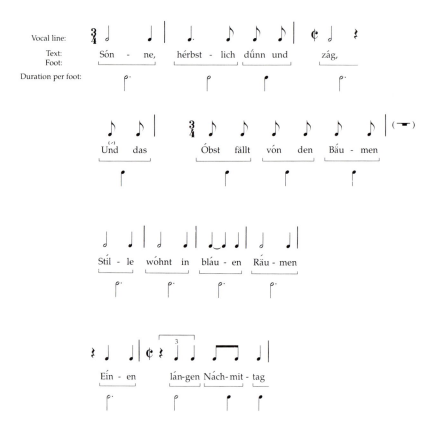

disjunct. The first two lines present two unconnected visual images, while the third and fourth lines bring in sound (or more accurately the lack of it, 'Stille') and also a sense of extended space and time ('Stille wohnt in blauen Räumen | Einen langen Nachmittag'). The declamation of the vocal line in Webern's fragment reflects the un-relatedness of these lines by giving each a distinct rhythmic profile (this is shown in Ex. 5.7). The second line is declaimed so fast (each poetic foot receiving one quarter-note's duration) that at the tempo implied by 'Sanft Bewegt (gently moving) ♩.' it would sound like the furtive whispering mentioned in the title. In contrast to this, Webern broadens out the third line until it is four times as long as its pre-decessor. The first line, 'Sonne, herbstlich dünn und zag', contains most of the other rhythms used in the fragment and therefore has a rather irregular declamation.

The relative freedom of the vocal part is counterbalanced by instrumental writing that is spare and metrically regular. The fragment begins with violin, cor anglais, and clarinet,[16] the latter see-sawing between C and A♭, almost creating an ostinato effect before it descends to G in m. 3. This figure resembles the opening measure of 'Der Tag ist vergangen' (Op. 12 No. 1, also from this year), which also features A♭–C as returning tones. In the earliest version of Op. 12 No. 1, however, there are 12 tones in 16 attacks,[17] while in 'Nachmittag' the accompaniment is virtually static for three measures. The vocal part is also repetitive; nearly every measure returns to a note used in the measure before. For example, the down-beats of mm. 6, 7, and 8 all sound the same pc, E, in half-notes. The sketch of 'Nachmittag' breaks off after several measures of two-part writing between violin and cor anglais. Here Webern seems to have changed his approach; each sonority uses a new pc and forms a new interval. The problem—the reason he didn't finish it—could be that he had not yet worked out how to maintain the total chromatic in a contrapuntal context.

For this type of free atonal counterpoint was new to Webern in 1915. His earlier miniatures are not contrapuntal, and could not be. Their effectiveness depends on the juxtaposition of non-overlapping musical ideas. The pieces are short, because the ear must be able to hold each gesture in the mind simultaneously and relate it to every other gesture.[18] In later songs, Webern was able to develop the kind of counterpoint he attempted in this fragment. In 'Ein Winterabend' (Op. 13 No. 4, composed 1918–22), for example, there is a passage of three-voice counterpoint in mm. 3–5 (at 'lang die Abendglocke läutet') that does not encounter the same problems as 'Nachmittag', because the separate lines are controlled harmonically by a vertical sonority. This sonority, made up of a tritone and a semitone (set-class 0,1,6), results from the conjunction of the three lines, and is heard almost every eighth-note. The tritone and semitone chord controls the counterpoint, just as tonal harmony does in a Bach fugue.

WHY ARE THEY FRAGMENTS?

Webern was only able to complete two pieces in 1915: 'Der Tag ist vergangen' (Rosegger, Op. 12 No. 1) and 'Schien mir's' (Strindberg, Op. 12 No. 3). The two Trakl fragments from 1915 remained incom-

---

[16] The stave above the instrumental parts is also scored up, presumably to allow space for more instruments.

[17] Later Webern revised this passage to consist of 12 tones in 14 attacks.

[18] Even in works that seem contrapuntal, such as Op. 5 No. 3, the parts function more as overlapping, quasi-independent layers than as truly interdependent polyphonic voices.

plete, as did his preliminary sketches for 'In der Fremde' (Bethge) and 'Wiese im Park' (Kraus), though the latter two were eventually taken up again and rewritten (as Op. 13 No. 3 and No. 1 respectively). The reasons could have been practical ones relating to Webern's military service and the turmoil of the war years. Another reason, in addition to the musical reasons already discussed, could have been the length of the poems he attempted; the two that were completed are by far the briefest.

The strict style of Trakl's early poems may have created a special problem; their regularity belies the near-anarchy of the images. While this tension between form and content can bring a written poem alive—indeed this is partly what makes Trakl's earlier poetry so powerful—it can cause difficulties in a musical setting. We have seen that Webern was always sensitive to the structure of a poem, mirroring its stanza and line divisions. He used a modified strophic form in music when necessary to reflect the strophic regularity of a poem, such as in 'Der Tag ist vergangen' (Op. 12 No. 1). At the same time, in these 1915 fragments Webern tried to give each particular image, such as 'Resedenduft' ('In der Heimat') and 'herbstlich dünn und zag' ('In den Nachmittag geflüstert'), a characteristic musical profile, either motivically or rhythmically. It is difficult to be equally responsive to both levels; the force of such an individual musical idea created to reflect a certain word or image can work against developing regular patterns of declamation and stanza-structure. Webern's free declamation of Trakl's highly metrical early poetry in fact disguises the poem's original rhythm beyond all recognition. His settings draw out the musical potential of Trakl's rhymed poetry by setting the vivid individual images and not their overall form, therefore 'liberating' the content from the restrictions of poetic convention. When Webern set Trakl in later years, he had the mature free verse poetry at his disposal, in which form and syntax are also irregular.

But the main obstacle to completion of the Trakl fragments was not the poetry, but instead Webern's musical language of the time—the language of the instrumental miniatures—which was not capable of supporting a piece of extended length. Vertical construction, often with symmetrical chords and brief juxtaposed gestures, is highly characteristic of the earlier aphorisms. In 'In der Heimat', Webern uses the same techniques to write an extended vocal piece; his solution is to tie the chords together with a unifying cell. But how long can one develop a fixed-pitch motive? The use of a motive which depends on the same pitch-classes for its identity is necessarily limited; given the basic assumption of Webern and his contemporaries that music must create variety within unity, one cannot structure a long piece without transposing and otherwise altering the motives. Perhaps the vertical force was stronger than the horizontal; in order to sustain an extended length, the piece would have needed either more linear, horizontal elements, or else, succumbing to the vertical mode, more isolated gestures to be developed through juxtaposition.[19] In the other fragment, 'In den Nachmittag geflüstert', Webern tried a more purely contrapuntal approach, but may have had difficulties avoiding too much pitch repetition. The two fragments aim to combine two genres, that of the instrumental miniature and contrapuntal song. The former technique, though powerful, was not the right one for composing an extended piece, while the latter was not yet developed enough. In his later songs, Webern was to find the solution, a synthesis of the two.

[19] Later, the concept of identity between material presented horizontally and vertically was to become an important part of Webern's thinking about his twelve-tone music. Regina Busch discusses this in 'On the Horizontal and Vertical Presentation of Musical Ideas', part 1, 2–10, and part 2, 7–15.

6. The Ostinato Fragments

> I am now hard at work. I think it is going well again. And I hope
> it will last. . . . I am gradually gaining clarity again. For that I
> thank your 'Pierrot'!
>
> (Webern to Schoenberg, 24 June 1917)[1]

> I have made good progress. Schoenberg confirmed it. Now I am
> writing very differently. . . . Closed (homogeneous) sound, in part
> long themes, something completely different from before the
> war.
>
> (Webern to Berg, 18 Aug. 1917)[2]

In the summer of 1917, Webern had become convinced that his music
had substantially changed. Two years earlier, he had already begun
to experiment with longer motives and time spans in several extended
fragments (including Trakl's 'In der Heimat' and 'In den Nachmittag
geflüstert'). And after serving two extended stints in the army and
experiencing the war first hand, he might well have approached
composition differently from before. But Webern's evaluation of his
music as 'something completely different from before the war' seems
exaggerated in the light of the published works from this year. The
piano songs, 'Die geheimnisvolle Flöte' and 'Gleich und Gleich' (Op.
12 Nos. 2 and 4), are hardly path-breaking; their musical language is
remarkably consistent with that of the other Op. 12 songs composed
two years earlier. Two other songs, 'Wiese im Park' (Op. 13 No. 1)
and 'In der Fremde' (Op. 13 No. 3), feature a slightly larger scale,
but their instrumentation, form, and motivic construction differ only
in degree from pre-war compositions such as Two Songs, Op. 8 or
'Die Einsame' (Op. 13 No. 2).

Webern's unfinished pieces from 1917, on the other hand, are so
extraordinary that his assertions about change seem understated. In
these fragments (listed in Table 8), he embarked on a series of

---

[1] 'Ich bin jetzt gut im Arbeiten drin. Ich glaube, es ist mir wieder was gelungen. Und ich
hoffe, es wird anhalten. . . . Ich gewinne allmählich wieder Klarheit. Das verdanke ich Deinem
"Pierrot"!' *Anton Webern 1883–1983*, 70–1.

[2] 'Ich bin auf gute Wege gekommen. Schönberg bestätigte es. Jetzt schreibe ich schon ganz
anders. . . . Geschlossener Klang, lange Themen zum Teil, überhaupt ganz was anderes als vor
dem Krieg.' *Anton Webern 1883–1983*, 71.

TABLE 8. Sketches with Ostinato

Name and film no. (PSS)	Date	Description
Trakl poems:		
'Verklärung' (103:0749)	1917	LH: repeated tritone (B–F); 6/8
'Verklärung' (103:0745)	[1917]	Upper voice, 3-note figure for 4 mm.; 6/8
'Amsel' ('new sketches', 2 pages, and 101:0600)	1917	Repeated chord, 3 mm. (7–10), two chords alternating (13a–15a)
'Siebengesang' (103:0752)	1917	Repeated chords, 3 mm. (6–9)
'Nachtergebung' (103:0755)	[1917]	Ostinato, marked by signs in LH
'Nachtergebung' (103:0756)	[1917]	Tritone ostinato in bass cl., 3 mm.
Unknown texts:		
Orchestra song, no text (103:0827)	1917	Repeated figure in harp, 5 mm.
Unknown, no text (101:0598)	[1917]	Entire pf. acc. is repetitive—drone sketches in bass. D major key signature

experiments with repetitive structures, especially ostinato. In many (including several incomplete Trakl settings), he explored the tonal implications that may result from repetition of a few pitches. The work of this summer formed a turning-point; Webern's efforts to superimpose ostinatos led to the development of the contrapuntal style that was to be the basis for almost all his future music. Remarkably, the changes do not result in a more 'advanced' musical language, but indicate instead an assimilation of earlier styles.

That Webern experimented with ostinato is not surprising in itself. The Second Viennese School's fondness for the technique can be observed in many works, including the first movement of Schoenberg's *Five Pieces for Orchestra*, Op. 16, the first scene of *Die glückliche Hand*, the first of Berg's *Altenberg-Lieder*, Webern's *Five Movements* for string quartet, Op. 5 No. 5, and many others. Ostinato in free atonal music provides aural coherence and at the same time articulates formal divisions.

The ostinatos in Webern's 1917 fragments differ, however, in several respects from those in his earlier works. Instead of drawing upon atonal ostinato technique, these fragments look back still earlier, to the tonal transition that occurred around 1908–9. One difference is that the fragments from 1917 unbalance the equilibrium maintained in earlier atonal ostinatos, such as that in Op. 7 No. 3. Here the recurring ascending figure in the violin seems unrelated to the melody

Ex. 6.1. 'Verklärung' No. 3, vocal line, mm. 1–5 (PSS, film 103:0745).

Wenn es   A - bend wird   ver-läßt dich   lei-se ein blau-es   Ant - litz   [ein klei- ner]

and to the sustained bass note, but the different layers complement each other by providing pitch-classes that the others lack. They are therefore balanced and interdependent; the relationship between them is not similar, but symbiotic.[3] An ostinato risks destroying the delicate balance between the twelve pitch-classes, and in 1917 Webern openly explores the possibilities of this disruption. By stressing certain pitches, sometimes to the point of creating tonal centres, the 1917 ostinatos recall techniques used in the first years of atonality. Second, the ostinato fragments are striking for their emphasis on the bass. While tonal music depends on the bass for everything from articulation of tonality to phrase-structure, atonal music commonly assumes that all registers function equally. In the atonal repertoire, a motive may appear horizontally or vertically, melodically or un-ordered, and in any register.

Other parallels to earlier styles can be seen in some of the fragments' vocal lines. In sketches for 'Nachtergebung' and 'Siebengesang des Todes' from 1917, voice parts are sometimes literally doubled, and at other times echoed by the instruments. In one of the 'Verklärung' fragments, to take just one passage, the vocal line often repeats pitches (shown in Ex. 6.1). After the G–F♯ at 'leise' is echoed down an octave at 'Antlitz', these two notes also begin the next phrase, 'ein kleiner Vogel'. This amount of pitch repetition is unusual, since by 1917 Webern's vocal parts were normally much less redundant.

Why did Webern return, even temporarily, to a musical language he had already left behind? By examining the following fragments and works, I hope to show how Webern deliberately worked through traditional techniques, restoring repetition, weighting of pitches, and hierarchical textures to his vocabulary. Though the experiment was short-lived, some of these elements found their way into some completed works, including Webern's first completed setting of a Trakl poem. Reconciling his 'modern' atonal language with aspects of the earlier one set the stage for the completion of Op. 14, whose character

---

[3] See Arnold Whittall, 'Webern and Atonality: The Path from the Old Aesthetic', *Musical Times*, 124 (1983), 733–7.

Ex. 6.2. Orchestra song, no text, mm. 1–6 (PSS, film 103:0827).

of 'Rückkunft ohne Zurückweichen' ('returning without retreating')
Adorno so trenchantly observed.[4]

AN APPARENT IMITATION OF *PIERROT LUNAIRE*

In an unusual fragment from the spring of 1917, Webern attempted a
quite conventional ostinato piece following a model by Schoenberg.
This fragment features a long ostinato passage, and, atypically, no
clear vocal line, though it is meant to be a song (the first six measures

---

[4] Adorno, 'Anton von Webern', 119.

are shown in Ex. 6.2).[5] The two ostinato chords repeat in ascending arpeggios, which maintain the same steady sixteenth-note rhythm for five measures. The ascending fifth (G–D), sounded twice in every measure, inevitably asserts a tonal centre no matter how much the upper voices contradict it. Webern even uses the harp in its traditional role of playing arpeggios, instead of his usual punctuating, percussive style for the instrument. Solo melodies played by flute and violin form the upper voices, whose rhythmic regularity confirms the ostinato's 6/8 metre.

Though its tonality is traditional, the fragment's steady metre, defined and reinforced by the ostinato, contrasts markedly with Webern's earlier atonal practices. In works such as Op. 5 No. 5, the layers are static, not forward-moving, and their interaction relies paradoxically on their being kept apart. Instead of distinct levels that interact but do not coincide, in the 1917 fragment all the parts articulate the metre together. The up-beat to m. 6, which is sustained by a fermata, even adds a 'Viennese' lilt to the ensuing down-beat.

The fragment closely resembles No. 20, 'Heimfahrt', from Schoenberg's *Pierrot Lunaire* (shown in Ex. 6.3). 'Heimfahrt' is a barcarole; its pizzicato arpeggios are very similar to Webern's harp part. Both ostinatos consist of sixteenth-notes in 6/8 time, with a bottom interval of an open fifth. In both pieces the ostinato lasts exactly five measures before changing. Webern even takes over the pitch and instrument of Schoenberg's first melodic note, $C\sharp^5$ in the flute, for the beginning of his melody.

The correspondences between the fragment and Schoenberg's piece go even farther, suggesting a direct imitation. For example, Schoenberg counteracted the tonal tendencies of his bass-line by providing the rest of the total chromatic in the upper voices. (The flute fills in one note lacking in the ostinato, and the first clarinet gesture provides the others.) Webern adopted the same strategy. The two ostinato chords together, in close position, create a nine-note chromatic space from C to A♭, with only C♯ and F♯ missing. The flute and violin sound these two notes, as well as the remaining three of the total chromatic, in the first measure. As in the Schoenberg piece, the upper voices of the Webern fragment complement the ostinato, therefore contradicting—without completely nullifying—the tonal implication of the fifth in the bass.

The method Webern uses to dissolve the ostinato is also Schoen-

---

[5] This is apparent from the blank stave with a treble clef above the instrumental staves, as well as a brief gesture at the bottom of the page marked 'Ges.' for 'Gesang'. The sketch is dated '1917, Hietzing'; the place-name indicates that it was made in the early part of the year.

Ex. 6.3. Schoenberg, *Pierrot Lunaire*, 'Heimfahrt', No. 20, mm. 1–3.

Ex. 6.4. Orchestra song, no text, two versions of m. 6 (PSS, film 103:0827).

bergian. In his first two attempts, he began the ostinato figure as before, then let it slide down chromatically in four-part chords (m. 6*a* is shown in Ex. 6.2, mm. 6*b* and 6*c* in Ex. 6.4). The third try breaks up the chromatic chords, using only half of them in a jagged, discontinuous reminiscence. Schoenberg called this technique 'liquidation', a word describing the dissolution of a motive by gradually stripping away the components that give it a characteristic profile; this is found often in Schoenberg's early music, particularly in the First Chamber Symphony and the Second String Quartet. Webern's own motivic technique is normally quite different; when he repeats or modifies motives, they are disguised, usually beyond immediate recognition. To make a verbal analogy, Webern's motives suggest and imply, while Schoenberg's narrate. It is surprising that Webern would try to copy the technique of 'liquidation'—so unlike his usual practices—as late as 1917.

Moreover, by trying to work within the conventional form of the barcarole, Webern avoided one of his most habitual practices. Unlike virtually every other song Webern wrote or sketched, in this fragment the vocal line is clearly subsidiary; it is not even part of the original conception. When he does sketch its rhythm at the end, the pitches are still undefined. The sketch disintegrates into a series of rhythmic notations. It is even possible that Webern had no specific text in mind. Since Webern's composition in this period was driven primarily by his encounters with and reactions to particular poems, and the vocal line—therefore the text—is usually the leading part in a sketch, the lack of a specific verbal impetus alone would have doomed the piece to its fragmentary status.

Webern's imitation was overt and evidently intentional. In a letter to Schoenberg, Webern wrote that he had brought along scores of *Pierrot*, *Erwartung*, and the *George-Lieder*: 'I am almost exclusively occupied with your music. Every day I play in these works.'[6] About a week later he wrote again to Schoenberg with an enthusiastic report: 'I am gradually gaining clarity again. For that I thank your "Pierrot"!'[7] And on September 12 the same year, he confirmed that, 'Now I have actually tried again to copy your "Pierrot" directly.'[8] Since Webern's 'barcarole' fragment was probably sketched in the spring of 1917, his comments from later that year show that his involvement with *Pierrot* was an ongoing preoccupation.

[6] '...bin fast ausnahmslos mit Deiner Musik beschäftigt. Jeden Tag spiele ich in diesen Werken.' Moldenhauer, *Anton von Webern*, 266 (Ger., 240).
[7] *Anton Webern 1883–1983*, 70–1.
[8] 'Erst heuer wieder habe ich doch eigentlich versucht direckt Deinen "Pierrot" zu copieren.' Moldenhauer, *Anton von Webern* (Ger.), 241.

But why would Webern need to imitate Schoenberg in order to improve his already mature technique? He had, after all, completed his studies almost ten years earlier. Schoenberg's psychological hold over Webern remained strong, however, reaching its peak the next year, when Webern followed Schoenberg to Mödling, ignoring the practical necessity of earning his own living. Another reason for the exercise might have been to develop his atonal contrapuntal techniques (for which *Pierrot* is a veritable catalogue), in order to be able to write longer pieces. In the same year Webern also completed the polyphonic 'Fahr hin, o Seel'' (Op. 15 No. 5) and 'Abendland III' (Op. 14 No. 4). As a strict double canon, 'Fahr hin, o Seel'' is the most contrapuntal of the six works completed this year; as Webern's first atonal canon, it takes a big step from the earlier double canon, the chorus 'Entflieht auf leichten Kähnen', Op. 2. The scoring—for five instruments and voice—resembles that of *Pierrot*, though its typically Webernian sound palette substitutes muted trumpet and harp for cello and piano. The day before Webern wrote to Schoenberg crediting *Pierrot* with his progress, he had completed 'Abendland III' (Op. 14 No. 4). While not strict counterpoint as in a canon, the tightly knit four-part texture in 'Abendland III' permeates every bar of the piece; there is also a prominent ostinato section. Its instrumentation—E♭ clarinet, bass clarinet, cello—also pays tribute to the *Pierrot* ensemble and contrasts with the many pieces for voice with large ensembles that Webern had written until now.

The fragmentary orchestra song from 1917 shows that the general influence of *Pierrot* that we see in works such as 'Fahr hin, o Seel'' (Op. 15 No. 5) and 'Abendland III' (Op. 14 No. 4) originated in Webern's explicit parody. His obsession with Schoenberg had become so intense that he tried to subjugate his own musical personality, even if only as a study. Though this gave him some useful ideas, in the published works from 1917 Webern ultimately assimilated the lessons of *Pierrot* without overt imitation.

PEDAL-POINT OSTINATOS

The barcarole fragment evidently inspired other experiments with ostinatos. In several other sketches, Webern experimented with simple pedal-points. In two drafts of 'Verklärung' and an untexted fragment, repetition and bass motion imply tonal centres.

'Verklärung' (No. 2)

This short fragment, one of six on this text, has two ostinatos, both functioning as pedal-points (the entire fragment is shown in Ex. 6.5).

Ex. 6.5. 'Verklärung' No. 2, entire fragment (PSS, film 103:0749).

1917

Their tonal function seems deliberate. Over the static bass is a chord
made up of a perfect fourth and major third: what in a tonal context
would be called a 6/4 chord (m. 1). This expands with a whole-tone
neighbour-note motion, then returns to the original chord. In the first
two measures of Ex. 6.5, the left hand of the piano plays a repeated
tritone B–F, and in mm. 5–6, a repeated F–Gb (both sounded in
registers 1 and 2). The first ostinato expands to Bb and G before
'resolving' up a fourth, to Eb, at the end of the phrase. The second
ostinato is followed by C in the bass with G above; this can also be
heard as the logical tonal goal of the original ostinato, B–F. Therefore the ostinatos of the first two bars of each phrase 'resolve' in the
last two. This creates the conventional phrasing of eight bars divided
into 4 + 4; also traditional is the harmonic rhythm, which is slow for
the first two measures, then accelerates for the cadence.

The harmonic motion is carried out by the bass. The vocal line and

Ex. 6.6. 'Eingang' (George), Op. 4/1 (1908–9), m. 1.

Ex. 6.7. 'Am Ufer' (Dehmel) (1906–8), mm. 5–6.

right-hand part of this 'Verklärung' fragment contradict rather than reinforce the tonal tendencies. While the bass asserts E♭ in mm. 3–4, the right hand, if played alone, clearly implies G major in the same measures. Similarly, the C emphasis in the last measure of the fragment is weakened by the voice's F♯ and D. The bass-line occupies its own world, separated rhythmically, registrally, and texturally from the vocal line and right-hand part. This seems at odds with Webern's other music from the time, which assumes an almost complete interchangeability of parts; by 1915, the motives that hold a piece together penetrate vocal and instrumental parts equally. In this 'Verklärung' fragment, Webern continues the earlier practice of separating the functions of each part.

The ostinatos, the implied tonality, and the near-quotation from his song 'Eingang' (Op. 4 No. 1; see Ex. 6.6) lend the fragment an archaic flavour. The striking resemblance between the ostinatos and those in Webern's Dehmel song from 1906–8, 'Am Ufer' (No. 2, mm. 5–7, shown in Ex. 6.7), and the slow movement of Schoenberg's Op. 11 suggests a conscious reaching back to these topoi of early atonal music. At the same time, Webern keeps all twelve pitches (unordered) in circulation. He sets up a chromatic field with one note missing; the absent note is then provided in a strategic place and functions like a resolution.[9] In the first phrase ('Wenn es Abend wird'), the pcs taken together form a set of eight notes, which can be grouped into two chromatic segments of four (8–6: 5,6,7,8,10,11,0,1). The pcs D, E♭, E, heard subsequently in the right hand, fill a gap between the two segments. The remaining note, A, is saved for the beat immediately before the 'arrival' on E♭, just as the ostinato is dissolved. In the second phrase, this happens again. The repeated pitches in the right and left hands taken together (mm. 5 and 6, with C and D♭ from the last beat of m. 4) form an eight-note chromatic group with a whole-tone gap (8–5: 1,2,3,5,6,7,8,9). The missing note, E, again sounds in the left hand immediately before the cadence.

Even though the two eight-note chromatic groups of the two phrases share five pcs (and any two eight-note groups must share at least four pcs), they sound different because the repeated pitches now have different functions. The notes that were in the voice part are now in the piano; what was in the right-hand chords is now (partially) in the ostinato, and the original ostinato notes (B–F) are stretched more than three octaves apart, from the bottom F in the piano to the B in the voice. Because of the changes in emphasis and function, the second phrase has shifted into a different tonal area.

'Verklärung' (No. 3)

Like 'Verklärung' (No. 2), this fragment was an experiment in combining ostinato with tonality (Ex. 6.8).[10] Given that the 'atonal revolution' emancipated rhythm as much as it did the dissonance, both fragments have unusually regular rhythm. Both are in 6/8, and both subdivide this metre clearly in eighth-notes. The down-beats are marked at least by attacks, and often more strongly by agogic or harmonic accents. The longest or highest notes of the vocal line often fall on the down-beats. In tonal music, knowing where the down-beat will come is a large part of comprehending a cadence; Wagner for example used this rhythmic predictability to simulate tonal arrivals when none actually occurs. In both 'Verklärung' fragments, the regular rhythm and metre reinforce the suggestions of tonality. Such

---

[9] Henri Pousseur describes the same procedure with Op. 9, in 'Weberns organische Chromatik (1. Bagatelle)', *Die Reihe*, 2 (1955), 56–65.

[10] This page is undated, but seems to belong with the other 'Verklärung' sketch because of their similar musical construction; in the two sketches, the same ostinato experiment is carried out twice with different results. They are also written on the same type of paper.

Ex. 6.8. 'Verklärung' No. 3, 2nd and 3rd systems (PSS, film 103:0745).

regularity is however unusual in Webern's music, in which the down-beat, indeed all strong beats, often seems consciously concealed.[11]

In contrast to the other fragment on this text, the ostinato in 'Verklärung' No. 3 is melodic while the pedal-point is chordal. This bass motion is even more overtly tonal than in the previous fragment. The prominent bass notes of No. 3 lead downwards in descending fifths: from E♭ (m. 1) to A♭ (m. 4) to D♭ (m. 7). The bass arrivals are all confirmed, to some extent, by the upper parts. In a steady chromatic ascent, the voice finally reaches E♭, doubling the first bass-note just before it slides away chromatically. Over the A♭ are two Cs; an E natural suggests the fifth of a possible augmented triad. In the last measure, the sonority over the D♭ bass is in fact a D♭ major seventh chord (spelled from the bottom: D♭–A♭–C–F (twice)–A♭).[12] In the voice are C and D, half-step neighbours of D♭. Webern revised the chord, weakening its tonal association, by crossing out the A♭–F in the treble clef and the C in the bass.

---

[11] One exception among the published works is 'Der Tag ist vergangen', Op. 12 No. 1, whose metrical regularity is clearly a response to the folksong-like text.

[12] I read the top circled note in the treble clef as A♭, because of the melodic figure, which alternates among the notes B♭, A, and A♭. The A♭ reading is supported by the natural sign on the second A of the last measure. Also, the bass-clef F could possibly be read as an F♭.

Throughout most of this brief fragment, the violin plays an ostinato of unordered notes: Ab, A, and Bb (mm. 1–3, 5–7). These circle around, and emphasize, A, which is a tritone away from the first bass-note Eb. This sets up an 'opposite pole' to the tonal arrival and helps to diminish its force.

One might question whether ostinato technique, with its characteristic 'sameness', is in fact appropriate for depicting such disjunct images as 'ein blaues Antlitz' ('a blue face') and 'ein kleiner Vogel singt im Tamarindenbaum' ('a small bird sings in the tamarind tree'). The slow ostinatos seem to evoke the atmosphere associated with the first line, 'Wenn es Abend wird' ('when dusk falls'), more than the others. Webern's strategy here is the opposite from the way he approached earlier Trakl poems, like the sonnet 'In der Heimat' with its regular metre and rhyme-schemes. There Webern neutralized the poem's structure by distorting its metrical framework. For 'Verklärung', a much freer poem, a setting in two four-bar phrases over a repetitious bass line might seem inconsistent with the poem's expressionistic qualities. But a subtly varied ostinato does bind together the disparate 'scenes' of the poem into a continuous musical texture.

Unidentified Ostinato Fragment with Key Signature

Possibly related to the other ostinato fragments is an unidentified vocal fragment that combines ostinato technique with a pedal-point (Ex. 6.9). This untexted six-bar fragment is remarkable because it carries a key signature of two sharps, and clearly implies D as a tonic. The fragment is undated, but is written on the other side of a sketch for 'Gesang einer gefangenen Amsel' (Op. 14 No. 6), which is dated 1918. Webern's latest published work to bear a key signature is 'Eingang' (Op. 4 No. 1), composed in 1908 or 1909.

A pedal-point (A), which maintains the same rhythm until the penultimate measure, sounds in the bass throughout. The right hand

Ex. 6.9. Unidentified fragment (PSS, film 101:0598).

presents an ostinato made up of three chords: one augmented triad and two major triads (in second inversion). The last chord in each bar is a D major triad, which therefore harmonizes with the A pedal. As we saw in one of the 'Verklärung' fragments, the tritone away from the tonic (G♯) is present in every bar; this partially neutralizes the tonal implications. The G♯ is also used to approach D; the pedal A moves through its chromatic upper and lower neighbours, then cadences, via A♭, on D. Though the vocal line does not participate in the ostinato, it insists repetitively on the note B. The line circles around this pitch until the last measure, where it descends to B♭. (From there it could easily descend a semitone to the dominant.) The tonal motion, though to some extent contradicted by the upper parts, is clear and unequivocal.

Because of the handwriting and general appearance of this fragment, it does not appear to have been written before 1908.[13] It could have been written as late as 1917 to 1919, around the time of the 'Amsel' sketch on the same sheet. The tonality of the fragment would seem to rule out the possibility of such a late date, but the techniques Webern uses here differ only in degree from those we know he explored in the two 'Verklärung' fragments and the untexted orchestra song sketched in 1917. In all of these, tonality is established with the help of bass root progressions, regular rhythm, and ostinatos. Although the untexted fragment has a key signature, it employs the same techniques as other fragments from these years. Webern could well have written it along with his other ostinato and pedal-point experiments. Seen in the light of the other Trakl fragments from 1917, this fragment may not be such an anomaly.

'Nachtergebung'

Not all of the fragments that have ostinato also imply tonal centres. A short fragment on 'Nachtergebung' (No. 2) sustains a tritone ostinato throughout its thirteen-beat duration (shown in Ex. 6.10).[14] Instead of centricity, the idea of chromatic completion is brought to the fore; the fragment breaks off after all twelve pcs have been heard. The first repetition of a pc (D) occurs in the fourth measure (D was also the first pitch heard outside of the ostinato). The pre-

[13] In early songs from 1904–8 (such as 'Aufblick'), Webern's handwriting has a noticeable backward slant; also the note-heads are bigger than in the manuscripts of the 1910s.

[14] The two undated 'Nachtergebung' fragments use types of ostinato very similar to those used in fragments dated 1917. Another fact pointing to a 1917 date is Webern's use of a baritone voice in the first 'Nachtergebung' fragment (PSS, film 103:0755). The only other use of this voice in Webern's output, except in the Second Cantata (1943), is in the Goethe fragment 'Gegenwart' from March 1917.

Ex. 6.10. 'Nachtergebung' No. 2, entire fragment (PSS, film 103:0756).

valence of pitches complementary to the E♭ and A of the ostinato reduces its force as a centre of gravity.

The pcs of the 'Nachtergebung' fragment are moreover all grouped symmetrically around an F♯–C axis. The ostinato notes E♭ and A, equidistant around F♯, set up the axis around which the other pitches revolve.[15] The trombone's first two notes, D–E, and the cello's B♭–A♭ in m. 2 are two whole tones equidistant from a still unheard F♯. The cello starts its first gesture with F (m. 1) and its second with G (m. 3), each a semitone from the axis. In the third measure, the voice enters on the axis pitch F♯, which has been withheld until now. The other axis pitch, C, sounded one beat earlier in the trombone. In spite of its resemblance to the 'Verklärung' fragments, this fragment's axial pitch construction and its symmetrical, static harmonies seem closer to the miniatures, such as the *Bagatelles*, Op. 9, than to any works written after 1917.

In another fragmentary sketch of 'Nachtergebung' (No. 1), Webern uses chordal ostinato instead of a pedal-point (shown in Ex. 6.11). The ostinato initially comprises two six-note chords, grouped into what appears to be right and left hands of the piano. By the second measure, Webern repeats only the bass-clef chords, shifted down an octave. These are now designated for trombone, bass clarinet, and double bass, crossing parts for the second chord (as in 'Eine blasse Wäscherin' from *Pierrot Lunaire*). The two chords are heard twelve (possibly thirteen) times throughout the ten-measure fragment.

If the vocal part is really meant to be read in treble clef as indicated, the range is astounding. Sustained singing on high C, D, and E♭[(6)] three octaves above the ostinato would sound very bizarre, in a way that does not seem consistent with the text or the accompanying parts. Moreover, the spellings are illogical as well as unusual:

---

[15] See David Lewin, 'Inversional Balance as an Organizing Force in Schoenberg's Music and Thought', *Perspectives of New Music*, 6 (1968), 1–21. Webern's choice of the pitches E♭ and A may also signify (e)S and A: Schoenberg's initials.

Ex. 6.11. 'Nachtergebung' No. 1, mm. 1–6, 9–10 (PSS, film 103:0755).

in the second phrase, E moves to F♭, while B and C are led to C♭ (Ex. 6.11, second system). If the vocal line is read in bass clef instead, the piece makes much more sense. Then illogical spellings are avoided, and the dark quality of the baritone voice blends with the low-register instruments such as bass clarinet, trombone, and double bass.

When the vocal line is read in bass clef, though, another peculiarity arises, namely unison doubling of the vocal line for two measures (Ex. 6.11, mm. 4–5). This robs the voice of any independence, as the line would be absorbed into the cello music.[16] Doubling of the voice is very unusual in Webern's music. The vocal line's dependence on the instruments is further confirmed by the fact that its entire first

---

[16] The two major thirds in the cello (m. 4) are derived from the first two 'right-hand' chords of the piece (m. 1). After drawing the major third B♭–G♭ from the inner voices, Webern tried to continue the parallelism with A–E, but then decided to preserve the major third interval, changing this to A–F.

phrase is a horizontal statement of the first chord (with two notes from the second):

chords m. 1, from bottom: C E B G♭ B♭ F/(A C♯)
first vocal phrase (reordered): C E B G♭ B♭ F A D♭

The ostinato chords do not simply repeat themselves in the bass, separated from everything else; instead they rule the piece, controlling the pitch organization in all the parts.

Such a unified statement in the music may result from Webern's response to the text. The poem 'Nachtergebung', like other Trakl poems, is made up of disjunct, unrelated images. The first two lines, both exclamations, are addressed to different objects:

1   Mönchin! schließ mich in dein Dunkel,
2   Ihr Gebirge kühl und blau![17]

The first line invokes a nun (literally, female monk), which is synonymous here with the night. ('Mönchin' is also a way Trakl sometimes referred to his sister.) Then follows a Hölderlin-like apostrophe to the cool blue mountains. If the chords represent the darkness, then the vocal line's absorption into them could represent the poet (as singer) surrendering to the night. The rather concrete word-painting continues. In the second verse ('Ihr Gebirge kühl und blau'), the perspective shifts from the night up into the mountains. Simultaneously the ostinato (in a varied form) moves up two octaves and is accompanied by the silvery sound of a viola note trilled, on a harmonic (Ex. 6.11, second system). The chords here have only two notes each instead of three; the thinning-out of the texture and the registral shift both give the impression of a shadow, or something partially remembered. The night—represented by the ostinato—is still there, but the poet's attention is now directed to the distant mountains, so he is less conscious of it.

FRAGMENT AS ANTECEDENT TO FINISHED WORK:
'SIEBENGESANG DES TODES' AND 'ABENDLAND III'

The only one of Webern's published vocal works with as much ostinato and repetition as the fragments discussed above is his first completed Trakl setting, 'Abendland III' (Op. 14 No. 4, completed 1917). Given the prominence of ostinato in the fragments of 1917, its use here is not surprising. The ways Webern had used this technique in the fragments—pedal-point, two or more ostinatos at once, dis-

[17] 'Nun, enclose me into your darkness, | You cool blue mountains!' DTV 93.

Ex. 6.12. 'Siebengesang des Todes', mm. 1–10 (PSS, film 103:0752).

solution—provided the technical fluency and the vocabulary for 'Abendland III'. One fragment specifically anticipates the ostinatos of 'Abendland III' as well as many of its other features.

Both 'Siebengesang des Todes' (hereafter, 'Siebengesang') and 'Abendland III' were composed during the summer of 1917, when Webern was living at Klagenfurt. Both texts were first published in *Der Brenner* in the spring of 1914, at a time when we know that Webern was reading the journal. They both also appeared in the Trakl volume *Sebastian im Traum*, which Webern owned.

A setting of 'Siebengesang' was a highly ambitious effort for Webern. The fragment, sixteen measures long in 4/4 time, extends only as far as the fourth line of the 27-line poem (its first ten measures can be seen in Ex. 6.12); if the rest of the poem were set with approximately the same time-scale as this fragment, it would have taken 144 measures! The large proportions are complemented by an instrumental ensemble of at least 20, possibly with tutti strings.

This is one of the largest ensembles Webern ever used.[18] If completed, 'Siebengesang' would have been more elaborate than any published song, and comparable in scale, among the vocal works, only to the two late cantatas. 'Abendland III', by contrast, is scored for three instruments and voice; at eighteen measures long, it is almost as long in its entirety as the fragmentary 'Siebengesang', less than one-quarter complete.

In spite of these differences of scale, there are many points of contact between the fragment and the completed piece. Both start with a gesture played by clarinet, and these gestures have similar contours. Both vocal parts lie in a low mezzo range.[19] The vocal lines develop similarly, approaching their high points in clear, semitone voice leading, and both draw their primary material from the instruments. The overall form of both pieces—apparent even in the fragmentary 'Siebengesang'—is modified strophic, a sort of varied repetition. Finally, Webern used multiple ostinatos (that is, more than one ostinato going on at the same time in different instruments) in both pieces to emphasize important moments in the texts.

Comparison of Ostinato Types

In 'Abendland III', ostinato could be considered the main idea of the piece. Ostinatos for all three instruments are sounded during the text 'Gewaltig ängstet | Schaurige Abendröte | Im Sturmgewölk' (in m. 11); here they seem to 'get stuck' and repeat their patterns. The bass clarinet continues its ostinato the longest; its ten and a half repetitions cease only at the text's climax, 'Im Sturmgewölk' (m. 13).

The 'Siebengesang' fragment also has multiple ostinatos. (The two ostinato passages are compared in Ex. 6.13a and b.) In m. 6, a repeating minor third in the bells (B–G♯) sounds during the next five measures. At 'Dunkles' (m. 8) two repeating chords in the low register begin, played by cello, bass, and bass clarinet. These two elements—bell and chords—are not in phase with each other rhythmically, and finally dissolve by becoming gradually more separated. In the first three statements of the 'bell ostinato', the B and G♯ are an eighth-note apart; then the unit begins to dissolve, until the last two statements are almost two beats apart. (The time between statements

---

[18] In the years 1917–19, only the continuity draft of 'Wiese im Park', with 23 instruments, exceeds this size.

[19] Webern often indicated a mezzo rather than a soprano voice in this period; see for example early versions of Webern's *Two Songs* Op. 8, whose first and second versions call for a 'mittlere Stimme' or 'Mezzosopran', 'Die Einsame' and 'Leise Düfte' (grouped together by Webern as 'Op. 7'), 'Schmerz, immer blick nach oben', as well as the two early Trakl fragments, 'In der Heimat' and 'In den Nachmittag geflüstert'.

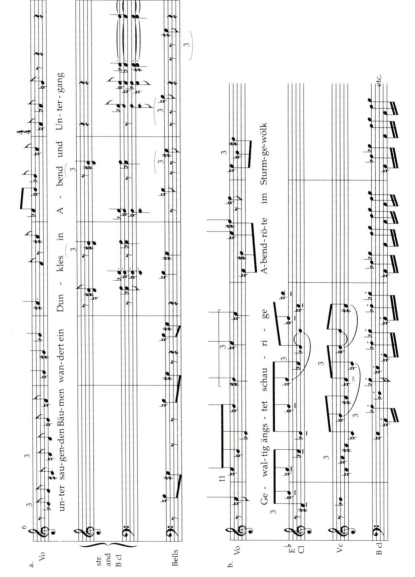

Ex. 6.13. Comparison of ostinato passages: (*a*) 'Siebengesang des Todes', mm. 6–10, ostinatos and voice only; (*b*) 'Abendland III', Op. 14/4, mm. 11–13, ostinatos and voice only.

of the minor third is not regular either, ranging from an eighth-note to almost two beats.) The two chords at 'Dunkles' also become progressively farther apart, until they are liquidated by chromatic contrary motion at the word 'Untergang'. The three ostinatos in 'Abendland III' are also out of phase with each other, coinciding only for about a beat. They are liquidated as well by a weakening of the regular surface rhythm in each part.

It is not surprising that Webern left 'Siebengesang des Todes' incomplete, given its potential length and ambitiousness. But this fragment was not a failure. He was able to extract from it useful techniques, which he refined and adapted to the much shorter and more suitable poem 'Abendland III'. From 'Siebengesang' Webern took the underlying musical ideas, not the surface features. He selected the vocal line's chromatic ascent, the strophic form, the fixed-pitch motives, and, most of all, ostinato; the completion of a vocal work with ostinato ended his several months' exploration of the technique.

WHAT OSTINATO ACCOMPLISHES

Webern's use of ostinato may have been motivated by the poems themselves as much as by musical technique. A musical setting establishes a hierarchy of relationships between the parts of a poem, by giving more emphasis to some lines than to others, and perhaps even bringing out aspects not explicit in the original poem. The 'unconnectedness' of Trakl's poetry gave Webern free rein to link the verses as he wished. By using ostinato, Webern binds together the juxtaposed, unrelated images in Trakl's poems. To make a theatrical analogy, an ostinato is like a painted backdrop, against which diverse 'scenes' can be played. In the poem 'Verklärung', for example, disparate events 'take place' at the same time (namely at dusk, 'Wenn es Abend wird'); here the ostinato provides a musical equivalent of the background time and place. Simultaneous events are difficult to imply in a single-voice setting, in which the text must be presented sequentially. A static 'background', however, gives the illusion of simultaneity by providing an unchanging focal point. The musical settings then reduce the ambiguity inherent in the original; Webern in some sense 'demythologizes' the poems by making them more concrete.

In the case of chordal or motoric ostinatos in 'Siebengesang' and 'Abendland III' there may be a more specific association. The ostinato passages in both settings occur at moments in the text that emphasize extremes of alienation: 'wandert ein Dunkles in Abend und

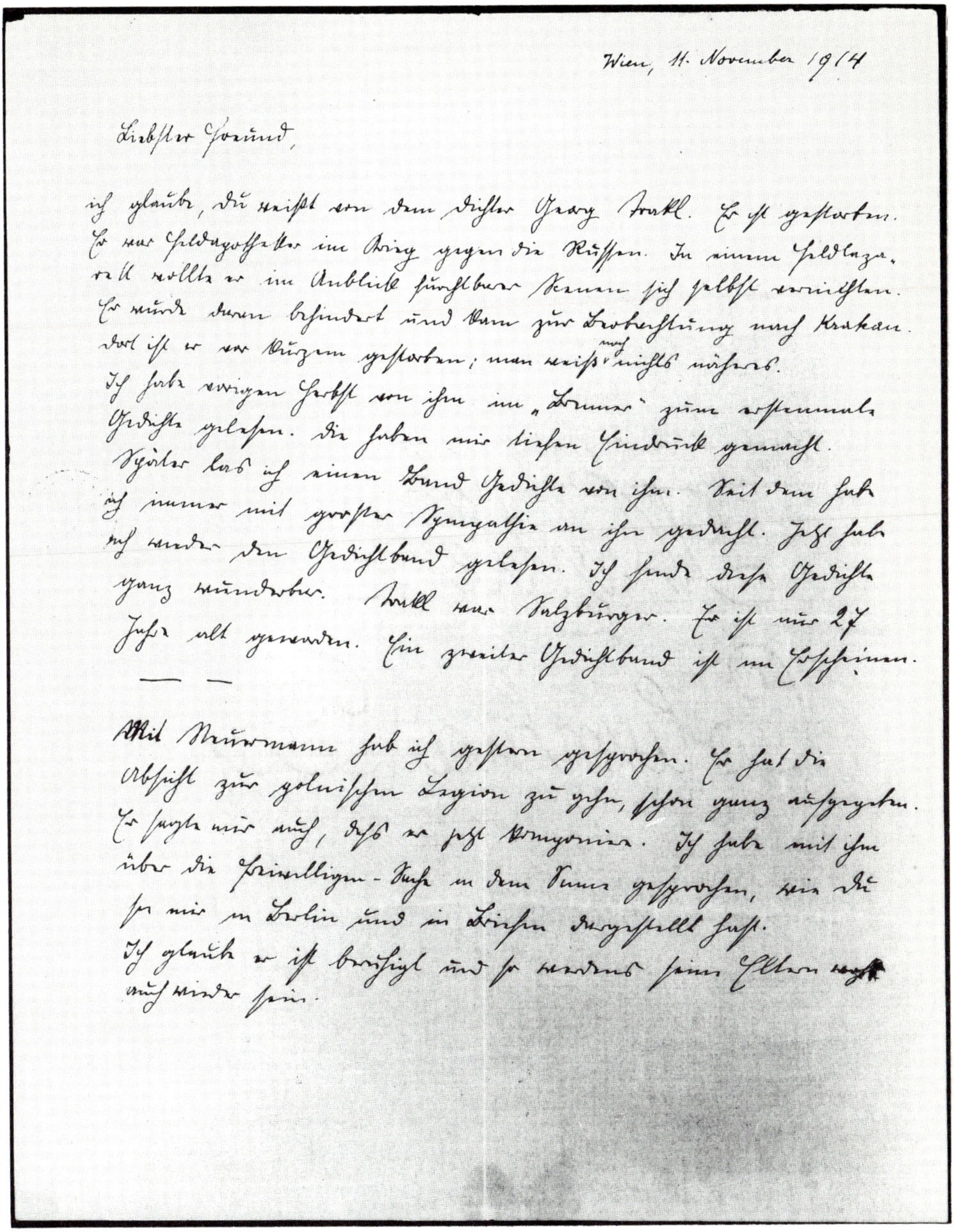

Wien, 11. November 1914

Liebster Freund,

Plate 1. Webern's letter to Schoenberg, 11 Nov. 1914. The Schoenberg Collection at the Library of Congress, Washington, DC.

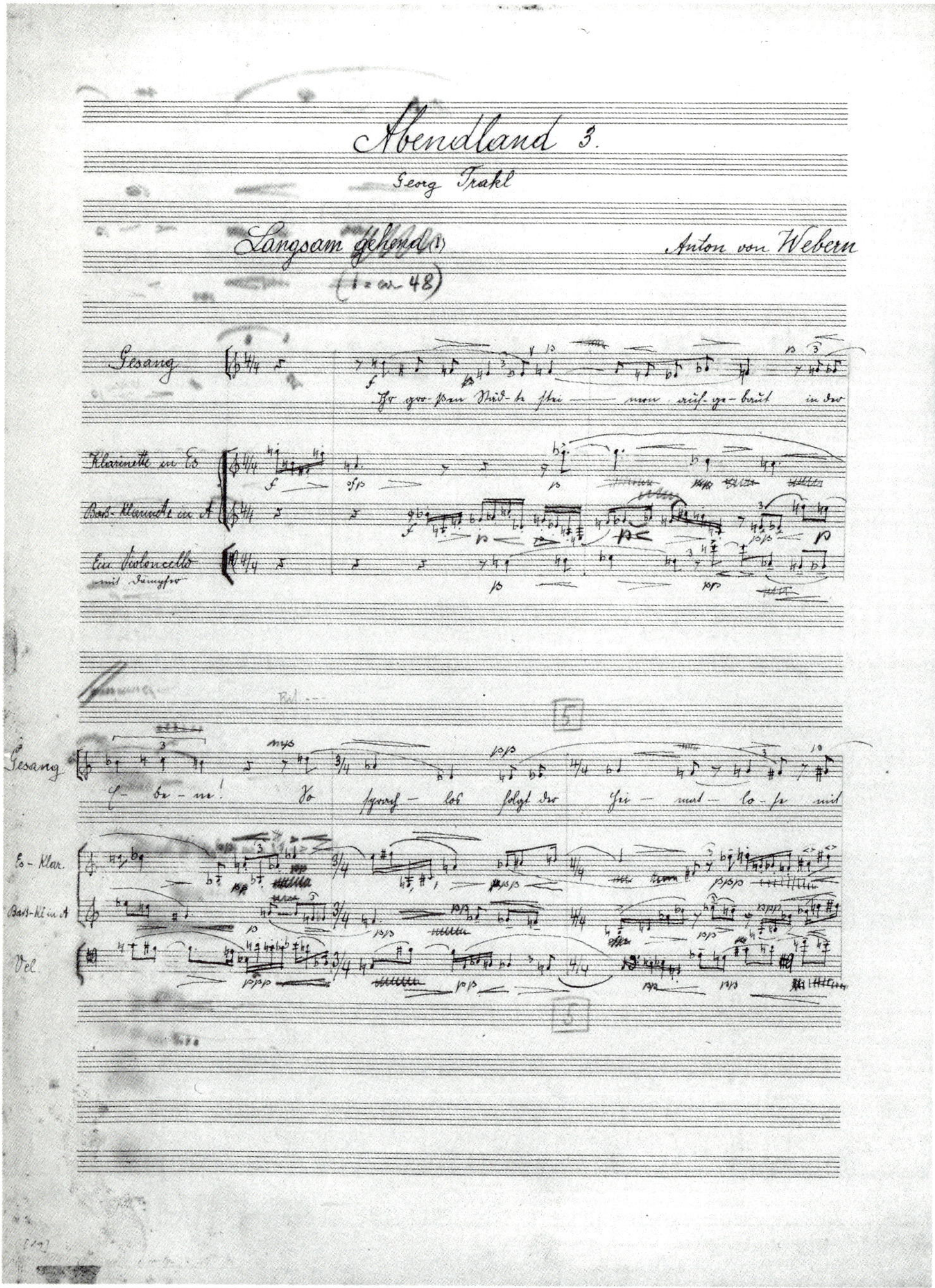

Plate 2. ‘Abendland III’ (Op. 14/4), fair copy, p.1.

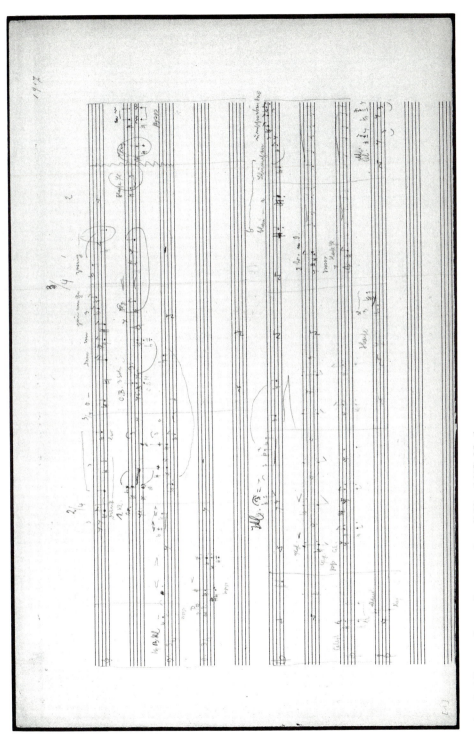

Plate 3. 'Gesang einer gefangenen Amsel' (Op. 14/6), No.1.

Plate 4. 'Nachts' (Op. 14/5), c.d. sketch, p. 2.

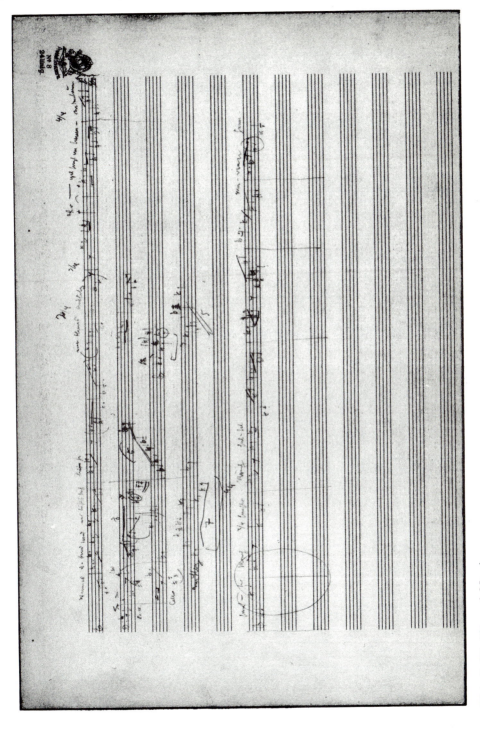

Plate 5. 'Verklärung', No. 4.

Plate 6. 'Abendland I', (Op. 14/2) c.d. sketch, p. 3.

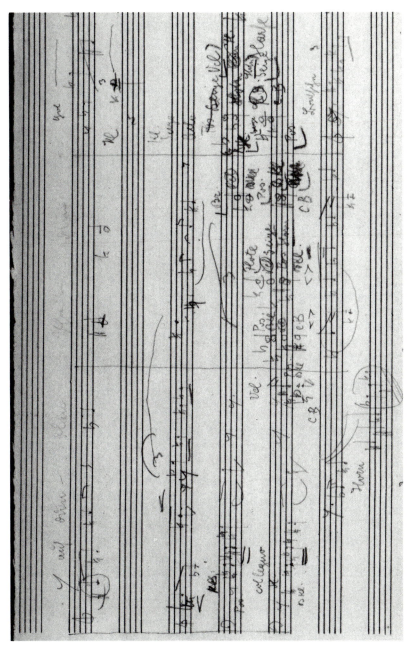

Plate 7. 'Ein Winterabend', (Op. 13/4) c.d. sketch, p. 2 (detail).

Plate 8. 'Gesang einer gefangenen Amsel' (Op. 14/6), No. 5.

Plate 9. Op. 14: title-page to the fair copy.

Plate 10. 'Gesang einer gefangenen Amsel' (Op. 14/6), c.d. sketch, p.1.

Untergang' (A dark thing wanders into evening and decline) or violence: 'Gewaltig ängstet schaurige Abendröte im Sturmgewölk' (The ghostly sunset stirs violent fear in the thunderheads). Webern may have associated the common theme of decline (*Untergang*) with the ostinato technique; if so, 'Abendland III' is the musical as well as the poetic apotheosis of the theme. In speaking of Webern's orchestra pieces, Op. 6 and Op. 10, Adorno pointed out how the percussion evokes the sounds of distant battle. In proclaiming Webern as a prophet of war, like Heym and Trakl, Adorno wrote, in one of his most perceptive and beautiful formulations, that Webern's pianissimos are not gentle, but instead are like a distant, powerful noise, like the guns of Verdun heard from the Waldchausee near Frankfurt.[20] The repetitive, rhythmic quality of the ostinato—which stands in stark relief to the rest of the music in both cases—underlines these emotions; this type of ostinato provided a kind of *affect* of violence and despair useful to a composer who was perhaps more comfortable in a more purely lyric vein.[21]

Although the slower, pedal-point types of ostinato with their evocation of tonal centres seem to draw Webern back to an earlier era, they are not entirely an 'alter Duft aus Märchenzeit'. Even though he and Schoenberg had used these techniques in their music of 1909 and 1910, by 1917 Webern again tried to incorporate them into the more 'advanced' aspects of his current writing, such as the constant circulation of the total chromatic. Perhaps Webern was trying to accomplish what Schoenberg had done with *Pierrot Lunaire* in 1912: a retreat from pure expressionism into a kind of 'neo-classicism'. Though Webern never attempted the ironic tone of *Pierrot*, he used other means to turn down the expressionist heat. Webern described this shift in a series of unusually detailed letters quoted at the beginning of this chapter. Rather than being general remarks, his comments could refer to actual music: his experiments during the summer of 1917. For example, 'more closed (or 'homogeneous') sound' ('geschlossener Klang') could mean the chordal ostinatos found in 'Nachtergebung' or 'Siebengesang des Todes'. 'Long[er] themes' ('lange Themen zum Teil') might refer to the barcarole melody that imitates Schoenberg's 'Heimfahrt'. 'I am gradually gaining clarity *again*' ('Ich gewinne allmählich wieder Klarheit'; emphasis mine) implies that he is returning to something he did before. It is certainly no overstatement that all of the fragments with pedal-point ostinatos

---

[20] Adorno, 'Anton von Webern', 118.
[21] Sketches for the passage 'gross ist unsrer Feinde Zahl' in Op. 18 No. 2 show that Webern considered a similar text-related use of ostinato here as late as 1925.

that tended, in various ways, toward tonality, were 'something completely different from before the war'.

Webern began this conscious change of style by imitating 'Heimfahrt' from *Pierrot*, a piece which is itself an imitation of a conventional form. In a series of attempts, he tried different ways to maintain
the balance between a repetitive figure and concurrently developing
motives. Later, with the chordal patterns of 'Nachtergebung' and
'Siebengesang', the material he used for ostinatos became more complicated. Through these experiments with ostinato, Webern refined
these techniques to the point that he was able to use them fluently in
his first completed Trakl setting, 'Abendland III'.

7. Different Readings of the Same Text: Sketches for 'Verklärung', 'Nachtergebung', and 'Offenbarung und Untergang'

While Webern was able to set some poems quickly from start to finish, others took much longer. He often returned to the same text many times over the course of several years. The incomplete settings that result reveal widely divergent approaches, as if he wrote down all spontaneous ideas that the text evoked rather than taking one thought and developing it. Between 1915 and 1921, Webern sketched different music to the same texts repeatedly; this tendency was especially pronounced with Trakl's poetry. Webern sketched his 'Gesang einer gefangenen Amsel' and 'Verklärung' each more than six times, completing 'Amsel' (as Op. 14 No. 6), but not 'Verklärung'. He also drafted several incomplete versions of Trakl's 'Nachtergebung' and 'Die Heimkehr', as well as a passage from the prose poem 'Offenbarung und Untergang'.

Multiple settings of the same text bring into question the extent to which intrinsic qualities of a poem, such as form, metre, or content, affect a composer's musical realization. In discussing text-setting, it is tempting to assume a kind of cause-and-effect relationship between poem and music. The text is supposed to exert a kind of force that elicits inevitable responses in the music; an 'appropriate' compositional response is deemed as 'faithful' to the text. Such a judgement usually validates after the fact the compositional relationships that exist. But what constitutes 'fidelity' to a text when a composer invents different music for the same poem? How can one judge whether and how the music 'reflects' the text when no single reading has been validated by completion? If the piece has been completed, do the divergent early versions then become superfluous?

One might start by asking what fragmentary settings for a given poem have in common. Although Webern's fragments differ substantially from one another, they all recognize the basic structure of the poem in some way. His settings always articulate poetic units, such as verses and stanzas and their punctuation. Moreover each fragmentary setting reflects the poem's metre and patterns of declamation. All the 'Verklärung' fragments, for example, extend through either the poem's first verse, first stanza, or first two stanzas; none breaks off in the middle of a syntactical or formal unit. Even in the fragments on 'Gesang einer gefangenen Amsel', which is not divided into stanzas, Webern follows the poem's sentence-structure. But beyond this treatment of poetic form—which is characteristic of all of Webern's vocal music—the fragments have very little in common with each other. A poem did not evidently suggest formed or concrete musical ideas to him.

I shall suggest that, rather than pursuing a single poetic–musical essence, Webern embarked upon a process of 'reading' the poem in different ways. We saw in Chapter 3 that the process of circling around a text was crucial for his compositional fluency. Each poem—and this is especially true of Trakl's complex verse—has many possibilities for realization. Whereas in one sketch Webern might try to illustrate a single powerful image, in another he might de-emphasize this image in favour of a broader interpretation of the poem's mood in the whole stanza or couplet. In either case the music renders in specific terms what may have been left open by the poet. Webern's fragments explore different readings of the text, just as an actor might try speaking with different inflections or rhythms to learn a part.[1]

This chapter will focus on the Trakl fragments 'Verklärung' (for which there are six fragmentary settings), 'Nachtergebung' (three fragments), and 'Mit silbernen Sohlen' (two fragments) (the special problem of 'Gesang einer gefangenen Amsel' will be treated in Chapter 10). Among the questions I shall ask are: what can the fragments tell us about how Webern understood Trakl's poetry? How did Webern balance attention to the poem's form versus its content? To what extent did he use text-painting and illustration, and how did this change over time? Why were the most detailed and full-fledged attempts never finished?

'VERKLÄRUNG': DIFFERENT INTERPRETATIONS OF FORM

Webern's six attempts to set 'Verklärung', listed in Table 9, range in size from a compact voice and piano setting to larger ones with chamber ensembles and percussion. While half of these were sketched in 1917, Webern returned to the poem in 1919, and perhaps even as late as 1921. The instrumentation of one of the fragments—No. 4,

---

[1] For this analogy I am indebted to David Lewin's article 'Auf dem Flusse: Image and Background in a Schubert Song', *Nineteenth-Century Music*, 6 (1982), 47–59.

TABLE 9. 'Verklärung' Fragments*

Portion Set and Film No.	No. of Pages	Instrumentation	Designated Date
1. vv. 1–5 103:0750, 0747	2	2 cl., b. cl., tpt., tbn., vn., va., vc., hp.	1917 Klagenfurt
2. vv. 1–3 103:0749	1	piano	1917
3. vv. 1–3 103:0745	1	vn. (others)	[1917]
4. 1st 2 stanzas 103:0746	1	b. cl., vc.	[1919–21]
5. 1st stanza 103:0748	1	ob., cl., b. cl., vn., vc., hp., tbn., cel., glock.	[1919–21]
6. v. 1 101:0557	1	cl., hp., va., tpt., vc.	[1919–21]

* I place the undated Fragment 3 in 1917 because of its use of ostinato technique (see Ch. 6). Fragments 4 and 5 are also undated; I include them in the years 1919–21 because both have the extremely high vocal range and the beamed notation characteristic of later songs. In addition, No. 4 calls for bass clarinet and cello, an ensemble similar to that of 'Abendland I', composed on 28 July 1919. Fragment 6 is found on the verso of p. 2 of the continuity draft of 'Die Sonne', Op. 14 No. 1, composed in 1921. The 'Verklärung' fragment was probably composed first, since Webern is more likely to have used the blank side of a fragment when writing a continuity draft than the other way around.

for bass clarinet and cello—is compatible with that of Op. 14; possibly Webern at one time considered including 'Verklärung' in this group.

'Verklärung', which was first published in Trakl's second volume of poetry, *Sebastian im Traum* (1915), does not relate a connected or unified series of images.[2] Even the religious images that recur throughout do not relate to each other strongly enough to tell us who exactly undergoes transfiguration, or how. The poem's 'characters'— the 'small bird', the 'gentle monk', the 'white angel', among others—exist on different levels of reality and unreality, just as its events take place on different perceptual planes. For instance, who is the 'you' mentioned twice in the poem? After the blue face softly leaves 'you', can he (or she) perceive the small bird singing in the next line? Where actually does the action take place? The third verse, 'ein kleiner Vogel singt im Tamarindenbaum', evokes a pure, realistic outdoors. Is it the same scene in which the blue face 'gently leaves you'? Or does this 'happen' in a non-real, dream world? Trakl

[2] For the text of 'Verklärung', see pp. 29–30 above.

does not give an answer; the images in his poems are contextually
ambiguous. The reader must construct the time and place of events,
as must a composer who wants to set these lines.

Trakl's images, though seemingly not ordered by narrative, are
bound together by the poem's structure. There are five stanzas of
three lines each, followed by a final couplet. While there is no rhyme-
scheme, the lines are often linked by similar vowel-sounds or allitera-
tion. Moreover, each three-line stanza (except the first) has the same
metrical organization: a short two-stress verse, followed by longer
verses with four or five accents. Two of the short lines share the
grammatical construction of indefinite article, adjective, masculine
noun ('Ein sanfter Mönch', 'Ein nächtiger Kranz'). Parallel forms
appear also at the end of stanzas 1 and 2: 'Ein kleiner Vogel' and
'Ein weisser Engel'. This sets up a refrain-like repetition, which
however is not continued beyond the third stanza.

In the third, fourth, and fifth stanzas (which Webern did not set),
stanzaic unity is achieved more by matching vowels than by parallel-
isms of grammar. For example, the last word of the third stanza,
'Schauenden', repeats the vowel-sound that ends the preceding line,
'Trauben', without making a true rhyme. The last two stanzas are a
complex of interlocking *o* and *u* sounds. These sounds are connected
in the three words that start with *m*: *Mund*, *Mond*, and *Mohn*, just as
the last word in the poem, 'Gestein', recalls the sound of the last
word of the fifth stanza, 'Gesang': these linking sonorities, in the
absence of a narrative or single point of view, lend coherence to the
poem's diverse images.

A composer might focus on one of two levels: the intense, morbid
images, or the strict, conventionalized form. Re-creating the powerful
images in music might distort the piece's form, as in fact happened in
Webern's highly impressionistic setting of Trakl's 'In der Heimat' of
1915. Too strict an observance of form would however neutralize the
force of the images. Webern's settings of 'Verklärung' show how he
first gave attention to one, then the other aspect. The fragments
range from the extremes of tone-painting of individual ideas to a
more controlled 'translation' of the poem's structure.

The first three lines of the poem are difficult to reconcile into a
single musical idea. Each line presents a different image: (1) a time
of day: at dusk, (2) the introduction of two 'characters': the blue
apparition and a third person besides the narrator, and (3) a bird
singing in a tree. Does the first line set the time and condition for the
rest? If so, when (or 'whenever', or even 'if') dusk sets in, then the
rest of the events in the poem can take place. During the evening,
the blue apparition disappears (line 2), the gentle monk folds his

hands (lines 4–5), and a blue flower sounds softly (lines 16–17).

In the sketches that only go as far as the first stanza (Nos. 2 and 3 of Table 9), Webern tried two ways of interpreting these lines. Both fragments use ostinato (as discussed in Chapter 6). By changing the ostinato at crucial points in the text, Webern interprets the poem in quite different ways. In No. 2, the ostinato breaks at the second line ('the blue face softly leaves you'), arriving at a stable point at 'Antlitz' (see Ex. 6.5 in Ch. 6). Then follows a short interlude between the second and third lines. During this interlude the pitch emphasis changes. The third line of text ('a small bird sings in the tamarind tree') enters over the new ostinato; now it is musically removed from the first two lines, creating the impression that the small bird and the tree are not physically near the evening and the blue face. The bird singing in the tree is part of the natural world of light and air, which when juxtaposed with the other world of dusky apparitions, appears more vividly 'real'. Yet the two parts of the fragment are closely related; both form four-measure phrases, and the ostinatos in both ultimately 'resolve' to more stable tonal areas. Although Webern distributes the text unevenly here (two lines in the first musical phrase, one in the second), the parallelism balances their weight. When the second ostinato begins, the music seems to start over again. In this reading, the third line, 'ein kleiner Vogel . . .', is framed with the musical equivalent of 'meanwhile', or 'at the same time'. In one world (perhaps an imaginary one), evening comes and a mysterious 'blue face' quietly leaves. Meanwhile, in the real world (or another imaginary one), a small bird sings in a tree.

Webern's setting in No. 3 interprets the relationship among the first three lines differently (see Ex. 6.8 in Ch. 6). In this reading, the first and third lines are musically connected, instead of the first and second. The second line is set apart by the break in the ostinato, which is otherwise heard in every measure. In addition to the absence of ostinato, the line 'Verläßt dich leise ein blaues Antlitz' is emphasized by the intensity of the vocal high point in m. 4 and the simultaneous arrival in the bass on a stable tone. One could hear this contrast as a pulling-back from the world of the ostinato into another realm. In this reading, we see a small bird in a tree in the evening dusk of the 'real' world, while in an internal or dream world, a mysterious blue face retreats. Although both 'Verklärung' fragments use ostinato, they allow the listener to visualize the three lines of the poem's first stanza in two different ways. The Trakl poem contains both possibilities; each musical setting chooses only one.

A longer fragment (No. 1), also from 1917, is one of only two 'Verklärung' fragment that extend into the poem's second stanza.

Ex. 7.1. 'Verklärung' No. 1, reconstructed transcription (PSS, film 103:0750 and 0747).

Webern has not abandoned ostinato completely, but only a passing one-measure reference to it remains. (A transcription, reconstructed from the somewhat messy original, can be found in Ex. 7.1.) In this fragment, Webern moves away from the level of individual lines, focusing instead on the larger musical structure. One problem is the abrupt shift of tone that begins the second stanza. One could introduce a new musical idea here, or connect the two parts with similar music. In 'Verklärung' No. 1 Webern opts for the latter, using material derived from the opening bars in both stanzas. (The other 1917 sketches, Nos. 2 and 3, may have been too specific, pertaining too closely to the mood of the first stanza.) In No. 1, Webern connects the two stanzas musically without giving each image a strong musical profile.

Webern further articulates the relationships among lines by separating them with instrumental interludes. In this fragment (Ex. 7.1), the third line is set apart by a one-measure interlude, the same length as that heard between the two stanzas. The first two lines of each stanza are moreover rhythmically merged, resulting in the following phrasing:

1   Wenn es Abend wird, (2) Verläßt dich leise ein blaues Antlitz.
3   Ein kleiner Vogel singt im Tamarindenbaum.

4 Ein sanfter Mönch (5) Faltet die erstorbenen Hände.
6 Ein weisser Engel sucht Marien heim.

This distribution of phrases brings out the grammatical parallelism between the first three words of lines 3, 4, and 6. This syntactical connection is mirrored in an intervallic 'rhyme-scheme' in the music; at the end of each line we hear a major seventh ('Antlitz' and '-rindenbaum') or its complement, a minor second ('Hände' and '-en heim') (the last line is in fact revised to achieve this). Moreover, the ends of lines 1 and 4 ('Antlitz' and 'Hände') use the same pitch-classes, E and F, drawing an aural connection between the two stanzas.

The poetic lines are further related by the recurrence of certain fixed pitch-classes. This technique is found in many other Webern songs and fragments (we have observed it in the fragments 'In der Heimat' and 'Siebengesang des Todes'). In this 'Verklärung' fragment, the recurrences are more disguised than, for example, the 'Resedenduft' motive of 'In der Heimat'. Table 10 shows excerpts from the piece with the pitches expressed, untransposed, in 'best normal order'. From this one can see the recurring invariant pitches C, D, E♭, and E, which form pc set 4–2, and its transpositions.

TABLE 10. 'Verklärung' No. 1: Some Elements of Pitch-Structure

Violin, mm. 1–3	B C D E♭ E F♯ G G♯	(8–19)
	C D E♭ E	(4–2)
	D E♭ E F♯	(4–2)*
	E F♯ G G♯	(4–2)
All instr., m. 4 ('. . . Abend wird')	B♭ B C D E♭ E F	(7–5)
	B♭ B C D	(4–2)
	C D E♭ E	(4–2)*
m. 7 (before 'ein kleiner Vogel')	F F♯ G A C C♯	(6–Z17)
	F F♯ G A	(4–2)*
m. 8 (down-beat)	C D E♭ E G	(5–11)
	C D E♭ E	(4–2)*
m. 11 (before 'ein sanfter Mönch')	C D E♭ E G G♯	(6–16)
	C D E♭ E	(4–2)
m. 12 ('ein sanfter Mönch')	A B♭ B C♯	(4–2)*
mm. 17–18 ('ein weisser Engel')	A B C C♯ D E♭	(6–2)
	A B C C♯	(4–2)
	B C C♯ E♭	(4–2)*
	B C♯ D E♭	(4–2)

* Ordered occurrence of 4–2.

The pitch-classes D, E♭, E, and F mark the beginnings of the grammatically parallel lines 'ein kleiner Vogel', 'ein sanfter Mönch', and 'ein weisser Engel', reinforcing Webern's rhythmic grouping of the phrase shown above. A group of intervallic relationships is also quite pervasive in the fragment, independent of fixed pitches. The set-class 4–2 (0,1,2,4) is a subset, multiply embedded, of all the larger sets listed in Table 10. It is also often heard in contiguous notes in the music (these occurrences of 4–2 are marked with an asterisk in Table 10). These groups, related by interval, bind the phrases together on a more background level, just as the recurring fixed pitches do on an audible surface level. Webern's solution is to relate the parallel but contrasting stanzas musically, while at the same time projecting a reading in which the third line of each stanza is differentiated from the first two.

Fragments, No. 4 and No. 5

At least two years (and up to four years) later, Webern tried again to set 'Verklärung', producing three more fragments (Nos. 4, 5, and 6). While in all three earlier attempts, he had used the 6/8 metre clearly suggested by the text's metre (and also the same rhythm for the first line), in the later fragments he experimented with duple and 3/8 metres. No. 4, like No. 1 discussed above, covers the poem's first two stanzas. No. 5, like the ostinato fragments, sets the first three lines of the poem. No. 6 is a two-measure fragment that only sets the poem's first line. In the two longer fragments (Nos. 4 and 5), Webern further explores a technique he had used in No. 1: 'musical rhyme', in which he analogizes intervallic repetition with verbal rhyme.

Ex. 7.2. 'Verklärung' No. 5, vocal line only (PSS, film 103:0748).

In 'Verklärung' No. 5, the first two lines of the poem both end with a descending major third. (Ex. 7.2 shows the vocal line of this fragment; below, the syllables set to a descending major third are italicized):

1   Wenn es A*bend wird*,
2   Verläßt dich *leise* ein blaues *Antlitz*.

By making the first two lines musically parallel, Webern links them poetically as well; in this reading, the dusk ('Wenn es Abend wird') would remain through the second line, providing the 'backdrop' for the action there, a blue face gently leaving. In this sketch, line 2 is further divided between 'leise' and 'ein blaues Antlitz' into two parallel phrases. This relationship is particularly strong in the first layer of the sketch, where not only are the two words 'leise' and 'Antlitz' set to the same interval, but the two halves of the verse have exactly the same rhythm.

The third line is set apart from the first two, with text-painting at 'Ein kleiner Vogel singt im Tamarindenbaum'. The voice in mm. 4–5 rises to its highest point so far, its B♭ surpassing the previous high point (A) at 'leise'. The ensuing dotted-sixteenth figure with wide leaps sounds like a depiction of bird-song.

In No. 4 (shown in Ex. 7.3 and Plate 5), Webern tries a similar strategy of intervallic linking to connect the first two lines. The third line is separated registrally and rhythmically from the other two.[3] Within the first couplet, the words 'Abend', 'leise', and 'Antlitz', major thirds in the other sketch, are here all minor thirds. Webern further associates 'ein blaues Antlitz' of line 2 with the first line, 'Wenn es Abend wird', by revising the vocal line so that it forms a loose retrograde of the beginning.

In this fragment (No. 4) Webern eschews tone-painting at the words 'ein kleiner Vogel'. Instead he incorporates this line into the overall scheme of rhyming intervals begun in the opening measures. Ex. 7.3 displays the entire vocal line of the fragment; this and Table 11 show how the repetition of intervals emphasizes the stanzaic structure.[4]

The corresponding lines in the two stanzas end with the same interval, and in the case of the first two lines, the same pitches as

---

[3] It is not possible to tell whether No. 4 or No. 5 was written first. It is tempting to claim that, since the longer fragment (No. 4) exploits the 'musical rhyme' found in the shorter (No. 5), the longer was written second, but it is of course possible that they were composed the other way around.

[4] In copying Ex. 7.3, I have used only the final versions of revised passages, and have also rearranged the vocal line on the page to match the poetic lines.

Ex. 7.3. 'Verklärung' No. 4, vocal line only (PSS, film 103:0746).

Wenn es A - bend wird

ver - läßt dich lei - se ein blau-es Ant- litz

[ein klei-ner] Vo - gel singt im Ta- ma- rin- den- baum

[ein] san- fter Mönch

fal- tet [die er- stor-bnen Hän - de]

[ein weis- ser En- gel sucht] Ma - ri - en heim

TABLE 11. 'Verklärung' No. 4, Intervallic Rhyme-Scheme

1	Wenn es *Abend wird*,	m3rd (Eb^5)
2	Verläßt dich *leise* ein blaues *Antlitz*.	m3rd (D–F, E–C♯)
3	Ein kleiner Vogel singt im Tam*arindenbaum*.	M7th
4	Ein *sanfter Mönch*	m3rd, M7th (Eb^5)
5	Faltet die erstorbenen *Hände*.	m3rd (E–C♯)
6	Ein weißer Engel sucht Mari*en heim*.	M7th

well. The third lines of both stanzas end with major sevenths; this intervallic identity connects the grammatically parallel lines, '*Ein* klei*ner* Vogel', etc. (as in No. 1). In the poem, line 4 takes a grammatical figure we associate with the end of a stanza and shifts it to the beginning ('ein sanfter Mönch'). Webern accordingly ends the fourth line with 'beginning' *and* 'ending' intervals: a minor third (as in the first line) followed by a major seventh (as in the third line). The next stanza of the poem begins with a verse of parallel construction, 'Ein nächtiger Kranz'. It might also have featured these intervals, had Webern got this far.

The parallelism between the two stanzas in No. 4 is reinforced by the matching contours and similar rhythms of their vocal lines. Both phrases reach the highest point in their third line, at 'Ein kleiner Vogel' (mm. 5–6) and 'Ein weißer Engel' (mm. 10–11). The rhythm in the two passages is also remarkably similar; 'Ein weißer Engel' can be heard as an expanded version, rhythmically and intervallically, of 'Ein kleiner Vogel'.

The rhyming pattern in these 'Verklärung' fragments represents a middle stage in Webern's effort to objectify the text. Begun in 1915 with the text-based motives of 'In der Heimat', this process culminates in the elaborate associations between word and sentence structure in the First Cantata, Op. 29, composed in 1938–9.[5] A consistent matching of word and interval might have proved too inflexible, since in the earlier atonal fragments, Webern's musical language does not normally feature the repetition of fixed patterns (as the twelve-tone method would do later). Perhaps Webern's 'Verklärung' experiments came too early; the published songs from Op. 14 do not parallel the poem's syntax and rhymes to the degree that we find here.

'MIT SILBERNEN SOHLEN': SETTING A PROSE POEM

Among the most remarkable of Webern's Trakl settings from the standpoint of relationships between musical and poetic structure are his two attempts to compose the last paragraph of the prose poem 'Offenbarung und Untergang'. This work, one of Trakl's last poems, takes up three pages of prose, and is divided into six large paragraphs. Most of the images in the text are drawn from other poems; the work can be considered a kind of condensed summary of Trakl's poetic language. Use of the first person throughout is, however, unusual; this lends the work a narrative quality and hints at its origins as a dramatic piece.[6] A long and unwieldy prose text may seem an odd choice for a musical setting, especially compared with the shorter, more structured poems that Webern was working on at the same time, but the very absence of a verse structure in 'Offenbarung' may have been part of its attraction. The prose organization allowed Webern to emphasize words and phrases unimpeded by the con-

[5] See Graham Phipps, 'Tonality in Webern's Cantata I', *Music Analysis*, 3 (1984), 125–58.
[6] There are two unpublished theatre fragments that apparently served as studies for 'Offenbarung und Untergang', in DTV 249–54.

straints of poetic structure. I shall suggest that the poem allowed Webern to articulate a correspondingly freer musical form, a kind of 'musical prose' far removed from his normal practice.

Trakl's 'Offenbarung und Untergang' presents on one level an account of a spiritual journey, which is described and even 'entitled' by the poem's first line: 'Seltsam sind die nächtigen Pfade des Menschen'. Over the course of the poem's six large sections, the first-person narrator encounters his home and family, sits drinking wine in a bar, walks along the edge of the woods and into a wilderness, and finally returns to the garden of his home and the room in which he began his odyssey. Yet the poem is not primarily a narrative. Each scene quickly fades into hallucinations which we see from the narrator's point of view. These visions are sometimes given a specific voice, as in 'scene' 2: 'Und es sprach eine dunkle Stimme aus mir . . .'.[7] Certain images, such as those of the sister and the young boy, recur in almost every section, each time transformed yet identifiable. The multiplication of an image does not serve to articulate it more clearly, or in the case of a person, to lend him or her a 'characterization'; rather they are altered perspectives that reflect the narrator's irrational state of consciousness.

The last section of the poem, the one Webern tried to compose, is parallel in many ways to the first section. Some of these correspondences are shown below:

Offenbarung und Untergang (Revelation and Decline)[8]

Part 6 (entire)

Mit silbernen Sohlen stieg ich die dornigen Stufen hinab

und ich trat ins kalkgetünchte Gemach.

Stille brannte ein Leuchter darin

und ich verbarg in purpurnen Linnen schweigend das Haupt;

und es warf die Erde einen kindlichen Leichnam aus, ein mondenes Gebilde, das langsam aus meinem Schatten trat, mit zerbrochenen Armen steinerne Stürze hinabsank, flockiger Schnee.

Part 1 (excerpts)

verklangen die Schritte der Schatten auf verfallenen Stufen,

Da ich nachtwandelnd an steinernen Zimmern hinging

und es brannte in jedem ein stilles Lämpchen, ein kupferner Leuchter,

und schweigend verbarg ich das Antlitz in den langsamen Händen.

Leise trat aus kalkiger Mauer ein unsägliches Antlitz—ein sterbender Jüngling—die Schönheit eines heimkehrenden Geschlechts. Mondesweiß . . .

_____

[7] DTV 96.
[8] DTV 95–7, trans. after *Twenty Poems of Georg Trakl*, trans. James Wright and Robert Bly (Madison, Minn.: The Sixties Press, 1961), 53.

Part 6, translation:
On silver soles I climbed down the thorny stairs, and I walked into the whitewashed room. A light burned there silently, and without speaking I wrapped my head in purple linen; and the earth threw out a childlike body, a creature of the moon, that slowly stepped out of the darkness of my shadow, with broken arms, stony waterfalls sank away, fluffy snow.

Part 1, translation of excerpts above:
The shadow's steps resonate on the crumbling stairs
Since I went sleep-walking in stony rooms
and in each burned a quiet lamp, a copper light,
and silently I hid my face in my slow hands.
Quietly an unspeakable figure entered from the limestone wall—a dying
      youth—the beauty of a race returning home. White as the moon . . .

The apparent return of the personae to the place of the first 'scene' does not function in a recapitulatory way. Instead they are part of a network of allusions that span the whole poem. The recurrence of certain phrases and their transformations gives the feeling of beginning again in an endless cycle rather than the resolution of events in a narrative. It is curious that Webern tried to set only the end of this long poem, which he evidently considered to be capable of standing alone. How can one cut the last paragraph off from the earlier parts of the poem that so closely resemble it? Can music fill in the crucial allusions left out of the truncated text?

There are two fragments on this passage, one of which covers the first sentence ('Mit silbernen Sohlen . . . Gemach'), and the other only three words. The shorter fragment presents quite an extraordinary idea: a brief plunging descent. It extends more than three octaves in a solo treble instrument (which is uncharacteristically not specified here) and an octave plus a tritone in the voice, all in the space of four beats (see Ex. 7.4). This gesture, apparently an anticipated illustration of the 'hinab' ('downward') that comes at the end of the phrase, might have been too extreme to be continued.

The longer fragment also alludes to the 'hinab' idea in its first measure, but mitigates it with seemingly contradictory upward motion on the word itself (see Ex. 7.5). A four-note chord in m. 2 slides up chromatically in all voices, recurring five measures later transposed up a tritone. This figure and the repeatedly transposed chord in m. 1 are repetitive to an unusual degree.[9] Each group of chords is

---

[9] The second of the four chords in m. 2 is not clearly notated; based on the context and the chord's recurrence in m. 7, I read it a semitone higher than the first. Of the five chords in m. 1, all but one are transpositions of a 0,1,4 set, arranged with a minor third on top and minor sixth on the bottom. The third chord forms a 0,1,5 set, arranged with a perfect fifth on top and major third on the bottom (in this context only a slight variant of the others).

Ex. 7.4. 'Mit silbernen Sohlen' No. 2 (PSS, film 103:0743).

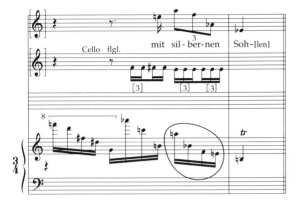

presented as an isolated gesture. Following the abrupt opening statement, which breaks off after one beat, they threaten to disrupt the
more continuous progress of the vocal line. In the second phrase
('und ich trat ins kalkgetünchte Gemach'), these roles are reversed.
The instruments proceed melodically, while the voice's declamation
is distorted. In the first phrase, 'Mit silbernen Sohlen stieg ich die
dornigen Stufen hinab' is sung in something approaching natural
speech-rhythms. In the second, the word 'kalkgetünchte' is extended
to almost four beats; the one word takes more than half the length of
the entire first phrase. The sustained low register (more pronounced
in Webern's first conception of the passage) also contrasts markedly
with the more registrally mobile first phrase.

    The amount of repetition, the flamboyance of the instrumental
gestures, and the exaggerated declamation lend this fragment an
almost operatic character.[10] Though Webern probably did not know
that Trakl first sketched this poem as a drama, he did take into
account the use of the first person, which gives the disjunct utterances
an immediate presence. Webern responded to this with ideas that for
him are quite extravagant. This can be heard in the orchestration,
which uses percussion freely (timpani, tam-tam, and xylophone). The
descending chords in m. 1 begin as string harmonics doubled by harp,
and continue with brass and timpani added. After 'Gemach', there is
a three-measure interlude before the word 'stille' (written without

---

[10] Webern had attempted two opera projects on Maeterlinck plays, *Alladine und Palomides*
in 1908, and *Die sieben Prinzessinen* in 1910, neither of which advanced beyond the most
preliminary sketches (Moldenhauer, *Anton von Webern*, 736–7).

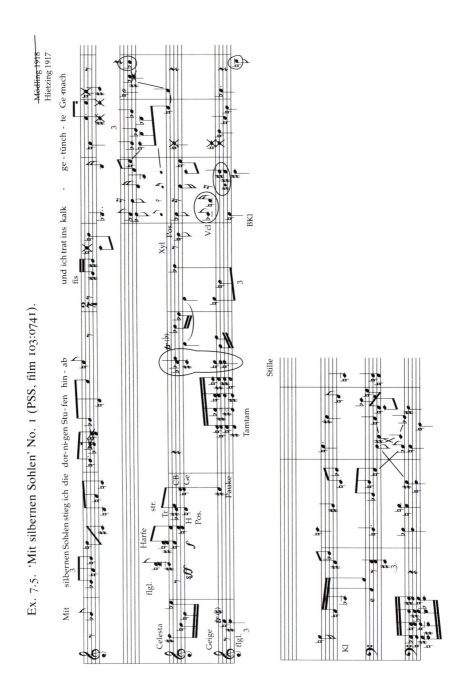

Ex. 7.5. 'Mit silbernen Sohlen' No. 1 (PSS, film 103:0741).

pitch), suggesting that the piece if finished would have been rather long.

Some early critics of Trakl claimed that his prose poems should be mentally rearranged as if they were in verse.[11] That attitude, fortunately now out of favour, would destroy the tension that results from the friction between heightened poetic language and the sentences and paragraphs of prose. Though Webern's fragmentary setting breaks the first line at the connective 'und' and inserts an interlude after the first sentence, this does not versify the lines. Instead the free declamation and unequal durations of the phrases indicate a 'musical prose' that was common with Schoenberg but at odds with Webern's usual practice (especially when we remember that the same year he worked out various schemes for 'rhyming' the lines of 'Verklärung', as shown above).[12] Setting a prose poem was a stretch for Webern. His partial solution is imaginative, and might have succeeded. To reflect the looseness of prose, he worked with small, movable units, such as chromatically ascending chords (m. 2 and m. 7). This figure seems to begin something by opening out, but it is first heard at the *end* of the first vocal phrase. The second time it occurs in a more 'logical' place: on a down-beat at the start of the interlude. With prose-like flexibility it can therefore signal both beginning and closing. This multiplicity of function can lead to ambiguity, however, making it difficult to structure a piece without the recurring patterns of verse.

'NACHTERGEBUNG': NEGOTIATING BETWEEN IMAGE
AND STRUCTURE

In 1920 Webern's text-setting took a turn towards further abstraction. First, he brought the vocal and instrumental parts closer together by 'instrumentalizing' the voice, which now features wide intervals and moves as rapidly as a clarinet part. At the same time, his musical language became more homogeneous; the primary interval in all parts is the semitone and its complements. Second (and paradoxically), Webern returned to rhymed poetry in strict forms, which in

---

[11] See Erwin Mahrholdt, 'Der Mensch und Dichter Georg Trakl', in *Erinnerung*, 86.

[12] Prose-like phrase-structure was an aspect of Schoenberg's music that Webern observed and admired early on. In an essay on Schoenberg's music, Webern wrote of Schoenberg's *Five Pieces* for Orchestra, Op. 16, 'Man könnte hier vielleicht von einer Prosa der Musik reden' ('Schönbergs Musik', in *Arnold Schönberg: Mit Beiträgen von Alban Berg* [et al.] (Munich: R. Piper & Co., 1912), 43). Schoenberg later articulated his ideas about musical prose and its historical antecedents in 'Brahms the Progressive' (*Style and Idea*, 414–16). See also Carl Dahlhaus, 'Musical Prose', in *Schoenberg and the New Music*, trans. Derrick Puffett and Alfred Clayton (Cambridge, New York, [etc.], Cambridge University Press, 1988), 105–19, and Hermann Danuser, *Musikalische Prosa* (Regensburg: G. Bosse, 1975).

his musical settings were declaimed in regular metrical subdivisions. This attraction to simpler poetry would ultimately cause him to stop setting Trakl in favour of anonymous folk- and religious poems, but for the time being he found two pieces of this type in the late Trakl: 'Nachtergebung' (Surrender to the Night) and 'Die Heimkehr' (Returning Home).

Nachtergebung (Surrender to the Night)[13]

Mönchin! schließ mich in dein Dunkel,	Nun! seal me in your darkness,
Ihr Gebirge kühl und blau!	You cool and blue mountains!
Niederblutet dunkler Tau;	Dark dew bleeds down;
Kreuz ragt steil im Sterngefunkel.	The cross towers steep in glittering stars.
Purpurn brachen Mund und Lüge	Purple broke mouth and lie
In verfallner Kammer kühl;	In the cool, mouldered room;
Scheint noch Lachen, golden Spiel,	Laughter still shines, golden play,
Einer Glocke letzte Züge.	Final strain of a bell.
Mondeswolke! Schwärzlich fallen	Mooncloud! By night
Wilde Früchte nachts vom Baum	Wild fruit falls black from the tree
Und zum Grabe wird der Raum	And the room becomes the grave
Und zum Traum dies Erdenwallen.	And this earth's pilgrimage the dream.

Trakl, like Webern, often produced multiple versions of the same work; 'Nachtergebung' exists in five different versions, although only the last was published. Apart from the aphoristic first version, which uses only fourteen words in all, the others present extended strict forms. Each of the four later versions has lines of four stresses within a rhyme-scheme; the third version, the strictest of all, uses only two rhymes over the course of its eight lines. The final version, which is the only one Webern would have known, features an ABBA rhyme-scheme in its first and third stanzas. In the middle stanza the line 'Scheint noch Lachen, golden Spiel' breaks the pattern by not rhyming with anything; this interruption parallels the disruption the line creates by its bright tone, which contrasts with the prevailing dark colours of the poem. Both first and third stanzas begin with a single-word exclamation, a feature found in 'Die Heimkehr' as well.

As in Trakl's earlier poems in *Gedichte* (1913), the form of 'Nachtergebung' seems barely to contain the extreme vividness of the images. For this poem is one of Trakl's most disjunct and least syntactical. Even the rhyme-scheme connects the fundamentally

[13] DTV 93, trans. after Lucia Getsi, 165.

Ex. 7.6. 'Nachtergebung' (PSS, not on film).

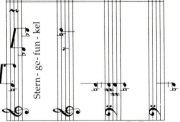

unrelated images only by sonic association. As discussed in Chapter 6, the frame of reference in this poem shifts dramatically in the first two lines alone. The rest juxtaposes related but not connected images: dark dew, a cross, a room, tolling of a bell, mooncloud, and fruits falling from a tree. The last couplet possibly alludes to Wagner's *Parsifal*: 'Und zum Grabe wird der Raum | Und zum Traum dies Erdenwallen'.

While Webern used ostinato to evoke the 'Dunkel' of the first line in his two earlier 'Nachtergebung' fragments (from 1917), in a longer fragment from 1920 he tried a different approach (see Ex. 7.6).[14] A comparison between the declamation in Webern's 1917 and 1920 settings of 'Nachtergebung' shows how his attitude had changed. In the earlier fragment, the poetic foot varies from a whole note to a quarter-note in duration within the first line alone ('Mönchin! schliess mich in dein Dunkel'; see Ex. 6.11). The second line presents a regular half-note pulse that contrasts markedly with the wild swings of the first line. Webern matched the poem's shift in perspective with a corresponding musical shift, first in the ostinato, and second in the declamation. In the 1920 fragment (Ex. 7.6), the predominant unit for the poetic foot is the quarter-note, which was the shortest duration in the earlier fragment. Certain important words, such as 'Mönchin', 'Tau', and 'Kreuz ragt', are lengthened slightly for emphasis. The result is an extremely rapid declamation; the preponderance of large leaps makes it moreover difficult to sing.

As in some of the 'Verklärung' fragments, in the later 'Nachtergebung' attempt Webern matched intervals to parallel parts of the text. Here both of the rhyming first and fourth lines begin with a descending perfect fourth (an interval anticipated both melodically and harmonically in the piano introduction). Beyond this surface motivic connection, the fragment's pitches are organized by small chromatic groups—with notes often registrally displaced—and their completion into unordered chromatic collections. After the first note, the vocal line presents a statement of the chromatic group between Bb and C♯. The second chromatic group starts with the G of 'Dunkel', and continues down to D. The third phrase, which corresponds to the third line of the poem, presents the group B–G, thus filling in the gap left between the first and second groups. The fourth phrase recalls the first phrase, not only in its repetition of the prominent perfect fourth of the beginning, but also by returning to the first phrase's chromatic group: Bb, B, C, Db. The piano meanwhile explores chromatic groups that complement the voice's. The piano

---

[14] PSS, 'Nachtergebung' fragment, verso of Op. 10 No. 4 draft (not on film).

introduction presents a series of three semitones, each one anticipating a different chromatic group from among those that will be heard in the first three phrases. Rather than illustrating each phrase with different music, as he had done earlier, in this fragment Webern composed out a basic musical idea that rules all phrases.

Over the years Webern moved away from a localized, immediate kind of text-setting to an approach that emphasizes continuity. Earlier fragments (from 1915 to about 1917; there are no distinct boundaries) featured metrical freedom reflecting every nuance of the text, word-painting, and an almost theatrical intensification of contrasts between stanzas and lines. Later (from 1917 to about 1921), sketches on the same texts elicited quite different responses, as Webern emphasized the poems' structure over their meaning. He simplified the vocal rhythms, constructed elaborate musical rhyme-schemes, and developed long-range pitch relationships that connect contrasting portions of text. The result is no less 'responsive' to the text than the earlier efforts. By allowing the words to be heard in regular metres, undistorted, Webern allows the poem to function as a text that communicates verbally, and at the same time as part of the musical argument. In the later approach (around 1920–1), the balance between poetic images and musical structure has shifted in favour of the latter.

By this time Webern had perhaps got to the point where he did not need dense multi-layered verse like Trakl's any more. As his music became more complex and 'constructed', he turned to simpler texts like chorales and folk-poetry, which were much less resistant than Trakl's poetry to submergence in primarily musical processes. His practice of sketching different settings of the same text, so common with the poetry of Trakl, Bethge, and Kraus, also became much less prevalent with the turn to simpler poetry.

Part IV
The Completed Works: Aspects of Music
and Text in Webern's **Sechs Lieder,** *Op. 14*

8. 'Abendland III' (Op. 14 No. 4):
Multiple Reference in Music and Text

Abendland III (The Occident, III)[1]

Ihr großen Städte	Ye mighty cities
Steinern aufgebaut	Built up from stone
In der Ebene!	In the plain!
So sprachlos folgt	Just as mute
Der Heimatlose	And with a darkened forehead
Mit dunkler Stirne dem Wind,	The homeless man follows the wind,
Kahlen Bäumen am Hügel.	Bare trees on the hill.
Ihr weithin dämmernden Ströme!	Ye distant twilit rivers!
Gewaltig ängstet	The ghostly sunset
Schaurige Abendröte	Stirs violent fear
Im Sturmgewölk.	In the thunderheads.
Ihr sterbenden Völker!	Ye dying peoples!
Bleiche Woge	Pale wave
Zerschellend am Strande der Nacht,	Breaking on the beach of night,
Fallende Sterne.	Falling stars.

Trakl's 'Abendland III' alludes directly to Hölderlin's 'Lebensalter':

Trakl	*Hölderlin*
1 Ihr großen Städte	1 Ihr Städte des Euphrats!
2 Steinern aufgebaut	2 Ihr Gassen von Palmyra!
3 In der Ebene!	3 Ihr Säulenwälder in der Eb'ne der Wüste,
	4 Was seid ihr?[2]

The Hölderlin poem begins with three statements using the oratorical second person plural, addressed to the mighty cities: 'Ihr Städte des Euphrats . . .'. Trakl's 'Abendland' echoes these statements with three exclamations interspersed throughout the poem:

> 1   Ihr großen Städte . . . !
> 8   Ihr weithin dämmernden Ströme!
> 12 Ihr sterbenden Völker!

---

[1] DTV 77, trans. after Lucia Getsi, 141.

[2] 'You cities of Euphrates, | You streets at Palmyra, | You forests of pillars in the desert plain, | What are you?' Friedrich Hölderlin, *Poems and Fragments*, ed. and trans. Michael Hamburger (Ann Arbor: University of Michigan Press, 1967), 368.

These apostrophes occur in increasing order of intensity: first, 'Ye mighty cities', then 'Ye distant twilit streams', culminating in the horrific address, 'Ye dying peoples'. Yet these parallel verses do not function as the beginnings of sections, and are not syntactically linked to other lines. Unlike the Hölderlin verses, Trakl's apostrophes spring up unexpectedly; his images flow in concentric circles rather than straight lines. The use of apostrophe contributes to this effect; Jonathan Culler has pointed out that apostrophe, through internalization, 'works against narrative and its accompaniments: sequentiality, causality, time, teleological meaning'.[3] The opening lines of 'Abendland III', 'Ihr großen Städte | Steinern aufgebaut', recall previous stone images that were associated with death, such as the rocky path of Part I of the poem and the crumbling wall of Part II. The stone is mute, as speechless as the homeless man with darkened forehead who wanders with the wind, or as speechless as the dead Elis. In the following lines, 'Gewaltig ängstet | Schaurige Abendröte | Im Sturmgewölk', the storm images of Parts I and II have been intensified; instead of the innocent spring thunderstorm, we see a stationary thundercloud rendered a ghastly red by the sunset. The third apostrophe is the most explicit: 'Ihr sterbenden Völker!' After having evoked this powerful image, Trakl dissolves the force of the poem into the disjointed images of pale waves breaking and falling stars.

For his first completed Trakl setting, Webern chose the last and most concise version of 'Abendland III'; a much longer version of the poem appeared in the magazine *Der Brenner* in May 1914. We know that he had begun reading *Der Brenner* by autumn 1913, and could well have encountered the poem here first (though there is no way to be sure). The early version of 'Abendland III' is more personal; its twenty-two stanzas ruminate, describe, and conjure in greater detail than the cryptic, compressed later version. Characters, such as a brother, sister, and mother appear often enough to give them a particular identity. There are whole 'scenes', involving meals, stony rooms, and angels, which Trakl does not retain in the final version of the poem. The early version also lacks the Hölderlin-like apostrophes; it preserves the narrative voice throughout.

In Webern's setting of 'Abendland III', a complex of motives associated with the opening lines of text recur and are transformed throughout the piece. Some of the variants are disguised, while others are closer to the model; some of these associations are literal enough

---

[3] Jonathan Culler, *The Pursuit of Signs: Semiotics, Literature, Deconstruction* (Ithaca, NY: Cornell University Press, 1981), 148.

so that they carry specific text associations, giving a voice to normally mute instrumental parts. As the vocal line unfolds, the instrumental parts comment on it with vocabulary drawn from both previous and subsequent events. Motives refer both forwards and backwards, and can even allude to more than one referent: I shall call this technique *multiple reference*. As a result, lines of the poem that were not linked by syntax—including the three apostrophes—are musically connected. Webern underlines the poem's high point with ostinato; the ostinato and the rhythms associated with it lend the poem a kinetic shape lacking in the words alone. Webern's reading of 'Abendland III' is therefore more directed and more concretely portrayed—and perhaps more pessimistic—than Trakl's own.

Opening Phrase

Webern begins with a staccato five-note figure in the Eb clarinet, which is immediately transformed into a vocal phrase that seems the opposite of the Eb clarinet gesture; the vocal line in m. 1 has narrow intervals instead of wide, eighths instead of sixteenths, and legato articulations instead of staccato. Yet the phrase, 'Ihr großen Städte',

Ex. 8.1. mm. 0, 1, 2. Opening phrase as motivic source.

is actually a modified repetition of the opening gesture, as shown in Ex. 8.1. The voice imitates the last three sixteenths of the clarinet: a descending fourth followed by a semitone: D–A–A♭, B–F♯–F (these form set-class 3–5, marked *x* and shown in brackets in Ex. 8.1). The repetition is disguised by means of slower note-values, transposition, and compression into a narrower range.

A further imitation is heard in the E♭ clarinet's next entrance: A–E–E♭. The note-values are slower still; the sustained, high register brings the imitation even farther away from the energetic opening gesture. The E♭ clarinet in mm. 1–3 forms set-class 4–5, a 'lyrical' version of its own opening gesture (in Ex. 8.1, set-class 4–5 is marked *y* and shown in dotted brackets). During these transposed but literal imitations, the bass clarinet line presents mirror images; most of its statements of the three-note motive are inversions of the original set (3–5: 8,7,2 and 10,9,4). The bass clarinet closes off the phrase (m. 2, second beat) by citing the set-class that began it (*y*, 4–5), in a version that shares three out of four pitches with the opening E♭ clarinet gesture.

Given the importance that the opening E♭ clarinet gesture is to take on during the rest of the piece, it is understandable that Webern would have had to draft it several times. Its pitches are fixed from the beginning; Webern revised the passage to achieve a motoric, staccato quality. His first try (shown in Ex. 8.2) entirely lacks the propulsive character of the finished piece. The E♭ clarinet begins in eighth-notes, revised to eighth-note triplets. The voice, apparently from the outset intended to proceed at half the pace of the clarinet, begins in quarter-notes, with the syllable 'Stä-[dte]' stretched out to a dotted half. Most remarkably, there is no rapid answer by the bass clarinet; the accom-

Ex. 8.2. C.d. sketch, p. 1, bottom layer (PSS, film 101:0575).

Ex. 8.3. C.d. sketch, p. 1, 2nd layer (PSS, film 101:0575).

paniment in m. 3 consists only of the four-voice chord F♯–A–C♯–G. It is not clear what the instrumentation would have been.

This chord resembles harmonies in the fragments of 1917 more than it does the final version of 'Abendland III'. Spelled and notated as an F♯ minor chord with added G, this chord occurs often in the early atonal repertoire of Schoenberg and Webern. With the voice's E and E♭ taken into account, the resulting six-note sonority is symmetrical (6–Z23: 1,3,4,6,7,9), and resembles the six- and seven-note symmetrical sets found in the fragment 'Siebengesang des Todes', a fragment that may have been composed soon before 'Abendland III'.[4]

In the next draft of the opening gesture (shown in Ex. 8.3), the note-values are now sixteenths, and the indications 'forte' and 'heftig' provide the character heard in the final version.[5] The C–D trill, *sfp*, in the first measure emphasizes the A♭–D tritone even more than the final version, which has no trill on the down-beat C. But this version has the even odder feature of a repeated three-note chord that would be the very first gesture. The notes A, A♭, and C (if read in treble clef), would duplicate three pitches of the E♭ clarinet figure at the beginning of the piece. If the imprecisely notated chord is to be read as A, A♭, and D, then the resulting sonority forms a 3–5 (0,1,6), a

[4] Compare the opening gesture (also clarinet) and the first vocal phrase of 'Siebengesang'; these both form symmetrical chords. (These pieces were compared in more detail in Ch. 6.)

[5] The word 'heftig' only appears here, and not in any fair copy of the score.

set-class featured prominently in the first phrase and in the rest of the piece. This three-note 'introduction to the introduction' is never visibly deleted, though the clarinet gesture is circled and corrected to its final version. That even at this stage Webern had not completely decided on the instrumentation is clear from the remarkable indication at the beginning of the cello part, 'Pos. m. D.' (Posaune mit Dämpfer) (corrected to 'Vcl. m. D.': Violoncello mit Dämpfer).

With the static repeated chord gone, the active E♭ clarinet gesture provides the initial impetus for the final version of the piece (and two of its basic set-classes); after m. 1, the voice is the *Hauptstimme* throughout. The instruments follow the voice, imitating and trans-forming its pitches and intervals. For example, the voice's emphasis on the chromatic space between E♭ and G♭ (mm. 1 and 2) seems to 'leak down' into the other parts; the E♭ clarinet breaks off its imitation and dwells on E, E♭, and F, in the same order as they appeared in the voice (a chromatically filled-in minor third is bracketed and designated *z* in Ex. 8.1). The cello line in the first two measures similarly consists entirely of semitone motion, broken only by a leap upwards of a major seventh at '[aufge]baut'. Even the rapidly moving bass clarinet responds to the chromatic 'pull' of the vocal line and breaks its sixteenth-note rhythm long enough to echo the E♭–F–E just after the voice's 'steinern auf[gebaut]'. Therefore all the parts respond to the vocal line's gravitational pull; they each imitate it and incorporate parts of it into their seemingly separate worlds. In the first phrase, the notes sung to the words 'Ihr großen Städte | Steinern aufgebaut | In der Ebene!' are echoed in the instruments: at first only in frag-mentary or disguised reminiscences, then in gradually lengthening statements. The ear following the brief 3–5 cell (*x*) in three successive statements—first E♭ clarinet, then voice, then E♭ clarinet again—will be presented with a graphic rendering of the first verse of the poem: 'Ye mighty cities, built up stonily in the plain!' As the motive stretches and elongates, the motion of sixteenths slows and finally ceases. By 'in der Ebene', all voices have slowed to the eighth-note; the vocal line has settled into constrained, chromatic motion, and the harmony has likewise 'congealed' into a series of piled-up fourths. Webern's change of harmony, from sonorities based on semitones to those based on fourths, adds a sense of death-like immobility to Trakl's more neutral image of cities built up of stone.

Motivic Connections with 'Ihr großen Städte'

Though most instrumental material is derived from the voice, the instruments do not cite the same vocal motives in tandem with the

TABLE 12. Op. 14 No. 4, mm. 0–1, voice and E♭ clarinet (the indications *x*, *y*, and *z* correspond to Ex. 8.1)

	5–9	(8,9,10,0,2): E♭ clarinet, mm. 0–1
	5–5	(11,3,4,5,6): voice, 'Ihr großen Städte'
x	3–5	(8,9,2): E♭ clarinet, m. 0
		(5,6,11): voice, 'Ihr großen . . .'
y	4–5	(8,9,10,2): E♭ clarinet, m. 0
	4–6	(4,5,6,11): voice, 'Ihr großen Stä[dte]'
z	4–1	(3,4,5,6): voice, '. . . großen Städte'
	4–9	(11,0,5,6): E♭ clarinet, m. 1 (C), with voice, 'Ihr großen . . .'

voice, or in conjunction with each other. The most pervasive 'multiple references' are those derived from the five syllables of the vocal phrase 'Ihr großen Städte' (which in turn comes from the opening E♭ clarinet gesture). They can take several forms; the most common are listed in Table 12. Motives drawn from these sets are heard in the voice or instruments (or both) in nearly every measure. Though I identify the various parts of 'Ihr großen Städte' with five different set-classes for convenience of labelling, I treat them as closely related because they all come from the same phrase. Although not formally equivalent, the sets displayed are functionally so because of their common origin.

In the second phrase (mm. 4–5), earlier ideas are transformed almost beyond recognition. For example, the voice at 'so sprachlos folgt der . . .' sounds a reordered and inverted version of the first phrase's 'Ihr großen Stä[dte]'. (The two statements of 4–6 are marked in Ex. 8.4.) The E♭ clarinet anticipates this with its own statement of 4–6 at the end of m. 3. In spite of sharing the same set-class, the clarinet and the voice do not sound alike here, nor do they noticeably recall that set the way it sounded at 'Ihr großen Stä[dte]'. More audibly related to the beginning are two statements of 4–5, the E♭ clarinet's opening gesture: by the bass clarinet, mm. 3–4, and the E♭ clarinet, at the end of m. 5 (these are marked *y* in Ex. 8.4). Both have the pitches A♭ and D in common with the original, and feature set-class 4–5 in its closest possible spacing.

When an instrument cites music from the vocal line, the text associated with that music may be recalled, subliminally or consciously. In these cases, the motives continue to carry associations of the words to which they were originally sung. At 'mit dunkler Stirne dem Wind', for example, the vocal line recalls the opening vocal phrase, filling in its B–F♯–F framework with A and G; the pitch A is heard for the first time in the voice (it also shares the same set-class as the

Ex. 8.4. mm. 3–5. Excerpts from voice, E♭ clarinet, and bass clarinet parts.

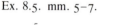

Ex. 8.5. mm. 5–7.

opening E♭ clarinet gesture; this passage is shown in Ex. 8.5). The E♭ clarinet, in mm. 5–6, sounds an inversion of the 'Ihr großen' motive (E–A–B♭), sandwiched between two statements of its own opening gesture, transposed and reordered (4–5: 8,0,1,2, end of m. 5, and 7,8,9,1, end of m. 6, the latter marked *y* in Ex. 8.5). At the same time, the cello plays the pitches it had in the beginning—a chromatically filled space between D♭ and A—reordered and, for the most part, an octave higher (marked *z* in Ex. 8.5).

The most obvious reference to the beginning in these measures, though, is almost buried in the dense texture. In m. 6, the bass clarinet plays the exact pitches of 'großen Städte' (4–1: G♭^{4}–F^4–E^4–E♭^{4}). While in the published score the bass clarinet is marked only *mp* with a *diminuendo*, in the autograph score it is marked 'forte' for two beats. In this guise the quotation from the vocal part would be emphasized more strongly.

This whole passage (mm. 5–7) is clearly a kind of restatement of the opening measures, but in what way? There are only fragments of literal repetition. Most citations are modified in some way, and moreover the opening material is recalled in the 'wrong' order. The instruments freely transform earlier material, either from their own parts, like the cello and E♭ clarinet, or from another's, in the case of the bass clarinet's literal repetition of a portion of the opening vocal line.

Though the music refers to the beginning, how does it relate to the words here: 'So sprachlos folgt | Der Heimatlose | Mit dunkler Stirne dem Wind' (lines 4–6)? The possible meanings of these lines resist a single definitive interpretation. 'Der Heimatlose' is more than a homeless man; it is someone who has lost his home, homeland, and all the other comforting things that the German word 'Heimat' implies. Mutely, he follows the wind and the bare trees on the hill. While in the poem the image of the homeless (or nationless) one, with dark forehead following the wind, does not directly refer to the opening lines about 'Ihr großen Städte', in Webern's setting they inhabit the same world because of the musical references. The instruments comment on the text by recalling earlier music, providing a subtext to the one being sung, musically reminding us that the 'mighty cities, built up of stone' can alienate the individual city-dweller.

If instruments can gain a voice by citing music earlier associated with a text, there can also be layers of vocal allusion, in which the earlier text is still 'audible' behind the one being sung. One such place is the climax '[Abendrö]te | Im Sturmgewölk' (mm. 12–13), where the voice uses the same pitches as at the beginning of the piece, at 'Ihr großen Städte' (this is shown in Ex. 8.6). The melodic character of the two places is quite different, however. Measure 1 is predominantly stepwise and in a low vocal register, while 'Im Sturmgewölk' (m. 13) is accented, disjunct, and at the top of the voice's range. Moreover, the motive goes across syntactical units, from the end of the vocal phrase '[Abendrö]te', to 'Im Sturmgewölk', which disguises its identity. Modified repetitions of motives associated with 'Ihr großen Städte' have occurred in virtually every measure so far. However, this is the first instance in which the vocal music from m. 1 recurs in the vocal line with the original pitch-classes.

Ex. 8.6. mm. 1 and 12.

The pitch-class identity and motivic congruence between 'Ihr großen Städte' and 'Im Sturmgewölk' does not 'replace' the latter's words with the former. Compared to other images in the poem—the stony cities, the homeless man, the pale wave and falling stars—the picture of a powerful, frightening, vivid red sunset amid thunderclouds is certainly the most visually immediate, which is probably why Webern placed the musical climax of the piece here. The high register and accented triplet rhythm of the vocal phrase at m. 13 sets it apart from its own previous music as well as from the instruments' ostinatos; the phrase clearly sets 'Im Sturmgewölk' yet alludes faintly to past verses. Some of this function is taken over by the instruments. The E♭ clarinet's eighth-note rhythm in m. 13 restates not only the rhythm of the immediately preceding vocal phrases '[Ge]waltig ängstet' and 'Abendröte', but also that of the bass clarinet's quotation of 'großen Städte' in m. 6 discussed above (and like the bass clarinet here, its pitches form a four-note chromatic set). The bass clarinet in mm. 12 and 13 is busy with an ostinato which itself is a reformulation of material from the opening bars. Therefore, this passage refers to the beginning in multiple ways: by pitch (vocal part), rhythm (E♭ clarinet), and motive (all instruments and voice). If one does not hear 'Ihr großen Städte' through the vocal force of 'Im Sturmgewölk', one will hear other allusions to it by the instruments, which are clearer even though non-verbal.

The congruence of these two places connects two significant moments in the piece and their texts. In Trakl's poem, the three apostrophes—of which line 1 is the first—are not overtly connected to the other lines; they function more like interruptions, by referring outside the third-person discourse. When reading the poem, we do not picture 'Im Sturmgewölk' as an actual thunderstorm in an actual city, but instead as a generalized image of destruction. Webern's reading of the poem, by motivically linking the two lines 'Ihr großen

Städte' and 'Im Sturmgewölk', articulates a more specific connection, one suggested but left unrealized in the text alone.

Ostinato Section

The passage leading up to the climactic m. 13 is at the same time the most active and the most static in the piece; active because of the rhythmic energy of all the parts, and static because they repeat fixed patterns of notes. The ostinatos heard in all instruments resemble the ostinato passage of a Trakl fragment, 'Siebengesang des Todes', and were quite possibly derived from it. The ostinatos also present the most radical reinterpretation of opening musical material in the piece.

The bass clarinet, beginning in m. 11 (as shown in Ex. 8.7), is the most ubiquitous, consisting of three sixteenths (A–A♭–B♭) grouped together, heard out of phase with the 4/4 metric pattern. The figure shifts by a sixteenth each time: from the second, to the first, then the fourth, etc. By the eleventh and final statement, the pattern has worked its way around to the strong beat again. Against this, the clarinet in m. 11 confines itself to the four notes F, F♯, G, and A♭ (a variant of the bass clarinet ostinato), while the cello in the same measure repeats another figure of only four notes. Even the vocal line repeats pitches to an unusual degree; in the 18 attacks since m. 8, it sounds only the seven pcs B♭, B, C, C♯, D, E♭, and E.

The instruments and voice congeal only gradually into their patterns of repetition, which are foreshadowed long before they solidify. The

Ex. 8.7. m. 11.

Ex. 8.8. mm. 0 and 1. Opening bars as source for ostinato passage.

bass clarinet ostinato is nothing more than an intensification of the repetitive sixteenth-note figures it has occupied itself with since the first measure. In the passage before the ostinato, the bass clarinet part seems to be searching for the 'right' notes; in mm. 8 and 9, the three notes (A, Ab, and Bb) occur often, but not in any particular order. Later, in m. 10, it settles on Eb, a tritone away from its goal, then 'finds' the right notes. At first they are out of order, then the bass clarinet focuses on A, Ab, and Bb, repeating them for ten more statements. These three pcs in this contour have been hinted at more than once since the beginning, for example by the bass clarinet in m. 2, and cello in mm. 3 and 4.

   The ultimate origin of the bass clarinet ostinato (shown in Ex. 8.8), however, is the Eb clarinet's first gesture (m. 0). The three ostinato notes Bb, A, and Ab are imbedded within it (Bb–D–A–Ab–C). Even the contour is the same as the bass clarinet in mm. 11–13. The opening measures are likewise a source for the other repetitive patterns. The Eb clarinet ostinato is a transposed and inverted version of the vocal line's continuation in m. 1, with the two pcs F and F♯ in common (m. 1: F♯–F–E–Eb, m. 11: F–F♯–G–Ab). The cello line in m. 11 is also derived from the beginning of the piece. By presenting 4–9 in the symmetrical form of two fourths separated by a semitone, at the pitch level B, F♯, F, C, the cello quotes the first four notes of m. 1, reordered. This reminiscence, played piano, with mute, is in the background, foreshadowing another more obvious statement of the opening cell, forte and accented, in the vocal part at 'im Sturmgewölk'.

   The sketch shows that the ostinato section, particularly the bass clarinet part (mm. 11–13), caused Webern some difficulties. The passage was written out twice. In one reading, all the features of the final version are there—repetition of a single short pattern, preceded by that pattern a tritone higher—but the rhythm is much more regular than in the final version (line b of Ex. 8.9), featuring Alberti bass-like figures that return to A on every eighth-note. On the other line of the sketch (marked a in Ex. 8.9), Webern notated the syncopated version that we find in the finished piece. While we might

Ex. 8.9. C.d. sketch, p. 2, excerpts (PSS, film 101:0576).

[B. Cl.]

Ex. 8.10. mm. 13–15. Voice and E♭ clarinet parts.

assume that the rhythmically regular version was the first attempt and the syncopated one was the second, the reverse is also possible. Perhaps after writing what became the final version, Webern then tried to simplify the figure, starting the ostinato earlier and making it more rhythmically predictable. Yet the pitches—A, A♭ (spelled G♯), and B♭—were never in question; Webern was undecided only about how they were to be rhythmically articulated and whether or not the pattern should be changed during the ostinato.

Transformed Reprise

A transformed return of the opening music is heard at 'Ihr sterbenden Völker', the third apostrophe (mm. 13–14, shown in Ex. 8.10). Yet this recollection of material, like others, refers simultaneously to different places. This passage is a good example of what I have called multiple reference. In the vocal line, one can hear the contour of the beginning, along with most of its exact pitches (G♭–F–E–[D]–E♭, at '[ster]benden Völker! Bleiche . . .'). The rhythms and contour, however, emphasize a transposition of the opening vocal phrase down a semitone (B♭–F–E–[E♭]–D). Also perceptible, though less obvious, is the opening music up a semitone (G–G♭–F–E, at 'Ihr sterbenden Völ[ker]'). All of these possibilities exist at the same time.

The E♭ clarinet recalls its opening gesture in yet another guise (marked *x* in Ex. 8.10), while the other instruments foreshadow, by anticipating the pitches of 'bleiche Woge' and 'fallende Sterne' (corresponding to z in Ex. 8.10), the vocal line ahead. Therefore the music of 'Ihr sterbenden Völker' (mm. 13–14) shares elements of the beginning as well as the end. As before, the individual parts do not recall parallel material at the same time or in the same order. While mm. 13–15 refer directly to the opening measures, this passage is clearly not a 'restatement' or 'recapitulation' of the beginning. 'Variation' is not the right description either, since that word implies a linear progression of events, while the music in this passage refers to different events, both past and future, simultaneously.

The exclamation 'Ihr sterbenden Völker' is the most emotionally intense moment in the poem. The third and shortest in a series of apostrophes of decreasing length, it parallels 'Ihr großen Städte' and 'Ihr weithin dämmernden Ströme'. The multiple possibilities inherent in the music at this place are also true of this verse. While grammatically similar to the two previous apostrophes, the *st* sound in 'sterbenden' recalls 'steinern aufgebaut', 'dunkler Stirne', and 'Im Sturmgewölk', as well as its counterparts 'großen Städte' and 'dämmernden Ströme'. Yet 'Ihr sterbenden Völker' is the verse that would have been the most immediately relevant to Webern in 1917, the third year of the war. By drawing direct motivic connections among 'Ihr sterbenden Völker', 'Ihr großen Städte', and 'Im Sturmgewölk', Webern articulates one of the implicit meanings of the poem: that the people will not be spared the violence done to the stony cities.

The Closing Measures: Dissolution of Ostinato Rhythm

After the last apostrophe, the last lines of Trakl's poem, 'Bleiche Woge | Zerschellend am Strande der Nacht, | Fallende Sterne', present a seemingly abrupt contrast. Is this to be read as a juxtaposition, in which the horrific image veers off into the apparently milder one of pale waves and falling stars, or as a continuation of the high tension that came before? Webern was at first undecided about how loud or how rhythmically active the closing should be. Though he never entertained thoughts of ending with a 'scream' (as at least one critic has suggested), his original closing was louder and more dramatic than the quiet final version.[6]

We can see this in the contour of the vocal line and the amount of

[6] Probably unaware of Webern's setting, Theodore Fiedler imagines the last lines of this poem delivered in a 'piercing scream'. See 'Hölderlin and Trakl's Poetry of 1914', in Emery E. George (ed.), *Friedrich Hölderlin: An Early Modern* (Ann Arbor: University of Michigan Press, 1972), 102.

Ex. 8.11. C.d. sketch, p. 3, excerpts (PSS, film 101:0577).

sixteenth-note motion present. Webern originally conceived the vocal line at 'fallende Sterne' in a high register, reaching F^5 on 'Sterne', leaping downwards to $F\sharp^4$ (this part of the sketch is shown in Ex. 8.11a). This would proceed naturally from the previous phrase, 'zerschellend am Strande der Nacht', which originally ascended to $E\flat^5$, for the first time since 'Im Sturmgewölk'. The resulting line $E\flat$–E–F in register 5 would result in the vocal line ending much higher than it began.

As first sketched, the bass clarinet part would contribute to the more intense effect of the high-register vocal line by continuing with a final sixteenth-note outburst. In the last two beats of m. 17 in the sketch, the bass clarinet responds to the sixteenths in the cello with a group of its own (Ex. 8.11a). This would carry the rapid motoric element of the piece all the way through the penultimate measure.

In the final version of the piece, the ostinato is gradually dissolved from 'Ihr sterbenden Völker' to the end (mm. 14–18). By doing this, Webern interprets the end of the poem as a loss of energy; in this reading, the vision of destruction is transformed and neutralized (Ex. 8.11b). The music reflects the shift in focus by dissolving the motoric, sixteenth-note rhythm, whose momentum has carried the piece along since the opening gesture. In the final measures (mm. 16–17), this

Ex. 8.12. mm. 1 and 18.

rhythm is heard with the weaker tone-colour of the muted cello in its high register. Finally reduced to **ppp**, it dissolves into tremolos, played *am Steg*, still sounding the bass clarinet's ostinato pitches Bb, A, and Ab. Even the voice receives some of the detritus of the motoric rhythm, when it sounds (in m. 16) the C♯–C–C♯ figure that had previously been the domain of the instruments. As we now expect, the instruments follow the voice's lead, playing their own versions of returning-note figures, now slowed down and legato. The last measure of the piece (m. 18) is purely instrumental; the voice has faded out, seemingly in exhaustion. The three instruments sound the six notes separately—and Webern notates the rhythm carefully to achieve this—but they are heard as one gesture. The instruments have abandoned their particular characters in order to sound a final fractured 'chord'.

The last gesture is yet another transformation of the beginning of the piece, now verticalized (m. 18 and its relationship to the beginning are shown in Ex. 8.12). The resulting simultaneity consists of two three-note chords related by interval-class 1 (from the top down: C–G–C♯, Db–Ab–D). These chords are versions of set 3–5 (marked *x* in the examples), and correspond to the first three notes in the

Ex. 8.13. mm. 17–18.

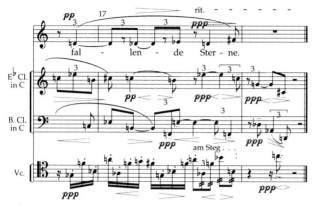

vocal line, 'Ihr großen'. Moreover, the final chord contains within it the set-class of the opening E♭ clarinet gesture (4–5, marked *y* in the examples). Even the spacing of m. 18 comes from the beginning. The opening gesture together with its 'echo' in the bass clarinet presents a symmetrical gesture built around A♭ and D. The bass clarinet in the final measure continues its thought from m. 1 by extending the tritone down to low D–A♭; these two pitches form the bass of the chord.

The final instrumental statement also took several stages to complete (Ex. 8.11*b*). First consisting only of the three descending notes in the bass clarinet, the E♭ clarinet's G–C♯ were apparently added as an afterthought. The symmetrical quality of the final chord is readily apparent in the next layer, where the E♭ clarinet plays the top three notes and the bass clarinet the bottom three. Finally, Webern gave the top note, C, to the cello, and arranged the rhythm so that no two notes are attacked together (the final version is shown in Ex. 8.13). Though its pitches are drawn from the beginning, the last measure is a quiet exhalation, far removed from the active, staccato gesture that began the piece.

'Abendland III' can also be heard as a fantasy on related musical ideas presented in two contrasting guises: one active and one static. The same motives recur, modified and transformed; the repetitions become more obvious until they finally 'congeal' into ostinatos. At the climax, 'Im Sturmgewölk', the active element has won out; the 'Ihr großen Städte' pitches are delivered in a forceful, staccato manner. After this, the momentum gradually slows until the energy of the ostinatos is finally spent. Webern captured the overall flow of the poem—a descending curve—with a similar burst of energy, which fades in intensity. By weaving together motivic references to the opening measures in virtually every measure of the piece, Webern's reading absorbs the three apostrophes beginning with 'Ihr' into the texture, instead of heightening Trakl's change of voice at these places.

Multiple Reference and Form

Motivic relationships to the material of the beginning are usually taken as evidence that an organic process of development is at work, expressed in terms implying that the whole piece 'grows from' the opening phrase. Yet in Webern's atonal music, the mere presence of relationships among elements does not mean that an 'organic structure' exists; such proof would depend on how connections unfold, and to what extent they are essential for determining and perceiving the form of the piece. In 'Abendland III' the motives are not transformed incrementally, nor do these references come in a linear or 'logical' succession. The sheer number and multiplicity of relationships among motives (both by pitch and rhythm) in 'Abendland III' blurs the faint outlines of ABA form that are implied; indeed the piece's force comes in part from the richness of possible connections and allusions, which cannot be (and should not be) reduced to a single sequence of ideas.

I have dwelt at some length on this piece because it represents a breakthrough in Webern's handling of motivic atonality. In his first completed Trakl setting, from 1917, Webern was able to break decisively from the miniature forms of his earlier music and employ a language capable of more extended development and breadth. He did this by changing how motives relate to each other, not the size of the units themselves. Still using a limited vocabulary of small cells as he had in his earlier works, Webern created his own version of Schoenbergian 'developing variation' based on multiple reference. As each verse in 'Abendland III' evokes other verses and words before and after, so does the music, with motives that can refer simultaneously to past and future musical events. These multi-referent qualities are shared by Trakl's poetry, which inspired Webern to create his own form of disjunct lyricism.

9. 'Abendland' II and I: New Variants of Formal Models

'ABENDLAND II' (OP. 14 NO. 3): EXTENDED
STROPHIC FORM

Abendland II (The Occident, II)[1]

So leise sind die grünen Wälder	So quiet are the green forests
Unsrer Heimat,	Of our homeland,
Die kristallne Woge	The crystalline wave
Hinsterbend an verfallner Mauer	Dying on a crumbled wall
Und wir haben im Schlaf geweint;	And we have wept in our sleep;
Wandern mit zögernden Schritten	Wander with hesitant steps
An der dornigen Hecke hin	Along the thorny hedge
Singende im Abendsommer,	Singers in the evening summer,
In heiliger Ruh	In holy peace
Des fern verstrahlenden	Of vineyards radiant in the
Weinbergs;	distance;
Schatten nun im kühlen Schoß	Shadows now in the cool lap
Der Nacht, trauernde Adler.	Of night, grieving eagles.
So leise schließt ein mondener	Thus quietly a moonbeam closes
Strahl	
Die purpurnen Male der	The purple wounds of sorrow.
Schwermut.	

The second part of Trakl's poem 'Abendland', to which Webern returned two years after completing Part III, forms a lyrical interlude between the two powerful outer sections of the poem. The lines 'So leise sind die grünen Wälder | Unsrer Heimat' begin the poem with a pastoral quality, invoking standard imagery of German romantic poetry. We find the stock figure of the Wanderer in the lines '[Singers] wander with hesitant steps', alluding possibly also to the 'Heimatlose' of Trakl's Part III. Unlike traditional wanderers, however, these are not travelling in a foreign land, but in their own, which none the less appears strange to them. Moreover, the narrators, after observing the beauty of the homeland, notice 'the crystalline wave dying on a crumbled wall', then remember that 'we cried in our sleep'. Even though we see 'radiant vineyards' and hear 'singing people in the summer evening', these are inflected by disturbing undertones: the

---

[1] DTV 76, trans. after Lucia Getsi, 139.

shadows of the seemingly peaceful night as 'grieving eagles', moonlight that helps only to 'close the purple wounds of sorrow'.

Webern's setting, with its 'langsam' tempo and the sentimental
downward glissando of the violin, parallels the lyrical quality of
Trakl's poem. The poem's middle part in particular (from 'Wandern
wir' to 'Weinbergs') avoids the shadow of decay that touches the rest;
correspondingly, Webern's unabashed ländler evokes a naïve outdoor
scene. In keeping with the neo-Romantic tone of the poem, Webern's
setting also preserves vestiges of traditional strophic form. It has
been radically reinterpreted, however; instead of succeeding stanzas
of a poem sung to the same music, recurring fixed pitches, particularly
D and Eb, mark boundaries and provide a framework for motivic
development. By recalling pitches and motives associated with words
such as 'So leise', 'hinsterbend', and 'verfallner Mauer', Webern
keeps them in consciousness. Therefore the text of one 'strophe' may
lurk in the background of the succeeding one.[2]

The change to 3/8 metre for the ländler section divides the piece
into three parts of 8, 12, and 9 measures each. The second and third
parts freely develop the first, with the third bearing a closer relationship to it than the second. The form can be outlined as follows:

Part 1 (mm. 1–8): a complete idea, inversional balance around D.
Part 2 (mm. 9–20): the idea taken apart, put together again in
    different ways, with different priority notes.
Part 3 (mm. 21–9): the original priority notes recur, along with many
    elements of the original idea, but completely reworked.

The division into sections corresponds to the poem's punctuation,
which suggests two subdivisions of five lines each (Webern's parts 1
and 2), followed by two couplets (Webern's part 3). In spite of the
poem's irregular metre, strophic form is implied here too, both
by the equal number of lines in the first two sections and by the
recurrence of the phrase 'So leise' at the beginnings of lines 1 and 13.
It reappears at the outset of the final couplet, just as the four-stress
line (like those of the beginning) re-emerges, suggesting the start of
another five-line 'strophe'. This expectation is however raised and
thwarted as the poem ends after only a couplet. Just as Trakl's poem
plays with the convention of strophic form, Webern's setting likewise
seems to break off in mid-phrase.

---

[2] With respect to the *Four Songs*, Op. 12, Edward Murray has described a 'kind of strophic
construction', or more specifically, 'model-and-variant procedure'. See his 'New Approaches to
the Analysis of Webern', 65 ff.

Fixed Pitches D and E♭

The first words of the poem, 'So leise' (So quiet), form a motive
that recurs often. The vocal gesture, a descending major seventh
(D–E♭), seems to have responded to the violin's glissando of the
same interval (C–C♯) that immediately preceded it. The four pitches
that make up the two gestures together fill in a minor third between
C and E♭, a chromatic area that will be explored further in the
following measures. But the four pcs, grouped into the two pairs
D–E♭ and C–C♯, gain significance in themselves as they form parts
of new motives, registral boundaries, even cadential tones (these are
diagrammed in Ex. 9.1, *a–g*).

   The first part of the poem is displayed below, with the words set to
D or E♭ highlighted:

        1   *So leise* sind die grünen Wälder
        2   Unsrer Heimat,
        3   *Die kristall*ne Woge

Ex. 9.1*a–g*. 'Abendland II', Op. 14/3, excerpts. Fixed-pitch motives.

4   Hinsterbend an *verfallner* Mauer
5   Und *wir ha*ben im Schlaf ge*weint*;

The third line (the second vocal phrase, m. 4) begins again with
D–E♭, now shifted into a lower register. A returning-tone figure on
'Die kristallne' emphasizes E♭^{4}. In measure 6 ('an verfallner') the
same returning-tone figure now emphasizes D^4, the other pc of the
pair (Ex. 9.1*b*). The end of the section (mm. 7–8) presents D and
E♭ in a dramatic expansion: E♭^{5}–D^4. The last note, 'geweint', repeats
the high E♭ (Ex. 9.1*c*). The note pair D–E♭ therefore marks the
beginning and ending of the section, as well as the beginnings of
smaller phrases within it.

The fifth line, 'Und wir haben im Schlaf geweint', is the first
straightforward declarative sentence in the poem, yet its meaning is
elusive. The 'we' referred to may be the same people to whom the
'green forests of *our* homeland' belong, yet it is not clear who
they are. It is also not explained why they cried in their sleep; the
statement simply informs of an unnamed pain, like the 'purpurnen
Male der Schwermut' of the last line. The fifth line's sudden shift of
tone and emphasis is reflected in the widest-ranging vocal part so far,
and set off by reduced activity in the instruments. At the same time,
Webern connects the violent leaps of this passage to earlier, more
placid music by referring to the opening vocal gesture D–E♭ (Ex.
9.1*c*).

The third section of the piece (which starts after the double bar at
m. 21) begins with the cello's recapitulation of the two original pitch
pairs: E♭–D–C–C♯ (Ex. 9.1*d*). As in mm. 1 and 2, these pcs are
heard as major sevenths; the cello sounds them in a chain of ascending
intervals that spans practically its entire range. Seeming to respond to
the cello, as it had the violin in m. 1, the voice in m. 22 recalls its
opening gesture exactly, D–E♭ in register (at '[Schat]ten nun').
Emphasis on first E♭ (m. 26, 'so leise'), then D (m. 27, 'mondener')
repeats the pcs emphasized in mm. 4–6 (Ex. 9.1*e*). Now that everything is condensed, we hear E♭ immediately after the D in m. 27,
again recalling the gesture associated with 'so leise'. This vocal passage
was also anticipated by a restatement of both opening gestures—of
violin and voice—in the clarinet in m. 24 (Ex. 9.1*f*).

The last word is saved for the clarinet, whose final solo gesture
includes both note-pairs C–C♯ (with E imbedded), and D–E♭ (with
F♯ imbedded: m. 29, Ex. 9.1*g*). In the sketches for 'Abendland II',
the pitches in the clarinet's last measure match the beginning more
closely than in the final version. In the continuity draft, the opening
violin gesture has three notes, not two; the C–C♯ is preceded by E^5.

Ex. 9.2. 'Abendland II', Op. 14/3, c.d. sketch, mm. 1–2, 7–8 (PSS, film 101:0569).

(This is shown in Ex. 9.2.) The resulting set-class, 3–3 (0,1,4), is found throughout the piece, in the vocal line alone at 'kristallne Woge', 'hinsterbend', and '[verfall]ner Mauer', among many other places. In both sketches and final version, the clarinet in the last measure presents this set at its original pitches—C, C♯, E—as well as the same set up a tone—D, D♯, F♯. Although Webern changed the piece's introduction, he did not change the reference to it in the last measure! However, by eliminating the E in the first measure, Webern strengthened the intervallic connection between the violin gesture and the voice's entrance; at a later stage he made their rhythms equal as well by rewriting 'leise' as even eighth-notes. In the fair copy, Webern added a violin glissando between C and C♯. An added vocal glissando between the two notes of 'leise' would be consistent with Webern's performance practice (given that, as discussed in Chapter 4, Webern added glissandos to other numbers of Op. 14 in the rehearsal score) and would connect the two gestures even more strongly.

While D occurs in several registers in the voice and instruments, E♭ is almost always fixed in register 4. Throughout the first six and a half measures, E♭ is heard five times in the vocal line, each time in its original register. At 'wir haben im Schlaf geweint', the opening gesture is turned upside down; E♭ (and its subsequent appearance, spelled D♯) is up in register 5 where D 'belongs'. In addition to the registral displacement of E♭, the ascending contour on 'geweint' contributes to the 'open-ended' quality with which the first section ends. In the sketch, Webern put E♭ into register 5, but with a descending contour $D\sharp^5$–E^4 instead of an ascending one (Ex. 9.2). After a couple of revisions, he replaced it with the final reading, creating a more jagged contour and leaving the section unresolved.

The pitch E♭ is not restored to the low register in the vocal part or in any *Hauptstimme* voice until mm. 21–2 ('Schatten nun'), corresponding to the several restatements of the opening gesture found there. In mm. 26–7 in the voice, the high E♭ is followed by D in the same register; with this, the 'too high' E♭ is finally resolved (see Ex.

9.1*e*). In m. 28, the clarinet restores E♭ to register 4; its final gesture also approaches E♭^{4} from D, only this time from below. Therefore E♭ is established in register 4 at the beginning of the piece, and shifted upwards at the end of the first section. Finally it returns, as if by force of gravity, to end the piece.

Multiple Text References in the Vocal Line

In the second and third sections of 'Abendland II', the vocal line restates the music of the first section in varied forms. In many cases, the restatements preserve the exact pitches or pcs; as we saw in 'Abendland III', references to earlier material can recall the text associated with those pcs. Here the more literal associations evoke the recurrence of freely transformed strophes.

The second section (mm. 9–12), with its 3/8 metre and the dance-like rhythmic figures in the clarinet, indicates a traditional ländler (something one would never guess from most performances). This sounds superficially quite different from the first section (mm. 1–8), which moves for the most part in steady sixteenths and eighths within a slow 2/4. Yet the middle section draws liberally upon earlier material. The voice's 'Wandern mit zög[ernden]' uses the same pitches, in order, as 'grünen Wäl[der]' from mm. 2–3 (shown in Ex. 9.3*a* and *b*). Several measures later, 'Singende im Abendsommer' recalls the same pcs as 'hinsterbend an verfallner Mauer' (Ex. 9.3*c*). The last phrase of the section ('des fern verstrahlenden Weinbergs') even shares the opening and closing interval and three pcs (D, F♯, and C♯) with the corresponding phrase of the first section ('und wir haben im Schlaf geweint'). The vocal line of the second section, therefore, freely restates that of the first, alluding to pcs and gestures but transforming metre and rhythms.

The instruments participate in the reminiscences in an even more fragmented way. Though the voice in m. 11 recalls only some of the words of the first line, the clarinet simultaneously provides the pitches that would complete the next part of the phrase: '[Wäl]der un[srer] Hei[mat]' (Ex. 9.3*b*). At the same time, the voice's A and D recall the violin's pitches at 'Wälder unsrer' (m. 3), while in m. 12, the clarinet and violin sound a reordered version of the cello gesture in mm. 3–4. Most of the material for mm. 10, 11, and 12 can in fact be traced back to the third measure of the piece. The overlapping text references for the whole piece are displayed in Table 13.

On the surface, the regular rhythms and frequent repeated notes of the ländler might describe 'wandering with hesitant steps'. The descriptive setting continues with the ecstatic, wide-ranging vocal

Ex. 9.3*a–e*. 'Abendland II', Op. 14/3, excerpts. Modified strophic organization.

TABLE 13. Abendland II, Musical References
(Note: there is no typographical division into stanzas in the original poem)

1. So leise sind die grünen Wälder	
Unsrer Heimat,	
Die kristallne Woge	
Hinsterbend an verfallner Mauer	
Und wir haben im Schlaf geweint;	
2. Wandern mit zögernden Schritten	(grünen Wälder unsrer Heimat)
An der dornigen Hecke hin	(Hinsterbend . . . Wälder)
Singende im Abendsommer,	(Hinsterbend an verfallner Mauer)
In heiliger Ruh	
Des fern verstrahlenden Weinbergs;	(und wir haben im Schlaf geweint)
3. Schatten nun im kühlen Schoß	(So leise . . . Die kristallne Woge)
Der Nacht, trauernde Adler.	(die grünen)
So leise schließt ein mondener Strahl	(So leise, Abendsommer)
Die purpurnen Male der Schwermut.	(haben im Schlaf geweint)
(Clarinet 'postlude')	(So leise)

part, at 'Singende im Abendsommer', emphasized by the performance indication 'warm'. At the same time, by recalling the first five lines of the poem, the voice superimposes those words on the second five lines. Behind 'Singende', there is another word: 'hinsterbend'. The dark images such as 'verfallner Mauer' are recalled through the music used to set positive ones, such as 'Abendsommer'. The threat is subconscious, because it is unstated, only implied, through the repetition of certain pitches.

The middle section's close relationship to the first opens up another level of text-setting. In this modified strophic form, the poem's middle lines are at the same time a contrasting section and a fractured repetition of the first. Yet if references to the first strophe capture the undertone of darkness that is present in those lines of the poem, then in Webern's reading, the second strophe is peopled by the same characters as the first. 'We', the ones who have cried in our sleep, are the ones who now wander with hesitant steps along the thorny hedge.

The third 'strophe' (mm. 21–9) sets up yet another layer of text references, since it refers to the second section as well as the first. The instruments figure prominently in this network of references. I have mentioned how the cello in m. 21, with its rising sevenths E♭–D–C♯–C, recapitulates the two opening gestures. Before the section begins, the violin's gesture over the barline also sounds the pcs of 'hinsterbend', and therefore, of 'Singende' (Ex. 9.3d). Which words do we hear?

By mm. 25–6, at 'So leise schließt', the transformation of earlier material is so complete that the original layer is almost gone. This passage is an exact transposition (down a tone) of 'Abendsommer', in m. 16 (Ex. 9.3*e*). 'Abendsommer' in turn had used the same pitches as 'verfallner Mauer' from the first section (m. 6). Yet 'So leise . . .' is much more audibly connected to 'Abendsommer', with which it shares register, contour, and intervals, than with m. 6.

Instead of proceeding with the modified reprise, the 'third strophe' is interrupted when the words 'So leise'—which previously marked a beginning—reappear in the middle of the strophe. Following Trakl's 'false recapitulation' here, the music seems to start over again with yet another set of references to the piece's opening measures (in addition to the vocal connection at 'So leise', the violin in m. 25 restates its first pcs two octaves higher; this is marked *Hauptstimme* in the fair copy of the score). The voice at this point alludes to both the words and the music of the opening gesture for the first time. The clarinet continues to present variations of its opening figure, until it ends alone with an inexact retrograde of its first four notes. The sketches show that Webern originally intended to include both cello and violin in this brief 'postlude', the latter recalling yet again the voice's opening pitch-pair, D–E♭, in their original registers. He removed this obvious reference, leaving the clarinet to end alone, abruptly broken off as if in mid-stream.

While in some respects the song's form resembles the traditional ternary ABA′ shape, Webern has merged into this a radical reinterpretation of strophic form. Both of these formal considerations are suggested by the structure of the poem. The vocal references to earlier melodies subvert the 'contrasting' middle section; these pc references, heard within the context of a ländler, at the same time draw us back into the first section. The third section is at first a purely musical conceit, a nod towards three-part song form, since the text does not imply a repetition at this point. When the poem does repeat its opening line in the last couplet—in the 'wrong' place—the music begins again with a new strophe. The 'reprise' is broken off and started again, but like the poem it also stops unexpectedly. Just as Trakl distilled a much longer earlier version of his poem 'Abendland' until its conventional features all but disappeared, Webern's setting likewise alludes to an earlier Lied-world of strophic repetition, compressed to its barest essentials.

'ABENDLAND I' (OP. 14 NO. 2): DRAMATIC RECITATIVE

If 'Abendland II' serves as the lyrical opposite to the ostinato-driven 'Abendland III', Webern's setting of Part I of the poem contains

elements of both. In 'Abendland I', the voice's free rhythmic declamation has loosened its ties with the poetic metre, creating tension
between the expected verbal rhythms and the vocal rhythm. Vivid
contrasts in rhythm and texture produce an almost dramatic effect.
Motives in both voice and instruments illustrate individual words
in the poem; figures used to reflect a particular word also come
unmoored and circulate throughout the texture. One can even hear
the piece as a drama in which two figures—one lyrical and one
active—are juxtaposed, their contrasting characters exaggerated,
not reconciled. The free recitative-like structure is controlled by the
recurrence of the (unordered) total chromatic at varying densities;
within this rotation, 'fresh' notes are placed at important points.

Abendland I (The Occident, I)[3]

Mond, als träte ein Totes	Moon, as if a dead thing emerged
Aus blauer Höhle,	From a blue cave,
Und es fallen der Blüten	And many flowers fall
Viele über den Felsenpfad.	Across the rocky path.
Silbern weint ein Krankes	Silver a sick thing weeps
Am Abendweiher,	By the evening pond,
Auf schwarzem Kahn	In a black boat
Hinüberstarben Liebende.	Lovers moving toward death.
Oder es läuten die Schritte	Or else Elis's footsteps
Elis' durch den Hain	Ring through the grove,
Den hyazinthenen	The hyacinth-like
Wieder verhallend unter Eichen.	Again fading under oaks.
O des Knaben Gestalt	Oh the boy's shape
Geformt aus kristallenen Tränen,	Formed from crystal tears,
Nächtigen Schatten.	Nocturnal shadows.
Zackige Blitze erhellen die Schläfe	Jagged lightning illuminates his temples
Die immerkühle,	Perpetually cool,
Wenn am grünenden Hügel	When on the green-growing hill
Frühlingsgewitter ertönt.	The thunder of spring resounds.

In the first stanza of 'Abendland I', Trakl presents four images,
some of which also recur in Parts II and III. In each a non-threatening
nature image is juxtaposed with one implying death or sickness. First,
the moon, a traditional romantic symbol of hope and love, is portrayed metaphorically as 'ein Totes'; the noun form is all the more
alienating as it is not a specific dead thing, animal, or person, but
something unknown and perhaps unidentifiable. The next lines contrast the natural scene of a rocky path with the dead flowers that fall

---

[3] DTV 76, trans. after Lucia Getsi, 139.

upon it. Similarly, the peaceful image of a pond at evening seems opposed to the 'sick thing' ('ein Krankes') weeping beside it. The stanza ends with the 'hinüberstarben Liebende', floating to their death on the same pond. Trakl does not paint the picture of decay as something to be feared, however. The poem's concrete language conveys the macabre images in a strangely dispassionate way, which only intensifies their horror.

The second stanza of 'Abendland I' introduces the character Elis. The legendary Elis Fröbom—whose story is said to be based on an actual event—fell into a mine and died on his wedding day; a generation later his body was found in a state of perfect preservation by his now aged bride. The subject of the ever-youthful Elis had been treated by others before Trakl, including E. T. A. Hoffmann (*Die Bergwerke zu Falun*, 1818) and Hofmannsthal (*Das Bergwerk von Falun*, 1906).[4] Trakl was fascinated with ideas that this theme offered: the falseness of mere appearances, death looking like life, and the dislocation of time and place implied by the Rip van Winkle-like tale. In addition to 'Abendland I', Elis also makes an appearance in several other Trakl poems, including 'Elis' and 'An dem Knaben Elis'.

At the beginning of the second stanza of 'Abendland I', which begins with the word 'Oder' (Or), Trakl seems to give us a choice. We can either consider nature as it is described in the first stanza, decayed and sick, or we can embrace the cold artificial 'life' of Elis. We first observe Elis passing, as the sound of his footsteps resounds through the grove, then fades. We see his face when lightning illuminates his icy temples, perhaps the same lightning that plays on the green hills in the spring thunderstorm of the last line. In line 13, the narrator breaks out of the third person voice for the first time. Here (at 'O des Knaben Gestalt'), with the first of a series of apostrophes that culminate in the three invocation-like apostrophes of Part III, we find out that Elis is only a creation of 'crystalline tears' and 'night-dark shadows'.

Chromatic Circulation and Form

The continual recurrence of twelve-tone groups creates a harmonic rhythm that marks off and shapes the large phrases of the piece, as shown in Table 14. The use of the total chromatic described here

---

[4] Lindenberger, *Georg Trakl*, 82. Francis Sharp discusses the Elis myth and its various realizations, in *The Poet's Madness*, 112–13. J. Stinchcombe compares the 'Elis' poems of Trakl with possible models, in 'Trakl's "Elis" Poems and E. T. A. Hoffmann's "Die Bergwerke zu Falun"', *Modern Language Review*, 59 (1964), 609–15.

TABLE 14. Phrase-Divisions and Chromatic Saturation in 'Abendland I'

1. Mond, als träte ein Totes Aus blauer Höhle, Und es fallen der Blüten Viele über den Felsenpfad.	predominantly 3/4, mm. 1–6 (12 pcs every *12* eighth-notes)
2. Silbern weint ein Krankes Am Abendweiher, Auf schwarzem Kahn Hinüberstarben Liebende.	predominantly 2/4, mm. 7–14 (12 pcs every *8* eighth-notes)
3. Oder es läuten die Schritte Elis' durch den Hain Den hyazinthenen Wieder verhallend unter Eichen. O des Knaben Gestalt Geformt aus kristallenen Tränen, Nächtigen Schatten.	predominantly 6/8, mm. 15–21 (12 pcs every *6* eighth-notes)
4. Zackige Blitze erhellen die Schläfe Die immerkühle, Wenn am grünenden Hügel Frühlingsgewitter ertönt.	3/4 and 2/4, mm. 22–7 (12 pcs every *8–12* eighth-notes)

should be clearly distinguished from the use of rows in the twelve-tone works, which began only after 1924. In 1919, Webern's goal was not to order the notes in a particular way, but rather to include them all without placing too much emphasis on any one note. He was paradoxically more sensitive to note-repetition in the atonal style than he was later with the twelve-tone method, since in free atonal music there is no built-in mechanism for ensuring that pcs be kept apart. Chromatic rotation as we find it in the Op. 14 songs is not a 'system' like the twelve-tone method, but still functions as a way of articulating phrases and sections.[5]

In 'Abendland I', clear division between statements of the twelve pcs separates the poem's first stanza into two phrases. Parallel features of the two sentences that make up the first stanza suggest such a division. Both have four lines and share a similar metrical scheme; moreover the first line of each ends with a formulation that Trakl used often: an adjective expressed in the form of a genderless, indeterminate noun, such as 'ein Totes', 'ein Krankes'. In the original version of the poem, the parallelism between lines 1 and 5 was

---

[5] William Benjamin discusses the role of chromatic rotation in atonal music in his review of Forte's *Structure of Atonal Music*, see *Perspectives of New Music*, 13 (1974), 170–90. Jonathan Dunsby and Arnold Whittall also discuss this phenomenon, in *Music Analysis in Theory and Practice* (London and Boston: Faber, 1988), 129–30.

even stronger because of matching metres and verb-forms: 'Wieder begegnet ein Totes' and 'Silbern weinet ein Krankes'.

	Early version[6]		*Final version*
42	Wieder begegnet ein Totes	1	Mond, als träte ein Totes
	Im weißen Linnen		Aus blauer Höhle,
	Und es fallen der Blüten		Und es fallen der Blüten
	Viele über den Felsenpfad.		Viele über den Felsenpfad.
46	Silbern weinet ein Krankes	5	Silbern weint ein Krankes
	Aussätziges am Weiher,		Am Abendweiher,
	Wo vor Zeiten		Auf schwarzem Kahn
	Froh im Nachmittag Liebende geruht.		Hinüberstarben Liebende.

In the final version, though the first lines of each quatrain match less closely, the parallelism between the two extends further, to the second lines of each section and (to a lesser extent) to the third and fourth lines. A cave and a pond, both round and deep objects found in nature, form parallel contexts for the active characters 'ein Totes' and 'ein Krankes'. The last two lines of both quatrains show traditional images, but with characteristically macabre distortions.

Corresponding to their parallel syntax, the first and second sentences of the poem's final version receive harmonically parallel settings. Each of the two sentences is shaped by the increasing acceleration of two or more discrete rotations of the total chromatic. In each phrase, the density gradually increases until the last measures are fully chromatic. In the first section, the twelfth pitch-class is not heard until the end of the third measure, when the bass clarinet's G completes the total chromatic. The end of the phrase compresses the leisurely time span of the beginning; in mm. 4–6, all twelve tones are sounded twice in the time it took before for a single statement. The second phrase has a similar harmonic rhythm. The first three measures (mm. 7–9) unfold a single chromatic set, while in the last four (mm. 10–13) the total chromatic is heard twice.

The process of acceleration occurs over the span of the two phrases as well as within them, aided by the acceleration resulting from the change from 3/4 to 2/4 time. While at the end of phrase 1, twelve tones sound in three beats (m. 5), at the end of phrase 2, the rotation has been compressed into two and a half beats (m. 11 and first beat of m. 12, also m. 13 and first beat of m. 14).

By circulating the total chromatic throughout each phrase, 'fresh'

[6] 'Again (one) encounters a dead thing | In white linen | And many flowers fall | Across the rocky path. | Silver a sick thing weeps | Leprous by the pond, | Where a long time ago | Lovers rested happily in the afternoon.' DTV 222.

notes are kept in the ear. The second phrase ('Silbern weint . . .'), for
example, begins on A^5, a pitch not heard before in that register. The
G♯ at 'weint' is a new pc altogether for the voice; its absence until
now gives special emphasis to this word.[7] Often one or two pcs
lacking from a twelve-tone collection are emphasized by their metric
placement. Measure 12 for example contains all pcs except B, which
is then sounded prominently in the voice on the downbeat of the next
measure.

The increasing density culminates in the third section of the piece,
'Oder es läuten die Schritte . . .' (mm. 15–21), where the total
chromatic is sounded in every measure. Here the metre shifts from
the 3/4–2/4 alternation of the first fourteen measures to the compound
6/8 (m. 15). This is one of the densest passages in all of Webern's
Lieder, consisting of four-voice counterpoint in steady eighths or
sixteenths, with few rests. While the wide leaps and fast note-values
in each part give the illusion of motion, the ultimate effect is static.
Whereas the instruments had moved freely between registers before,
here each part seems locked into its own registral space, returning
constantly to the same points. The parts overlap, creating a succession
of similar harmonies.

The change in the music in m. 15 reflects the poem's shift of
emphasis at this point. While the first eight lines present images of
death and decay, the ninth line suggests an alternative: the artificial
ice-world of the figure Elis ('Oder es läuten die Schritte Elis' ').
Although in the poem, Elis—and the world around him—looks alive
and real, Webern's setting allows no illusion. He sets the word 'Oder'
in m. 15 to the same two pcs as 'Totes' ('a dead thing', m. 3) in
opposite registers, revealing them as literal alternatives. Each part of
the four-voice texture outlines repetitive, endlessly circling patterns.
The music is frozen still, just like the lifelike body of the frozen Elis.

In m. 22, the bass clarinet announces the return of the freer, more
dramatic music. With the arrival of 3/4 time, Webern also returns to
the slower harmonic rhythm of the first two sections. After three
measures of incomplete twelve-tone collections, m. 25, the climax of
the phrase and of the piece, presents the total chromatic.

Declamation and Drama

'Abendland I' features two types of gesture that are opposite in
contour, rhythm, and character. These gestures remain distinct from
one another until the end of the piece, when the boundaries between

---

[7] In the sketches, Webern first assigns the 'new' G♯ to the first word of the phrase, 'silbern',
then changes it to A. The early reading would have started the second phrase with a new note
in a new register, but the change delays the entrance of the new pitch.

them start to blur. One of the two is developed throughout by the instruments; only at the very end of the piece is it taken over by the voice. The other is heard both in voice and instruments from the beginning. We have noted that in other Webern songs, when instrumental gestures are derived from vocal material, verbal references associated with that material may remain, implied by the music though not actually uttered. What about when the situation is reversed? Perhaps the words, in articulating a gesture that previously belonged only to the instruments, lend verbal meaning in retrospect. A sketch for 'Abendland I' documents Webern's crucial moment of realization that a word can be anticipated instrumentally. The sketch shows Webern allowing this instrumental anticipation—a disorderly outburst—to interrupt and irreconcilably alter the course of his original, more straightforward conception of the piece.

One of the two gesture-types in 'Abendland I' occurs often throughout Webern's music: a descending figure of three to five notes. (Well-known examples include the last measures of Op. 7 No. 4, and Op. 10 No. 4.) In 'Abendland I' the descending gestures use different pitches and intervals; they have in common only contour and rhythm (eighth-notes, often landing on a strong beat). The first statement of the 'descending figure' is heard in the violin in m. 4; it is clearly derived from the first two notes in the voice, Eb–C (Ex. 9.4a). Here, the violin's role is descriptive, foreshadowing the voice's descending gesture that illustrates the next line, 'und es fallen der Blüten'. At the beginning of the second phrase ('Silbern weint', m. 7), the voice and bass clarinet both articulate different versions of the gesture (Ex. 9.4b), while two measures later (mm. 9–10) the violin echoes it twice (Ex. 9.4c). The cello joins in with its own descending figure in answer to the violin in m. 12 (Ex. 9.4d). The figures have been heard increasingly closer together; the culmination is reached in m. 13, where all four parts sound descending figures at once (Ex. 9.4e).

The 'descending figure' almost ceases during the third ('Elis') section, appearing only to mark the interjection 'O des Knaben Gestalt' (violin, m. 19) (Ex. 9.4f). It returns, however, in intensified form in the recapitulatory fourth section. Here, the violin sounds two extended descending gestures which are connected for the first time, unlike the smaller, separated ones heard before (m. 23, Ex. 9.4g). The larger gestures prepare for the climactic vocal statement in m. 25, where the voice descends from its highest point in the piece, B (Ex. 9.4h). Moreover, the intervals used in the descent—minor third, minor ninth—match exactly those of the gesture the first time it was played, by the violin in m. 4. The words at m. 25 refer to Elis. In the

Ex. 9.4*a*–*h*. 'Abendland I', Op. 14/2, excerpts. Descending gestures.

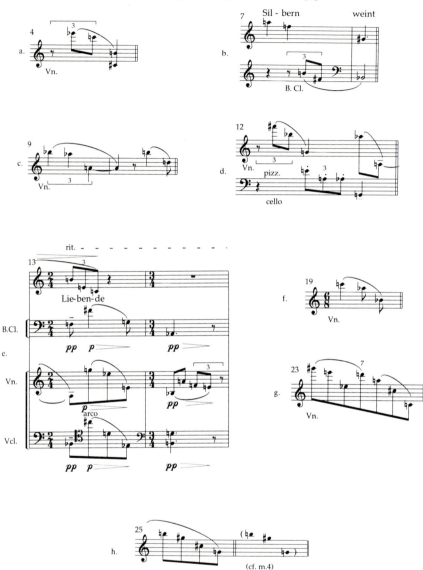

poem, though it is night, a flash of lightning illuminates him for a moment, we realize for the first time that his temples, 'die immerkühle', are frozen and lifeless. Webern's setting for the words 'die immerkühle', by using the same gesture previously associated with 'ein Totes', 'es fallen der Blüten', and 'hinüberstarben Liebende', conveys the full horror of that realization, emphasized by the very top of the singer's range.

Although tone-painting is not an acknowledged feature of Webern's songs, it is prominent in 'Abendland I'.[8] While places such as the passage 'es fallen der Blüten' in this work have been acknowledged, other obvious ones have not. One such passage is 'Frühlingsgewitter ertönt', a rapid burst of notes in the last measure (shown in Ex. 9.5a). Here seven syllables are compressed into one quarter-note beat; even with the 'ritard.', this is by far the fastest music for the voice in the piece. While the vocal 'lick' at the end clearly illustrates the suddenness and chaos—if not the noise—of a spring thunderstorm, this can also be heard as one of a family of related gestures that have been developed since the beginning of the piece.

The predecessors to the 'Frühlingsgewitter' gesture are instrumental, not vocal: the bass clarinet's two outbursts of rapid notes in mm. 11 and 22 (Ex. 9.5c and d). Both outbursts are rhythmically distinct from their surroundings, subdividing the beat into 6, 7, or 8. The bass clarinet gesture in m. 22 is dramatically exposed, and is almost unplayable at the 'accel. . . . lebhaft' tempo indicated. These gestures are also related to other rapid staccato figures, such as those in mm. 3 and 26 (Ex. 9.5b and e). All four of them anticipate the 'Frühlingsgewitter' figure to come; the bass clarinet in m. 22 specifically foreshadows the voice's 'Zackige Blitze', musically connecting 'lightning' with the later 'thunderstorm' music.

The continuity draft sketch for 'Abendland I' shows how one of the 'Frühlingsgewitter' figures helped Webern continue the sketch after he had broken it off (see Plate 6). At m. 21 Webern sketched the phrase 'nächtigen Schatten' in forceful eighths and sixteenths, emphasized by an unusual 5/8 measure, 'rit.', and 'forte' dynamic. He then indicated that the bass clarinet would accelerate into the next part of the piece. In this reading, 'nächtigen Schatten' would be heard as part of the 'Elis' section, indeed as its culmination. This conforms to the syntax of the poem here, which describes both 'kristallenen Tränen' and 'nächtigen Schatten' as characteristics of 'des Knaben Gestalt'. The bass clarinet's vigorous music would then lead into a new section of even greater intensity, appropriate for the words 'zackige Blitze'. Webern then continued to sketch the rhythms

---

[8] An exception is Rolf Urs Ringger, who has identified three different kinds of tone-painting, which he calls 'Sprach-musikalische Chiffern', in Webern's songs with piano: 'Sprach-musikalische Chiffern in Anton Weberns Klavierliedern', *Schweizerische Musikzeitung*, 106 (1966), 14–19.

Ex. 9.5a–e. 'Abendland I', Op. 14/2, excerpts. 'Frühlingsgewitter' gestures.

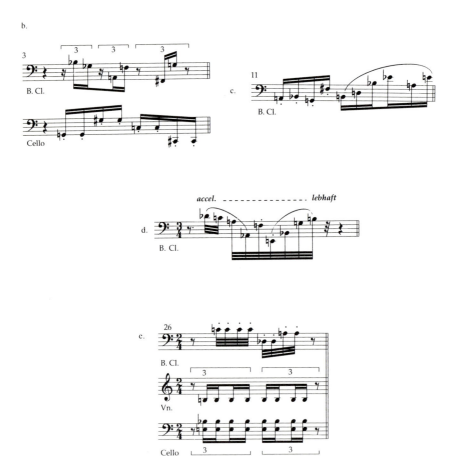

of the vocal line to the end; these rhythms produce a 'normal' declamation that corresponds to the natural rhythms of the words.

Webern's conception of this passage changed substantially, but only after he had finished sketching the whole piece. First, he sketched the transitional bass clarinet figure again in a new metre; instead of the 3/8 that had linked it to the previous passage in compound time, he turned to a contrasting 2/4 metre and wrote the new figure in regular sixteenth-notes. The rest followed in a form remarkably similar to the final version; the vocal line freely disregards the strait-laced rhythms Webern had sketched on the previous page. The piece ends with the outburst of fast music (a sixteenth-note septuplet) illustrating the words 'Frühlingsgewitter ertönt', followed in the sketch by a further outburst from the instruments.

At this point, Webern went back to the crucial juncture between sections 3 and 4 (mm. 21–2) and worked the vocal 'Frühlingsgewitter' gesture back into the piece *with instruments*. Disregarding what he had written, he began to sketch a new 'nächtigen Schatten' in the blank instrumental staves, this time in a lower register. Then follows the rewritten rapid bass clarinet figure of m. 22, now notated in sevens, which is exactly the same rhythm as 'Frühlingsgewitter ertönt', and marked 'frei' (later, he changed the rhythm to seven thirty-second notes, an imperceptible difference). With this stroke, the previous division into sections is dissolved. The phrase 'nächtigen Schatten' now belongs with the following 'zackige Blitze'. The bass clarinet, which before provided a smooth transition between sections, now interrupts the progress. Only after Webern had realized the setting for 'Frühlingsgewitter' did he use this figure to bring earlier music into its world.

Even though they are rhythmically disruptive, we might expect that the 'Frühlingsgewitter' gestures relate, at least in terms of pitch, to other passages. There was, for example, originally a pitch connection between 'Frühlingsgewitter ertönt' and the first measure, but Webern eliminated it when he revised the beginning. Ex. 9.6*a* and *b* displays the first measure as it appears in the continuity draft sketch and fair copy. Here the first note in the voice is C♯, not E♭, and the violin plays a trilled E♭–E, instead of a single note. Such a variant in the first measure of a piece is rather unusual; Webern's alterations occur far more frequently near the end. One feature of the original reading is that the C♯ in the voice and G♯ in the bass clarinet match the last two pitches of the piece exactly: $C\sharp^5$ and $G\sharp^4$ (on the word 'ertönt', marked in Ex. 9.5*a*). The sketch's E♭–E trill in the violin has its counterpart in the E♭–E trill in the bass clarinet, three octaves lower. By removing the trill and changing the voice's first note from C♯ to E♭, Webern considerably reduced this connection.

This is not necessarily a weakness. By minimizing the link between the first measure and the 'Frühlingsgewitter' gesture, the latter is further isolated. This supports the role of the 'Frühlingsgewitter'

Ex. 9.6. (a) 'Abendland I', Op. 14/2, c.d. sketch, mm. 1–3 (PSS, film 101:0563); (b) 'Abendland I', Op. 14/2, mm. 1–3.

gestures, which is not to connect with other parts of the music, but to interrupt them. Their rapid rhythmic profile is conspicuous and disruptive; the 'Frühlingsgewitter' gestures are not meant to 'fit in'. Wherever the explosions of rapid notes are heard, they disrupt the smoother rhythmic textures around them, just like the text's unexpected thunderstorm.

Whereas in earlier songs each poetic foot receives—on average— the same metrical length, that relationship had begun to weaken by 1915, in the fragment 'In der Heimat'. In 'Abendland I', it has been almost completely dissolved. The vocal line's declamation at the beginning shows that the piece will be neither predictable nor smooth. The violent shock of the opening chord—in a metrically ambiguous position and marked *sfpp*—is followed by a vocal rhythm that does

Ex. 9.7. 'Abendland I', Op. 14/2, mm. 22–7. Declamation in the third section.

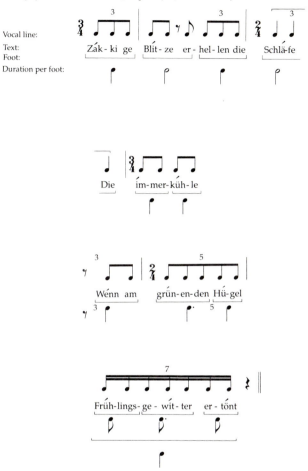

nothing to establish a perceptible metre.[9] The declamation continues to be irregular; the moments in which a text accent is matched to an even quarter-note pulse stand out as exceptions (these include the passages 'Viele über dem Felsenpfad', mm. 5–6, and 'Am Abendweiher', m. 10). In the last section of the piece, the voice engages in a continuous acceleration, until it finally achieves the speed of the instrumental gestures. (The declamation of this section is shown in Ex. 9.7.)

[9] The rhythm associated with 'Mond, als träte ein Totes', perhaps not coincidentally, matches exactly the rhythm and contour of a gesture in 'Der Dandy' (No. 3) of Schoenberg's *Pierrot Lunaire* (mm. 28–30).

The drama of 'Abendland I' lies in the friction between two gesture-types—the 'descending figure' and the 'Frühlingsgewitter' outbursts—which are not reconciled, but instead coexist in an uneasy balance. Though one gesture-type is more characteristic of a vocal line, and the other of an instrumental line, they are not confined to those roles, rather they move androgynously between the voice and instruments. The instruments therefore take on some of the characteristics of a recitative, namely the ability to exclaim and to interrupt. The voice, freed of the necessity to be 'vocal' and legato, is able to illustrate and reflect the vivid individual images in the poem by adopting 'instrumental' characteristics. The three 'Abendland' songs—which Webern considered as a unit but composed in reverse order—can be heard together as a kind of extended aria. The first ('Abendland I'), which has the character of a dramatic recitative, is followed by a cantabile (II), with a fast contrapuntal finale (III) to end.[10]

[10] Webern used a similar metaphor when describing a later song, 'Das dunkle Herz' (Op. 23 No. 1): '. . . in musical form it is really a kind of "aria": consisting of a slow section and a faster one . . . which nevertheless bears the tempo indication "ganz ruhig" (quite calm).' In *Letters to Hildegard Jone and Josef Humplik*, 25.

10. 'Gesang einer gefangenen Amsel' (Op. 14 No. 6): A Two-Year Preoccupation

Webern worked longer and more intensively on 'Gesang einer gefangenen Amsel' than on any other Trakl poem. Between 1917 and 1919, he sketched nine distinct drafts, the last of which became Op. 14 No. 6 (these are shown in Table 15). The 'Amsel' sketches document years of experimentation. Calling for instruments ranging from a trio of flute, viola, and bass clarinet to a large chamber orchestra, they range in length as well from a single phrase to a setting of the whole poem.

The musical variety of Webern's 'Amsel' fragments allows us insight into his two-year-long preoccupation with this short poem. Given that the settings differ in contour, pitch, metre, and instrumentation, a 'core meaning' common to all would be hard to find. (Even the 6/8 suggested by the poem's dactylic metre is not shared by all the sketches.) As with the 'Verklärung' fragments, Webern's 'Amsel' settings place the lines of the poem in various relationships to each other, essaying different 'readings'. At first, Webern was attracted to the sonorous words of the poem's first line: several fragments present beautifully descriptive settings of the words 'Dunkler Odem im grünen Gezweig', then break off. Vestiges of tone-painting at these words remain even in the final version. As he sketched the text again and again, his focus shifted from illustrating individual words to a more generalized organization that encompassed more of the poem.

Gesang einer gefangenen Amsel (Song of a Captured Blackbird)[1]

Dunkler Odem im grünen Gezweig.	Dark breath in green branches.
Blaue Blümchen umschweben das Antlitz	Small blue flowers suspended around the face
Des Einsamen, den goldnen Schritt	Of the lonely man, his golden step
Ersterbend unter dem Ölbaum.	Dying away under the olive-tree.
Aufflattert mit trunkenem Flügel die Nacht.	Night flutters up on drunken wings.
So leise blutet Demut,	Meekness bleeds gently,
Tau, der langsam tropft vom blühenden Dorn.	Dew, dripping slowly from the blossoming thorn.

---

[1] DTV 74, trans. after Lucia Getsi, 135.

TABLE 15. 'Gesang einer gefangenen Amsel' (Op. 14/6): Fragments and
Continuity Draft Sketch

Portion Set and Film No. (PSS)	No. of Pages	Instrumentation	Designated Date
1. vv. 1–5 2 pp., 104:0426, 0427, 101:0600	3	fl., cl., b. cl., 2 tpt., 3 tbn., va., vc., 3 d.b., hp., cel., mand., glock.	1917
2. v. 1 101:0493, 0492	2	solo d.b., strings	1917 [before July 4]
3. vv. 1–4 1 p., top, 104:0428	1	fl., cl., tpt., va., vc., d.b.	Mödling 1918 (Herbst)
4. vv. 1–4 1 p, bottom, 104:0428	1	cl., b. cl., tpt., vn., va., vc., d.b., hp., cel., glock., b. dr.	Mödling 1918 (Herbst)
5. v. 1 101:0597	1	picc., cl., tpt., vn., vc., hp.	1918
6. v. 1 101:0599	1	cl., tpt., hn., vn., vc., hp.	[1918–19]
7. vv. 1–3 101:0595	1	fl., b. cl., vc., d.b.	1918
8. vv. 1–4 101:0601	1	fl., va., b. cl.	[1919]
9. entire (continuity draft) 101:0590–0592	3	cl., b. cl., vn., vc.	11.7.19

Strahlender Arme Erbarmen	Compassion of radiant arms
Umfängt ein brechendes Herz.	Enfolds a breaking heart.

This poem, like all of Trakl's, allows many different readings.
Several phrases are cryptically isolated, requiring the reader to make
his own connections. The first line, which ends with a period, sounds
more like an ending than an opening line. The phrase is highly
condensed, as if it were distilled from a longer statement, such as
'and I saw the dark breath of the blackbird, entangled in the green
branches', for example. (This kind of compression in fact occurred
between Trakl's first and last versions of 'Abendland'.)

Then follows the image of a certain 'lonely one', whose face is
surrounded by blue flowers, and whose footsteps die away under the
olive-tree. The lonely man is not related narratively to the first line;
the two passages can be associated only by the recurring image of
something encompassing or surrounding: the blue flowers and the

green branches, in which the 'dark breath' is caught. These images anticipate the explicit 'surrounding' depicted in the last line, 'Umfängt ein brechendes Herz'.

The poem's nine lines are arranged symmetrically around a mid-point, 'Aufflattert mit trunkenem Flügel die Nacht'. This line interrupts the previous dactylic metre and describes a new spatial direction as well. As Zenck has noted, the rest of the poem uses images that imply either downwards or horizontal directions: 'umschweben', 'unter', 'blutet', 'tropft', 'umfängt'.[2] Line 5, with its vivid depiction of upward motion, is the central axis of the poem; literally, because it is preceded and followed by four lines, and figuratively, because of its contrast with—and interruption of—the other images.[3]

While the bare content of 'Amsel' may be, as Zenck suggests, that a dying man bleeds at night in the forest, and is caught, collapsing, by helping arms, others have suggested alternative meanings.[4] Ludwig von Ficker, Trakl's friend and the editor of *Der Brenner*, read the poem as a religious drama, in which the 'lonely one' is a Christ-like figure, and the 'Ölbaum' an allusion to the Mount of Olives. In this reading, lines 6 and 7 refer to the Crucifixion with the arresting image of thorns (alluding to the crown of thorns), which bleed humility. The story of redemption is completed in the last couplet, 'Strahlender Arme Erbarmen | Umfängt ein brechendes Herz'. Ficker, to whom the poem is dedicated, also relates a personal incident: in the spring of 1914 he was sitting with Trakl in a café at sunset, and noticed him spellbound by the song of a bird perched on an olive-branch.[5] Ficker believed this to be the actual event that inspired the poem; but, as Preisendanz rightly points out, the image of the Amsel turns up in many earlier poems.[6] Other images, such as 'thorns', for example, are prevalent as well, and have multiple implications. In addition to an allusion to the Crucifixion, a thorn in Trakl's poetry can be a biblical reference to the sting of death, as well as an erotic symbol. Moreover the words and images can function independently of a direct referent, like motives in Symbolist poetry. In this sense, the 'Amsel' does not refer to an actual blackbird or to any other poetic

---

[2] Martin Zenck, 'Indifferenz von Ausdruck und Konstruktion in Anton Weberns Trakllied "Gesang einer gefangenen Amsel" (Op. 14, nr. 6)', in *Kunst als begriffslose Erkenntnis: Zum Kunstbegriff der ästhetischen Theorie Theodor W. Adornos* (Munich: Fink, 1977), 215.

[3] Preisendanz has pointed out that, from the earliest poems, Trakl often fashioned a strict outward form, such as a sonnet or overall symmetry, in order to organize the otherwise conflicting images within. See 'Auflösung und Verdinglichung', 243–4.

[4] Zenck, 'Indifferenz von Ausdruck und Konstruktion', 213.

[5] *Erinnerung an Georg Trakl*, 203.

[6] 'Auflösung und Verdinglichung', 253.

blackbird, but is what Killy calls a 'wiederkehrende Chiffre' (recurring cipher).[7]

'Gesang einer gefangenen Amsel' shares some independent images with the 'Abendland' poems, such as footsteps ('Schritte') and trees ('Ölbaum', 'Eichen', 'kahlen Bäumen'). Trakl's 'Amsel' also bears a strong resemblance to his 'Elis' poems. Particularly suggestive is the image of footsteps dying away, 'den goldnen Schritt | Ersterbend unter dem Ölbaum', which in other poems is associated with the character Elis. In 'Abendland I', we find:

> 9   Oder es läuten die Schritte
> 10 Elis' durch den Hain . . .
> 12 Wieder verhallend unter Eichen.[8]

'An den Knaben Elis' contains a similar image:

> 7   Du aber gehst mit weichen Schritten in die Nacht,[9]

The Elis poems also contain images of thorn-bushes, which 'act' with verbs not normally used with stationary objects, such as 'tönt', as for example in 'An den Knaben Elis':

> 10 Ein Dornenbusch tönt,
> 11 Wo deine mondenen Augen sind.
> 12 O, wie lange bist, Elis, du verstorben.[10]

and 'Elis':

> 19 Ein blaues Wild
> 20 Blutet leise im Dornengestrüpp.[11]

These lines from earlier poems foreshadow the following lines in 'Amsel': 'So leise blutet Demut | Tau, der langsam tropft vom blühenden Dorn.' The beginning of 'An den Knaben Elis' even evokes the Amsel:

> 1   Elis, wenn die Amsel im schwarzen Wald ruft,
> 2   Dieses ist dein Untergang.[12]

These connections suggest another possible narrative for 'Amsel': this poem could tell the Elis story too, even though his name is never mentioned.

---

[7] Killy, *Über Georg Trakl*, 28.

[8] 'Or else Elis' footsteps | Ring through the grove, | . . . Again fading under oaks.' DTV 76.

[9] 'But you go with soft footsteps into the night,' DTV 50.

[10] 'A thornbush rings, | Where your moon-like eyes are. | Oh, how long ago have you died.' DTV 50.

[11] 'A blue deer | Bleeds softly in a thicket of thorns.' DTV 51.

[12] 'Elis, when the blackbird calls in the black forest, | This is your destruction.' DTV 49.

But to look for a single coherent narrative in this or any other Trakl poem would be to limit its effectiveness as a locus of many such connections and narratives. 'Amsel' does not tell a specific story, but instead juxtaposes images about being captured or enclosed in general. The religious imagery and 'Elis' allusions reach across to other poems and refer to several mythologies without articulating a single one. Webern's multiple attempts to set this poem can be seen as his recognition of this, rather than as failed attempts in which he groped towards a definitive solution.

TONE-PAINTING IN THE 'AMSEL' FRAGMENTS

Webern's settings often depict the image of 'darkness' in the poem's first line with low-register instruments. Sometimes there are also tremolos or trills in the opening bars, which could illustrate either the fluttering of a bird's wings as it tries to escape or the waving of the branches. Both the bass emphasis and the fluttering sounds are present in a 1917 fragment on 'Amsel' (No. 1). A melodic figure played by bass clarinet (formerly by double bass) is accompanied by three trombones who play a flutter-tongued chord. In another attempt (No. 2), scribbled on the back of a sketch for Op. 13 No. 3, Webern filled a whole page with sketches for a solo double bass introduction to the first verse. Each gesture uses the lowest note on the double bass (without an extension), E, which as an open string and therefore non-vibrato, would produce a very dark sound. After the double bass solo is finally worked out, the voice enters over tremolo strings and trilled double bass. The final layer of this fragment, which breaks off after the first verse, is shown in Ex. 10.1. In 1918 Webern continued with the double bass idea in fragment No. 7, whose three-measure introduction features solo double bass with bass clarinet (Ex. 10.2). The 'dark' colour of the opening measures is continued with bass

Ex. 10.1. Fragment, No. 2, end of sketch (PSS, film 101:0493–0492).

Ex. 10.2. Fragment, No. 7, mm. 1–5 (PSS, film 101:0595).

Ex. 10.3. Fragment, No. 5, mm. 1–5 (PSS, film 101:0597).

clarinet (or cello) trills and sixteenth-notes during the first vocal phrase.

After writing music appropriate for 'Dunkler Odem', it perhaps became difficult to continue the sketch when the text demanded an immediately contrasting mood. One 'Amsel' fragment from 1918 (No. 5) achieves a contrast between the first and subsequent lines, though it does not proceed vocally beyond the first verse. After an initial violin gesture, a clarinet in its low register, trilled, and low harp accompany the first line of text (Ex. 10.3 and Plate 8). The following measure explodes with rapid piccolo and muted trumpet figures that change the orchestral colour and mood and anticipate the next line, 'Blaue Blümchen umschweben das Antlitz'.

What is probably Webern's earliest sketch for 'Gesang einer gefangenen Amsel' is also the longest, covering the first half of the poem (to the end of line 5, 'Aufflattert mit trunkenem Flügel...') (No. 1; mm. 1–9 are shown in Ex. 10.4). This fragment is unusual

Ex. 10.4. Fragment, No. 1, mm. 1–9 (PSS, film 104:0426).

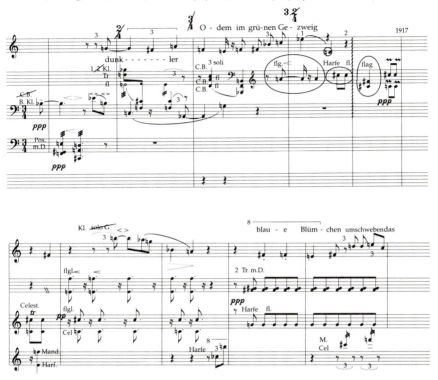

because of its use of vocal melismas, which Webern normally avoided. Here the regular dactylic metre of the line is obscured by the elongations on 'Dunkler' and 'Gezweig'; the voice's entrance on the last third of a triplet and continuation into an inserted 2/4 measure further conceal the notated metre, which becomes clear only at the vocal high point of '[Ge]zweig' on the down-beat of m. 4.

Tone-painting is also prominent, not just for the first line but throughout all sixteen measures. As in other fragments, 'Dunkler Odem' is illustrated with low-register instruments. At the word 'Odem', three solo double basses are heard, first playing harmonics in the treble clef, then descending into registers 1 and 2. As well as painting 'Dunkler Odem', the music depicts footsteps: the 'goldnen Schritt' of line 3. In Ex. 10.5a (first system), three-voice chords fall just after the beat. The fragment originally displays five-voice chords, which are then trimmed to a simpler, returning-note idea played by

Ex. 10.5. (*a*) Fragment, No. 1, mm. 12–15 (PSS, film 104:0427); (*b*) Fragment, No. 1, mm. 11–14 (PSS, film 101:0600).

cello, trumpet, and violin. The 'footsteps' sound earlier in the piece as well. In the instrumental interlude between the first two lines, chords falling one sixteenth after the beat (here in a higher register) can be heard as a 'pre-echo' of the 'goldnen Schritt'. Rhythmically regular chords occur in the second measure of the page, at 'Einsamen', as well as in Ex. 10.4 (second system), the interlude between the first two lines of the poem. This interlude rather pointedly recalls the fourth movement of Webern's *Six Pieces* for orchestra, Op. 6 (Funeral March), in which the delayed chords depicted the footsteps of a weird, post-Mahlerian march. In this 'Amsel' fragment, Webern uses similar march music to depict the 'goldnen Schritt' of Elis.

On another sketch page, Webern again revised 'den goldnen Schritt | Ersterbend unter dem Ölbaum' (Ex. 10.5*b*, second system), making the footstep tone-painting even clearer. Whereas before the 'Schritte' consisted of only three chords, now the idea has been expanded to seven chords, which extend from 'goldnen Schritt' to the end of the sentence at 'Ölbaum'. The one-measure interlude between 'Einsamen' and 'goldnen Schritt' has been eliminated, making the connection between the chords with 'Schritt' and the chords with 'Einsamen' more immediate. Most notably, the chords have been moved down an octave (Ex. 10.5b, mm. 12–13). The glockenspiel takes over a modified version of the previous bass clarinet part, two octaves higher.

The instrumental chords are now solely responsible for the tone-painting, since the voice's rhythm has been changed. In the first draft (Ex. 10.5a), the voice's steady eighth-notes helped to evoke the rhythm of footsteps; this rhythm was even anticipated by the clarinet in the previous measure. Webern then changed the rhythm of the clarinet figure, making its connection with the voice less obvious. In the second draft (Ex. 10.5b), the vocal line has been changed to dotted rhythms. Perhaps it would have been too repetitive for the voice to continue in eighth-notes as well, when the instruments had taken on the 'footstep' role for themselves.

This reading connects two phrases of line 3 that Trakl had left ambiguous. The object phrase 'den goldnen Schritt' has no subject (it could have been something like 'Man hört den goldnen Schritt'). Only because of the context might it refer to the steps of the 'lonely one'. In his first draft Webern takes the grammatical construction literally and separates the two parts of the verse by an interlude. In the second draft, he puts the two phrases together; by using the same pitches for 'Einsamen' and 'den goldnen Schritt', the footsteps are interpreted as specifically those of the lonely man.

Tone-painting is less prominent in two other long drafts of 'Amsel' from a year later. Both are found on a single large page (Nos. 3 and 4) and dated 'Mödling 1918 (Herbst)'. Webern resists a prolonged illustration of 'dunkler Odem'; the fragment at the top of the page begins almost immediately with the voice, preceded only by harmonics in cello and viola. The second line ('Blaue Blümchen') is separated from the first only by a brief viola solo. The rest of the fragment consists of the voice alone, whose syncopated rhythm at 'goldnen Schritt' does not suggest march rhythms or footsteps.

A more elaborate draft at the bottom of the page (No. 4) extends through the poem's first four lines; there are no interludes to break up the verses (portions of this draft are shown in Ex. 10.6). Even though Webern employs many instruments, he does not use the rich palette illustratively, except perhaps for a single low-register chord that precedes the voice's entrance on 'dunkler'. His goal was rather to create one large phrase, organized primarily by inversionally balanced groups of pcs. At the beginning and end of the phrase,

Ex. 10.6. Fragment, No. 4, mm. 1–5 complete, and mm. 6–17, vocal line only (top layer) (PSS, film 104:0428).

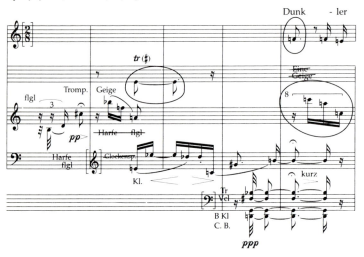

there is a strong tendency towards balance around D. The note-pair F–B between the voice and clarinet is especially prominent, as are the pairs F♯–B♭ and E♭–C♯ in the instrumental introduction.[13] Starting with a wedge-shape, the pitches of the middle octave are gradually filled in. At 'den goldnen Schritt', the voice escapes the middle register with its first leap above the stave. In the last measures of the fragment the voice again emphasizes its starting pitch, F, closing off the phrase with F–B, the same pair with which it began.

[13] This approach was developed by David Lewin (with respect to Schoenberg's music) in his article 'Inversional Balance as an Organizing Force in Schoenberg's Music and Thought'. Others have shown pc symmetry to be a crucial aspect of Webern's music as well, notably Peter Johnson, 'Studies in Atonality: Non-Thematic Processes in the Early Atonal Music of Schoenberg and Webern' (D.Phil. thesis, Oxford, 1978).

COMPARISON OF FRAGMENTS WITH FINAL VERSION

Although the musical surface differs among the 'Amsel' fragments, they and the published song share a basic structure; there is a break after the first line of the poem, then a larger break after line 4, 'Ersterbend unter dem Ölbaum'. Only one fragment gets beyond this point; in most cases the period at the end of this sentence seems to have blocked further progress. Evidently, whatever other musical variables there were, the overall grammatical structure of the poem was not to be tampered with. But in addition to phrase-structure, the 'Amsel' fragments have certain musical techniques in common with the finished song: these include pitch-class symmetry, the chromatic unfolding of a small interval, and an emphasis on certain fixed pitches.

Inversional Balance

The final version of 'Amsel' tends prominently towards pitch symmetry. The vocal line of the first nine measures is clearly balanced around D^4. The voice unfolds chromatically in a wedge-shape, emphasizing the pitch-pairs $C\sharp^4$–$D\sharp^4$ and E^4–C^4. These pairs are all equidistant from D^4, which is sounded on the down-beat of m. 1. Measures 7–9 ('den goldnen . . . Ölbaum') go through the same process again; starting with D, now registrally displaced, the line widens out with the symmetrical note-pairs C♯–D♯ and E–C. This marks the end of the first large section of the piece. The next verse begins at m. 10, with an abrupt change at 'Aufflattert mit trunkenem Flügel die Nacht'. The phrase from mm. 1 to 9 is therefore tonally 'closed', marked by a return to the same axis of symmetry with which it began. Many fragments also share this feature. In No. 6, Webern even corrects the vocal line to achieve pc symmetry (Ex. 10.7). The notes C and E♭ are prominent in both versions, but in the revision, they are arranged in the note-pairs C–E and C♯–E♭, pointing to a symmetry around D.

Two other brief fragments hint at symmetry around F♯ instead. The opening gesture of No. 5 contains the notes G♯–E, G–(D)–F, and F♯–B (with the first note in the vocal line). The symmetry becomes weakened by the second measure, however. In No. 8, the flute outlines a wedge-shape that is at least partially symmetrical around F♯^{4}; this is emphasized by the opening G♭ in the voice, and gains further resonance with the voice's E–F♯–F in m. 3 (Ex. 10.8).

The extended 'Amsel' draft, No. 1, also displays overall pitch symmetry. (Portions of this draft were shown in Exx. 10.4 and 10.5.) The opening instrumental gesture implies four of the five possible note-pairs symmetrical around G and C♯, with the axis note C♯

Ex. 10.7. Fragment, No. 6, mm. 1–5 (PSS, film 101:0599).

Ex. 10.8. Fragment, No. 8, mm. 1–3 (PSS, film 101:0601).

sounded in the bass. In mm. 2–3, all twelve tones are sounded, including *ipso facto* all five note-pairs. A continuation of hearing the G and C♯ symmetry is encouraged, however, by the vocal line, which begins with the axis note G and unfolds to the pair F♯–A. The end of the phrase, at 'ersterbend unter dem Ölbaum', is similarly balanced around G; the line creates a reverse wedge, F–A narrowing to F♯–G♯, then G. The result is a closed musical unit corresponding to the first four lines of the poem.

Chromatic Sets

In the published version of 'Amsel', the voice unfolds chromatically over the first nine bars. The same chromatic process is at work later

Ex. 10.9. Opening vocal lines of three fragments: (*a*) No. 5 (PSS, film 101:0597); (*b*) No. 4 (104:0428); (*c*) No. 7 (101:0595).

in the piece; at the climax, 'Strahlender Arme', the disjunct vocal phrase can be reduced to a chromatically filled-in space, like the opening vocal line. A similar chromatic unfolding also occurs in several of the fragments.

Three fragments employ a chromatic set for the opening vocal phrase ('Dunkler Odem im grünen Gezweig'); these three also use an ascending contour on 'grünen Gezweig', a feature found in many of the fragments. They all, incidentally, end on the same note (Ex. 10.9). In No. 5, the pitches of the vocal line compressed into one octave form a filled chromatic space of a fifth, from G♯ to D♯. A more stepwise presentation of a chromatic set is heard in No. 4. Its vocal line in the first four measures unfolds all the pitches between D and G, starting in the middle. A third example is No. 7, whose vocal line consists of chromatic pitches between G♯ and D♯. Though Webern did not adopt the contour of these fragments in the final version, he did evidently retain the idea of an opening gesture made up of a chromatic set.

Fixed Pitches

It is curious that so many of the 'Amsel' fragments emphasize the same pitch-classes, even though their melodic lines are quite different. In the published song, B in the bass clarinet initiates a chromatic progression of C, C♯, and D in the voice. The vocal line of No. 2, which does not superficially resemble the final version (the line is much more jagged, defining two active registers rather than one), like the finished piece is made up almost entirely of the three pcs B, C, and C♯. No. 5 highlights the same pcs in a different way. The notes B, C, C♯, and D are the 'corners' of the line; they occur at the relative low and high points of the melody. (These vocal lines can be compared in Exx. 10.1 and 10.3.) One might also note the pre-dominance of F and F♯ for the words 'blaue Blümchen', found in several fragments. Webern evidently used certain pitch-collections as building blocks, experimenting with their contour, rhythm, and in-strumentation over the course of several drafts.

'AMSEL' CONTINUITY DRAFT AND FINAL VERSION

On 11 July 1919, two years after his first attempt, Webern fashioned a complete musical realization of the poem for the first time. Though the continuity draft sketch differs yet again from any of the other 'Amsel' sketches, ideas from some earlier ones filter through. The first page of the continuity draft begins like many of the fragments, with a score system neatly set up in pencil (see Plate 10). Its scoring, for B♭ clarinet, cello, bass clarinet, and violin, is a combination that resembles the ensemble used in the other Op. 14 songs composed previously (Nos. 2, 3, 4, and 5); this shows that Webern here con-sidered an 'Amsel' sketch as a potential member of the Trakl cycle for the first time. When he added the violin, this became the only song in Op. 14 to use all four instruments.

As one would expect, the vocal line is entirely syllabic; Webern had abandoned melismas after the first attempts with this text in 1917. The 6/8 metre is also familiar from many of the earlier frag-ments; indeed it suits the poem's dactylic metre well. The elongated first syllable ('Dunk[ler]') is a feature Webern had used in some of the earliest fragments, but not in the most recent ones. He had never before used the syncopated rhythm at 'grünen Gezweig', on the other hand, though several fragments have the more conventional variant. (Part of the vocal line of the continuity draft is displayed in Ex. 10.10b.)

The most striking difference between the continuity draft and the fragments is the contour of the vocal line; in all but one of the

Ex. 10.10. (a) Fragment, No. 8 (PSS, film 101:0601); and (b) c.d. sketch, mm. 1–3 (101:0590).

fragments, the first phrase ascends on 'Gezweig', and the second phrase, 'blaue Blümchen', starts on a higher pitch than any previous one. A typical instance is shown in Ex. 10.10a, which displays the fragment that is probably the immediate predecessor of the continuity draft. In the final version, Webern keeps both phrases in the low register, abandoning the upward leaps to 'Gezweig' as well as a high vocal register for 'blaue Blümchen'; this results in a speech-like delivery in which the words are more readily understood. In fact one of Webern's concerns in the continuity draft seems to have been when and how to introduce the verbally disrupting high register in the voice.

Vestiges of Text-Painting

The cello harmonics in the first measure of the continuity draft (like the final version, m. 1) are a subtle reminder of other attempts to illustrate 'Dunkler Odem', alluding particularly to the similarly rapid viola harmonics in the fragment sketched just before this. We might also expect to find an illustrative treatment of the phrase 'den goldnen Schritt | Ersterbend unter dem Ölbaum' as before, but all that remains here is regular eighth-notes in the voice at 'den goldnen Schritt'. In the sketch the violin plays even sixteenths throughout mm. 7 and 8; if these are meant to depict footsteps, then the 'Schritt' has been speeded up to a jog. (Ex. 10.11 shows this passage in the continuity draft.)

Rather than depict the specific words 'goldnen Schritt', Webern

Ex. 10.11. C.d. sketch, mm. 7–9 (PSS, film 101:0590).

Ex. 10.12. Final version, chromatic unfolding in the vocal line.

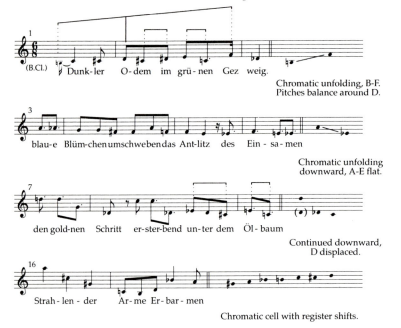

analogizes the more abstract image of 'Ersterbend unter dem Ölbaum'
with an increasingly sparse texture. In the sketch, the clarinet, cello,
and violin in mm. 7–8 have the character of soloistic display; in the
fair copy these parts are thinned out and separated until they are
reduced to isolated pointillistic gestures. The note-values gradually
slow as the phrase ends (mm. 8–9), corresponding to the image of
dissolution in the poem. This contrasts with the sudden burst of
activity at the next line, 'Aufflattert mit trunkenem Flügel die Nacht'.
The voice reaches the high register here for the first time, clearly
depicting the upwards fluttering image in the poem.

Although the middle line shifts abruptly from what came before, it
also functions in the context of the chromatic unfolding around which
the pitches are organized. First, the opening phrase of the vocal line
unfolds in a wedge-shape inversionally balanced around D^4, filling
the tritone-sized chromatic space B–F. (These steps are displayed in
Ex. 10.12.) In verse 2 a different tritone, A–Eb, unfolds downwards
by semitones. Next, in mm. 7–9, the pitches of the first gesture—a
chromatic scale balanced around D^4—are repeated, but now some
notes are shifted into their upper registers, which anticipates the
higher vocal range of the phrase to come. The end of the phrase is a

kind of compressed restatement of the first, with its opening wedge around D; the fourth phrase ends on C, where the first began. As in several of the fragments, Webern enfolds the poem's first four verses, from the beginning to 'Ölbaum', into a large musical unit. The resulting large phrase is tonally coherent, starting and ending with pitches inversionally balanced around D.

In the continuity draft, Webern's revisions at 'Einsamen, den goldnen Schritt' (mm. 6–7) show how he worked out the tonal plan. In the original reading of 'Einsamen', the vocal line has the same pcs as in m. 1 (D, Db, and C), only now in reverse order and up an octave (shown in Ex. 10.13). Perhaps thinking that these pcs would be too obvious a reference to the beginning, Webern transposed the passage to the lower-register F, E, and Eb. Since these pitches continue directly from the chromatic descent begun in m. 3, the new reading connects the syntactically joined phrases 'Blaue Blümchen umschweben das Antlitz' and 'Des Einsamen', which had been separated by Trakl's verse-division. The instrumental parts in mm. 6–8 display their own chromatic unfolding, which is carried out with more directness in the sketch than in the more disjunct final version.

Changes in the continuity draft show that decisions about register were also important to Webern. Knowing already that the climax of the vocal line would be in a high register, he needed to prepare this with some earlier high notes. As we have seen, he first tried to interject the high register at 'Des Einsamen'. This he changed so that it remained in the low register to complete the chromatic descent begun in m. 3 (Ex. 10.12 illustrates this). Webern's solution in the next phrase, 'den goldnen Schritt', shifts upward in register, but at the same time lets the descent continue with the notes lacking since the first phrase, D and Db⁴.

With the phrase 'Aufflattert mit trunkenem Flügel . . .' (m. 10), the continuity draft ventures beyond all the fragments but one. Even in the continuity draft, there is a physical break at this point; Webern starts a new page for line 5, reworking m. 9 ('Ölbaum') in the process. The line 'Aufflattert . . .' comes at the midpoint of the poem, and interrupts it like a sudden interjection. Webern treated this line as an interruption in the music as well. Along with a sudden increase

Ex. 10.13. C.d. sketch, at 'des Einsamen' (PSS, film 101:0590).

in density and dynamics comes a new vocal register. The phrase repositions the opening pcs C and C♯ into register 5; it is as if the chromatic unfolding of the first section were about to begin again, now an octave higher. But instead of continuing the ascent, the vocal line returns to register 4 after only two measures. This disruptive phrase divides the piece as well as the poem exactly in half; the first and last four lines each take nine measures, symmetrically surrounding the central two-measure pivot.

The last nine-measure section replays the process of chromatic unfolding carried out in the first; in fact the second half (mm. 12–20) has so much in common with the first (mm. 1–9) that it appears to be a recomposition of the same material. (The result is an interesting variant on the modified strophic form found in other songs.) The last section of 'Amsel' begins by varying the opening gesture; the vocal line at 'So leise' uses the same two pcs with which the voice began, in reverse order (D♭, C). Though the D♭ sounds in the same register as the opening C♯, the vocal line goes on to explore the upper middle of the octave (G♯–A–B, m. 12), an area which was avoided in the first phrase.

The chromatic webs unfolded from phrase to phrase extend over longer spans as well. After the opening vocal phrase gradually expands from C to A, there is a sense of unfulfilled expectations; completion of the rest of the octave—in the vocal line—seems necessary. This registral 'resolution' comes at 'Tau' (m. 13), where the B♭—a new pitch for the voice—picks up exactly where the first expansion left off; Webern emphasizes this by giving this word one of the longest durations in the vocal line. He continues to employ as many new notes as possible. At 'Strahlender', the top A^5 and low B^3 are both new pitches (in their registers), as is the F^5 at 'brechendes'.

In the continuity draft, the next step is a routine composing-out of this idea; the next two measures to fill in the remaining chromatic space between B and A♭ (mm. 14–15, 'vom blühenden Dorn'; the two versions are displayed in Ex. 10.14). There is a lot of pitch repetition in this version, however, particularly of B, which is heard on successive down-beats. Hearing B♭–A twice in mm. 14 and 15, as indicated in the sketch, would also reduce the freshness of the same pitches at 'Erbarmen' in m. 17; Webern normally avoided repeating the same pitches in register within such a short time. This passage was revised in the second layer of the fair copy. Here Webern changed the voice part at 'blühenden Dorn' so that it ascends to its highest point in the piece so far. The soaring gesture is also beautifully picturesque; we find similar gestures in 'Ein Winterabend' (at 'golden blüht'), 'Die Sonne' (at 'Himmel'), among many others (and its

Ex. 10.14. (a) C.d. sketch (PSS, film 101:0592); (b) final version, mm. 14–15.

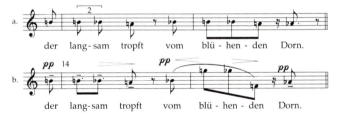

presence here is surprising given that Webern rejected other forms of tone-painting in this piece). The revised version fills in more of the chromatic space, while at the same time expanding the vocal range and avoiding pc repetition. (The total pc collection in mm. 13–15 fills a tritone chromatically, B down to F, instead of only a minor third as in the sketch.)

The expanded range also helps to prepare the large leaps in the voice at 'Strahlender Arme Erbarmen', which would otherwise form too vivid a contrast following three measures with such a narrow range. This passage is the climax of the poem and of the piece. Though it might appear unrelated to what came before, it can be heard as a culmination of the process of registral expansion begun in the first measures. Spanning almost two octaves and attaining both the vocal high point and low point of the piece (low B to high A), the pitches in the voice part can be reduced to a chromatically filled tritone, G♯–D (this is shown in Ex. 10.12). The music therefore summarizes the materials of the opening, but radically transformed. The chromatic tritone stated at the beginning in close position returns, but it has been transposed and distorted, its notes scattered over a wide area. The registral shifts used sparingly in the opening measures are here brought to their most extreme possible state: expansion over the entire vocal range.

The piece's chromatic unfolding does not establish all twelve tones equally; some pitches receive greater emphasis than others. The pc C is prominent; we have already noted its role at the beginning and ending of the first section (as part of a scheme of inversional balance around D). It is emphasized even more in the last section of the piece; first, C is sounded on the down-beat in *each* of mm. 17, 18, and 19 (and in m. 16 just after the down-beat, in its highest octave). The last note of the piece, a pizzicato low C in the cello, sounds like a down-beat even though it occurs on the last sixteenth of a 3/8 bar. In the continuity draft, Webern first gave C even more attention; it

Ex. 10.15. (*a*) C.d. sketch (PSS, film 101:0592); (*b*) final version, mm. 19–20.

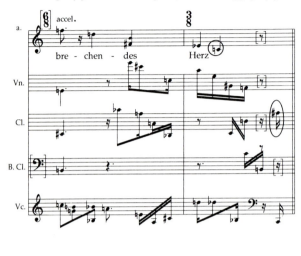

sounds four times in the last measure alone, including the last note in
the voice! (The last two measures of both the sketch and final version
are shown in Ex. 10.15.) This C would recall that note's role in the
first phrase; Webern's original idea may have been to strengthen that
focus by emphasizing C more. Of the many occurrences of this pc in
the last five measures, Webern preserved all but those in the last

measure; the revision gives other notes to the voice and the bass clarinet, but keeps the cello's low C.

In Webern's completed setting of 'Amsel', chromatic unfolding and registral balance offer a musical equivalent to the poem's images of 'surrounding'. The poem's images, as we saw earlier, are not related by theme or subject, but are linked instead by the recurring idea of verbs having to do with surrounding or enclosing: 'umfangen', 'gefangen', 'umschweben'. Both the image of green branches sur-rounding the dark breath, as in line 1, and that of merciful arms enclosing the breaking heart, in the last line, depict encircling or en-closure. Likewise pitches are surrounded horizontally, by inversional balance, and vertically, by registral symmetry. Even on the largest scale, the proportions of both poem and music balance around a central midpoint. The first phrase unfolds chromatically, 'circling' a D axis. Then, eight measures later, the first section ends balanced around the same pitch axis. On the level of the whole piece, the proportions comprise sections of equal length 'surrounding' a shorter central one. These musical effects are all horizontal; there are vertical 'enclosures' as well. The high and low points of the vocal line in mm. 16 and 17 are equidistant around Bb^4 ('Erbarmen'), as are the re-gistrally extreme points of the instruments in m. 16. 'Strahlender Arme . . .' would then be the culmination of this process, with the most intense poetic version of this image set to the most widely spaced chromatic group.

These last lines are crucial for the interpretation of the piece. It has been suggested that Webern in fact misinterpreted Trakl's poem; though the text implies that the dying man is redeemed, Webern's music depicts a terrible fall instead.[14] Adorno described it thus: 'With the outbreak at the end of the last song, the musical soul crashes in on itself.'[15] Both Adorno and Zenck respond to the undeniably shat-tering effect of the last measures with their extreme dynamics, where the piece's final gestures form a dramatic descent, and Webern paints 'brech-endes' with a madrigal-like gasp. This is a cataclysmic end to the whole Op. 14 group as well.

In one sense, of course, Adorno is right; the piece's final gesture forms a dramatic descent of unrivalled intensity. Yet Webern was able to portray the meaning of 'brechendes Herz', while at the same time grasping the essence of the poem, apart from the force of any single image. The redemption that Zenck thinks Webern overlooked

[14] Zenck, 'Indifferenz von Ausdruck und Konstruktion', 221.
[15] 'Mit dem Ausbruch am Ende des letzten Liedes stürzt das musikalische Innere in sich zusammen.' Adorno, 'Anton von Webern', 119.

is present in musical processes spun out from the piece's beginning. The 'Strahlender Arme Erbarmen' of the closing measures is illustrated by the music's structure, not its surface; every bar contains audible evidence of balance and symmetry. Webern's complex atonal language allowed him to illustrate a crushing fall at 'brechendes Herz', while at the same time composing out mitigating elements also present in the poem, such as 'Erbarmen' and 'umfängt'.

Webern's virtuosity lies in his ability to grasp the essence of the poem while simultaneously capturing the force of single images. With the sketches for 'Gesang einer gefangenen Amsel' and other fragments (particularly 'Verklärung'), we have seen that Webern's settings often start with the specific and illustrative and proceed with more abstract analogies between music and words. This process parallels a similar development in Trakl's poetry. The early poems often contain detailed and descriptive narratives, as does, for example, the first version of 'Abendland'; later this was reduced to a pared-down, allusive statement. Webern, by gradually dispensing with text-painting, constructs musical figures analogous to images in the text. As the music mirrors the poem's structure rather than its specific images, the text gains autonomy. At the same time both poetic and musical structures are deeply interrelated.

11. 'Nachts' and 'Sonne'

'NACHTS' (OP. 14 NO. 5): RETURN TO APHORISM

One week after ending his two-year struggle with 'Gesang einer gefangenen Amsel' in July 1919, Webern quickly completed another Trakl poem, 'Nachts' (At Night) in only a sitting or two. With this two-page continuity draft, Webern returned to the aphoristic dimensions of much of his pre-World War I music. Yet within the piece's approximately 30-second duration we do not hear the subtle whispers of the earlier miniatures; instead, Webern builds a dense four-part texture in which each instrument and the voice are stretched to their practicable extremes of range and flexibility.[1] Webern's setting undermines the strict, symmetrical four-line structure of the poem by blurring the 'frame' of beginning and ending, and by avoiding clear parallels between words and images in the service of a powerful musical idea.

Webern probably read Trakl's poem 'Nachts' in *Der Brenner*, where it first appeared in the spring of 1913.[2] The aphoristic style of the poem pays homage to Karl Kraus, for whom aphorism was a favoured genre and a particularly potent form of satire. Possibly in response to Trakl's poem, Kraus, in at least two subsequent issues of *Die Fackel*, gave the title 'Nachts' to groups of aphorisms; moreover he later published a collection of aphorisms under the same title.[3] The juxtaposition of opposites in Trakl's poem results in a characteristically Krausian kind of word-play.

'Nachts' compresses five distinct images into four lines, creating a stylized, almost artificial, structure. The colour-words 'blue' and 'red' occur in lines 1 and 3 and 2 and 4 respectively. At the same time, possessive pronouns divide the poem a different way; lines 1 and 2

---

[1] With regard to 'Nachts', Kurt von Fischer notes perceptively that 'It seems as if he wanted to compress his (and Trakl's) emotions by a kind of time-accelerator'; see 'A Musical Approach to Georg Trakl (1887–1914): A Study of Musical Settings of German Twentieth-Century Poetry', in Claus Reschke and Howard Pollack (eds.), *German Literature and Music: An Aesthetic Fusion: 1890–1989* (Munich: Fink, 1992), 11.

[2] The next volumes of *Brenner* after this featured the celebrated 'Rundfrage über Karl Kraus', which Berg at least is known to have read, and therefore Webern probably did too. See Rode, *Alban Berg und Karl Kraus*, 393.

[3] See *Fackel* 381/382/383 (19 Sept. 1913), 69–74, and 389/390 (mid-Dec. 1913), 28–43; and Karl Kraus, 'Nachts' (Leipzig–Munich: Verlag der Schriften von Karl Kraus, 1918).

are about 'my', lines 3 and 4 about 'your'. Still another grouping is suggested by the near-rhymes that link the outer and inner lines: 'Nacht' and 'Umnachtung' (lines 1 and 4), and 'Licht' and 'Sinkenden' (lines 2 and 3). The use of the past tense throughout provides a layer of distance between the narrator and the two losses that he describes: first a loss of identity, then of reason. These relationships are diagrammed below:

my	*blue*	Die Bläue meiner Augen ist erloschen in dieser Nacht,
my	*red*	Das rote Gold meines Herzens. O! wie stille brannte das Licht.
your	*blue*	Dein blauer Mantel umfing den Sinkenden;
your	*red*	Dein roter Mund besiegelte des Freundes Umnachtung.

> The blue of my eyes is extinguished in this night,
> The red gold of my heart. O how still the light burned.
> Your blue robe surrounded the sinking one,
> Your red mouth sealed the friend's derangement.[4]

Though the lines are arranged symmetrically, the personae of 'I' and 'you' are not equal; the 'I' is only acted upon, while the person addressed as 'you' is an active agent. In the first two lines, the narrator cannot even completely describe what happens to him: the sentence that begins 'Das rote Gold meines Herzens' is left incomplete, though its parallel structure with the first line implies the same continuation: 'ist erloschen in dieser Nacht'. Instead, the second utterance trails off, juxtaposed with a reminiscence of 'das Licht'; perhaps he remembers the reflected light from his own eyes and his heart, that is, his ego before it was destroyed. The last two lines, unlike the first couplet, relate two events in the form of complete declarative sentences. The night, in the guise of a 'blue robe' belonging to the unnamed 'du', surrounds 'the sinking one' and then a 'red mouth' propels him into madness (literally, possession by night: 'Umnachtung'). The masculine objects in these lines, which recall the previous 'I', confirm the narrator's helplessness and passivity.

Motifs of darkness and night are prominent in practically all of Trakl's poems. Often 'the night' represents a feminine figure as well, as the first line of 'Nachtergebung' makes explicit: 'Mönchin, schliess mich in dein Dunkel'.[5] The concept of night in Trakl's poetry also carries with it the Wagnerian association (most notably in the second act of *Tristan und Isolde*) that night represents the irrational, the erotic, and the creative. Trakl however subverts the traditional romantic dichotomy between night as irrationality and day as rationality, since his images of light are just as demented as his nocturnal ones.

---

[4] DTV 56, trans. after Lucia Getsi, 99.   [5] DTV 93.

In 'Nachts', light represents the narrator's personal identity, which is dissolved (literally, 'erloschen', extinguished) by the encroaching Night. The unexpected exclamation in the second line, 'O! wie stille brannte das Licht', is therefore not only a syntactical and structural interruption; it wrenches the narrator back to a time before the events he is describing, into a moment of dispassionate reminiscence of his intact ego.

The most striking feature of Webern's setting is the extremely high vocal register of the beginning. Though Webern had written high B♭s and Bs for the voice before, they usually serve as the climax of a line and are approached incrementally, by step or by leap. The remarkable—if treacherous—opening gesture of 'Nachts' starts as if in the middle of an imaginary gesture that has just reached this high point; it overwhelms the words, which cannot be clearly pronounced in this range, with sheer vocal intensity. At 'Augen' (m. 3), the voice plunges an octave and a half downwards (Webern had first considered the more manageable leap of a major seventh). This starts a series of gestures that descend rapidly and almost violently, occurring throughout in voice and instruments (the E♭ clarinet had anticipated this contour in mm. 2–3). Through the destabilizing quality of these gestures, Webern's reading of the poem seems to re-enact the over-powering force of Night or madness rather than the narrator's passive acceptance of these.

After the arresting opening vocal gesture, the voice can proceed only in short gasps; the phrase 'ist erloschen' is separated from what came before and from what follows ('in dieser Nacht'). The end of the phrase is marked by a plunge of more than two octaves in the bass clarinet (mm. 4–5) and by a faster figure in the E♭ clarinet that also descends more than two octaves (m. 5; this was apparently an afterthought, since it appears in the margin of the sketch). These gravity-succumbing figures continue in spite of the efforts of the second phrase to reverse the direction with ascending gestures (mm. 6–7). The violin in m. 12 and mm. 15–17 covers its entire three-octave-plus range in two descending gestures, both marked *Hauptstimme*. In m. 15 the voice surpasses its previous high notes with a high C, the first Webern ever wrote for the voice. The high C begins a phrase that ends in a violent descent more than two octaves lower. In the sketches, Webern repeatedly shortened the closing gesture, until it became a stark unaccompanied leap of a minor ninth downwards, vividly illustrating the word 'Umnachtung' (see Plate 4).[6]

[6] In the next work Webern composed this summer, 'Abendland I', he also organized the piece around a series of descending gestures, although these, unlike 'Nachts', originate in the instruments.

Instead of following Trakl's symmetrical four-line structure, Webern essentially turns it into a five-line poem. He separated the phrase 'O! wie stille . . .', and shifted it to the exact midpoint of the piece (which falls on the first syllable, 'O', in m. 8). The 'new' phrase forms an oasis of balance within the strongly directed motion of the outer sections. Set apart by a slower tempo and softer dynamic, the vocal line's pitches are loosely balanced around a central B♭^{4}, which ends the phrase, extended by a fermata (the high point, G, and the low point, C♯, are each a major sixth away from B♭). The violin provides a relaxed echo of the previous descending figures (and two of the pitches of the first vocal gesture) with a long glissando from A^6 to B♭^{4}, marked 'espr[essivo]'. The next two lines of text are declaimed without pause and compressed into seventeen beats (the first couplet took twenty-one). To replace Trakl's four-line schema, Webern creates his own symmetry of maximum tension balanced by an interval of repose. Rather than reflect specific verbal connections such as the colours blue and red, or the pronouns 'my' and 'your', Webern's brief setting is devoted to the projection of one idea: the massive, overwhelming loss of control that the poem describes.

While it would be exaggerated to speak of any configuration of pitches in this piece as 'stable' or 'unstable', there is one motive that Webern uses particularly to create the impression of continuous motion and total instability: this is an ordered chromatic set (of any size). The chromatic scale is the most basic element of atonal music, but as such is not often used in its raw form. Whether descending, as in the opening phrase in the voice, or ascending, as in the E♭ clarinet in m. 9, a figure made up of adjacent semitones moves quicksand-like without destination or end. Whereas in 'Gesang einer gefangenen Amsel' Webern arranged chromatic cells in wedge-like or other symmetrical shapes, in 'Nachts' he allows the more elemental chromatic sequence of pitches to create an extremely unstable effect.

The motive in the opening vocal phrase (m. 2: B–B♭–A–G♯) reinforces the sense of free fall already communicated by the plunge from the high register; in Webern's original sketch, the entire phrase was to be made up of a continuous chromatic chain (see Ex. 11.1). Echoes of the chromatic descent remain in the violin part in this phrase (m. 3, third beat, m. 4, third, and m. 5, first beats). In mm. 9–10 the E♭ clarinet presents an ascending chromatic group with displaced octaves (mm. 9–10: F♯–G–G♯–A); appropriately for a contrasting middle phrase, this motive is a registrally balanced version of the opening gesture, and therefore its opposite in character (and as a transposed retrograde, motivically opposite as well). Direct chromatic descent returns illustratively at the word 'Sinkenden' (m.

Ex. 11.1. 'Nachts', Op. 14/5, c.d. sketch, p. 1, vocal line, mm. 2–5 (PSS, film 101:0585).

Die Bläu - e mei - ner Au-gen ist er - lo-schen in die-ser Nacht

13: Bb–A–Ab–[G]). The last phrase likewise consists of the descending chromatic pitches D–Db–C–B with octave displacements (mm. 16–17). In the sketch, the chromatic descent takes place in close position: D^4–Db–C–B^3. There is also a remarkably impractical '8ve' sign *under* the voice's C^4, which was (probably immediately!) deleted. The poem's last word, 'Umnachtung', is therefore set to a transformation of the opening cell (mm. 2–3: 'Die Bläue meiner Au[gen]'). Both chromatic sets unfold from the note B, each in a different direction. By ending two octaves lower than it began, the vocal line's overall motion repeats the plunging downwards motion articulated in the first phrase.

This piece marks the beginning of the kind of vocal writing that Webern was to cultivate in later works, from *Five Sacred Songs*, Op. 15 (1921–2) to the *Three Songs*, Op. 18 (1925), and which is considered typically 'Webernian' in spite of the relatively small number of works in which it appears. This vocal style, characterized by large leaps, extreme range, and predominance of intervals made up of compound semitones, has been described as 'instrumental', and indeed Webern does require an instrumental agility and virtuosity of the voice in these pieces. It is misleading however simply to consider the voice as another instrument. As the text-bearing part, the voice can never hide inside the instrumental texture; moreover the vocal sonority itself has such a strong presence that (without conscious manipulation) it will always be heard as the *Hauptstimme*. Intrinsic to the force of Webern's extreme gestures in the voice is that fact that they are vocal; the palpable sense of difficulty and effort is essential to their effect.[7]

We have seen with respect to other Webern songs that the interplay between voice and instruments can go two ways; either the voice takes over a motive from the instruments (usually one presented in the introduction), or—more commonly—the instruments adopt and transform bits of vocal material throughout. In 'Nachts', both of

---

[7] Webern was acutely aware of how difficult this song was to perform (see the letter to Jalowetz quoted in Ch. 4, n. 16).

these happen, but in an unusual way. Instead of immediately taking material from the instruments, the voice presents a new figure at the beginning of the piece. Because of its range and contour, this figure is more characteristically 'instrumental' than vocal. At the same time, the instruments play 'vocal'-type material that will in fact later be adopted by the voice. The E♭ clarinet part, for example, never rises above C^6, also the highest vocal pitch. In the first half of the piece, the E♭ clarinet twice specifically foreshadows the vocal climax in m. 15, where the high C is reached, approached by G♯ (m. 2: C–G♯, m. 5: C–G♯). The violin also stays in an uncharacteristically low range until m. 8; this phrase (mm. 6–8) incidentally begins and ends with the same note-pair, C–G♯, that marks the vocal climax and the clarinet's anticipations of it. In the second half, the violin finds the high register it had avoided. The voice, in approaching its high point (mm. 14–15), adopts the dotted rhythm as well as several pitches from the E♭ clarinet in m. 3, and finally achieves the high C 'suggested' to it earlier. The interchange of roles between voice and instruments in the two outer sections of the piece mirrors the poem's two-part symmetry, with its shift from 'my' to 'your'. In Webern's setting of 'Nachts', like the poem, hyperexpressive free material is mediated within a highly structured form. The free-association construction of the pre-war miniatures has been recast; musical aphorism has been redefined in terms very close to Kraus's verbal aphorisms.

'DIE SONNE' (OP. 14 NO. 1): PAST AND FUTURE

Webern's last Trakl setting from 1921 ultimately became the first song of his Op. 14. 'Die Sonne' uses the most advanced idiom of the group, although the complexity found here differs only in degree from that of the other Op. 14 songs. In the six years that had elapsed since Webern first began to set Trakl's poetry, his musical language had evolved from contrapuntal, horizontal organization to a more pointillistic, hypercharged intensity. In 'Die Sonne', voice and instruments are more evenly balanced than in the earlier songs, and both require more extravagant virtuosity. The vocal line's declamation is freer, with prominent pitch accents often falling on unaccented syllables.

Die Sonne (The Sun)[8]

| Täglich kommt die gelbe Sonne | Daily the yellow sun comes over |
| über den Hügel. | the hill. |

---

[8] DTV 73, trans. after Lucia Getsi, 132.

Schön ist der Wald, das dunkle Tier,	Beautiful is the forest, the dark animal,
Der Mensch; Jäger oder Hirt.	The man; hunter or shepherd.
Rötlich steigt im grünen Weiher der Fisch.	Redly the fish glides upward in the green pond.
Unter dem runden Himmel	Under the round heavens
Fährt der Fischer leise im blauen Kahn.	The fisherman softly sails in a blue boat.
Langsam reift die Traube, das Korn.	Slowly ripen grape and grain.
Wenn sich stille der Tag neigt,	When day descends into stillness,
Ist ein Gutes und Böses bereitet.	A good thing and an evil is prepared.
Wenn es Nacht wird,	When night falls,
Hebt der Wanderer leise die schweren Lider;	The wanderer gently lifts his heavy eyelids;
Sonne aus finsterer Schlucht bricht.	Sun breaks from the dark gorge.

In *Sebastian im Traum*, of which Webern owned a copy, the poem 'Die Sonne' is printed on the page facing 'Gesang einer gefangenen Amsel'.[9] (He could also have read it in *Der Brenner* a year earlier.) One can see why Webern would have been attracted to this poem; here nature is presented as a peaceful, almost bucolic landscape, and therefore complements the dark mood of 'Untergang' and decay found in so many of Trakl's other poems. The concise twelve-line poem is divided into four stanzas of three lines each; this recalls the similar structure of 'Verklärung', which as we have seen inspired Webern to experiment with parallel musical structures. The beginnings of the first three stanzas of 'Die Sonne' have a parallel construction: each takes the form adverb–verb–singular subject ('Täglich kommt die . . . Sonne'; 'Rötlich steigt . . . der Fisch'; 'Langsam reift die Traube'). This pattern is then varied within the stanza, often by multiple subjects:

> *1 Täglich kommt die gelbe Sonne . . .
> 2 Schön ist der Wald, das dunkle Tier,
> 3 Der Mensch; Jäger oder Hirt.
> *4 Rötlich steigt . . . der Fisch
> *7 Langsam reift die Traube, das Korn.
> 9 Ist ein Gutes und Böses bereitet.
>
> (* = beginning of stanza)

This presentation of alternatives is familiar from other Trakl poems, as we saw in the use of 'oder' in 'Abendland I', only here there

---

[9] *Sebastian im Traum*, 66–7.

are no connectives; the alternatives, even ones loaded with emotional connotations like 'Gutes und Böses', are stated as neutrally as possible.

The word-order pattern is broken when the last line of the second stanza begins with the verb instead of the adverb: 'Fährt der Fischer leise . . .' (imagine how repetitious 'Leise fährt der Fischer im blauen Kahn' would sound, especially when followed by the next line, 'Langsam reift die Traube . . .'). In the third stanza, a further permutation occurs with 'Wenn sich stille der Tag neigt' (instead of the irritatingly predictable 'Stille neigt sich der Tag'); the 'when–if' construction anticipates the last and more significant disruption of the syntactical pattern that begins the fourth stanza: 'Wenn es Nacht wird'. Line 11, 'Hebt der Wanderer leise . . .', then echoes the first alteration of the pattern from line 6 ('Fährt der Fischer leise').

The last line presents the only subject–verb succession in the poem: 'Sonne . . . bricht'; the verb is also the only active one that is not modified by an adverb. The resulting directness of expression—intensified by the absence of the article 'die'—jolts the reader with the vivid image of the sun breaking out from the dark gorge. The first line's gentle image of the sun rising daily over the hill has been transformed; now it does not shine in the sky realistically, but instead is streaming from a dark place surrealistically, since it is night. Perhaps it radiates from the eyes of the Wanderer, a character also familiar from the 'Abendland' poems, as he opens his 'schweren Lider'.

An Early Fragment

Webern had attempted to set 'Die Sonne' three years before successfully completing the piece in 1921.[10] The two-page sketch extends through the first six lines of the poem, stopping short at the same place that gave Webern trouble in the final version: 'Langsam reift die Traube . . .'.[11] The 1918 fragment, which calls for a mezzo range instead of a high soprano and an ensemble of nine instruments instead of three, bears little resemblance to the final version. Perhaps

[10] PSS, film 104:0423 and 101:0596. The early draft of 'Die Sonne' is not listed in Moldenhauer's works list, though he does mention it in the text (Moldenhauer, *Anton von Webern*, 268). Manfred Angerer, 'Das Umkreisen der Sonne: Zu Anton Weberns Trakl-Lied, op. 14/1', *Melos*, 49 (1988), 94–117, does not mention this fragment.

[11] The Paul Sacher Foundation previously possessed only the second page of this sketch, which was unidentified. The only word of text on the page is 'Kahn'. With the help of the Trakl concordance (Heinz Wetzel (ed.), *Konkordanz zu den Dichtungen Georg Trakls* (Salzburg: Otto Müller, 1971)), I ascertained that only 'Die Sonne' had the proper number of syllables and stresses to fit the existing vocal line. In October 1987, the Paul Sacher Foundation acquired a one-page manuscript of 'Die Sonne' that turned out to be the first page of this draft.

the most striking difference, however, is the texture. While the final version of 'Die Sonne' is highly contrapuntal, in Webern's earlier attempt block chords of three to five voices are predominant.

With the early fragment (on the verso of the second page) is a sketch for the beginning of 'Amsel'. There is another brief sketch for 'Amsel' on the back of the first page, which appears to connect with the other 'Amsel' sketch.[12] The result is interlocking drafts; on one side of the two sheets, a sketch for 'Die Sonne', and on the other side, a sketch for 'Amsel'. The 'Die Sonne' sketch is dated 'Mödling 1918'; this suggests a similar date for the undated 'Amsel' fragment.

Two aspects of the 1918 'Die Sonne' sketch are immediately familiar from other sketches and fragments from this time: first, the relationship between the instrumental introduction and the voice, and second, the returning-note chords. (Ex. 11.2a displays the beginning of the 1918 sketch.) The opening flute line begins a four-note chromatic descent from B to G♯, while the violin and clarinet carry out another from F♯ to D. The 'gap' between the two chromatic segments is G, which is filled by the first note in the voice. The second note, C, completes the total chromatic. This note is prominent because of its high register—it connects to the flute's first chromatic span—and its role as the only one of the first six notes not belonging to the C♯ whole-tone collection.

We have found the same technique of chromatic unfolding in many other of Webern's pieces and fragments from these years. In 'Verklärung' (No. 2), for example, the bass and right-hand notes together form chromatic collections with missing notes, which are then provided in a strategic place. There is a sense of expectation of the total chromatic; it is imperative that gaps be filled. In the early sketch of 'Die Sonne', the vocal line of the first phrase also operates on the principle of chromatic unfolding; its ten pcs lack D and B♭, which are provided by the two upper notes in the accompanying chord.

In mm. 3–4 we find one of the most familiar 'progressions' of atonal music: returning-note chords moving stepwise in contrary motion. The middle chord of 'Die Sonne' (Ex. 11.2a, m. 4) is unstable, because of its subordinate rhythmic position, and perhaps also because the number of pitches it shares with the vocal part reduces its independence.

The most striking difference between the 1918 draft of 'Die Sonne' and the final version is the declamation of the vocal line. In the early version, the second and third lines of text are declaimed in a regular

---

[12] PSS, film 104:0423 and 101:0596.

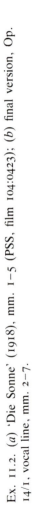

Ex. 11.2. (*a*) 'Die Sonne' (1918), mm. 1–5 (PSS, film 104:0423); (*b*) final version, Op. 14/1, vocal line, mm. 2–7.

Ex. 11.2 (cont.)

pattern of alternating half-notes and quarters in 3/4 metre, with a
particular emphasis on the word 'Mensch'. These lines ('Schön ist der
Wald . . . Hirt') are unfolded at the leisurely pace of 21 beats in the
early version. The 1921 version, however, distorts a 'normal' reading
of the verse's metre. The passage 'Schön ist der Wald . . . Hirt' is
compressed into half the time of the earlier version (see Ex. 11.2a,
b). Unaccented words like 'ist' and '[o]-der' receive the agogic
emphasis of high-register notes. The comprehensibility of the words
is obscured by the extreme vocal range (in mm. 5–6 alone it covers
two octaves, see Ex. 11.2b). Although the two versions employ the
same pitches on the words 'Mensch' (Eb^5) and 'Hirt' (C^4), the two
kinds of vocal delivery create totally different effects.

   The differences between the 1918 and 1921 vocal lines are characteristic of Webern's evolution on the whole during these years. In the
1918 draft, the opening phrase in the vocal line draws mostly on the
C♯ whole-tone collection, except for C, the first note, and F♯ later
in the phrase (all versions of the vocal lines are compared in Ex.
11.3). Such whole-tone emphasis is very common in Webern's and
Schoenberg's earlier music, especially that from the first years of
atonality. Three years later Webern's original idea for this passage is
also surprisingly conventional; the voice part in m. 1 forms the set 6–
Z19 (0,1,4,5,7,8). These notes are registrally separated to form two
major triads on C and D♭; the C triad is placed in the upper register,
the D♭ in the lower. Webern revised the line immediately, probably
to eliminate the overt triadic sonorities. The result of the change was
to create a symmetrical set, 6–7 (0,1,2,6,7,8).

   Some time after the sketch was completed, Webern revised the
opening bars yet again. From the standpoint of the vocal line, the
revision has a small but significant effect. The final version forms a
set very similar to the first one he sketched: 6–5 (1,2,3,4,7,8). It is
registrally divided as before, only now, instead of emphasizing triads,

Ex. 11.3. 'Die Sonne', opening vocal phrase. Comparison of vocal lines in four versions.

Täg- lich kommt die gel- be Son - ne . . .

the registral fragmentation produces two pentatonic segments, between 'white-key' and 'black-key' notes.[13] In its final version, the vocal line also has the advantage of sharing five out of six pcs with the opening clarinet gesture. The main result of the revision, however, is to replace a symmetrical set with an asymmetrical one.

Final Version: Musical Rhyme and Assonance

By settling on the exact shape of the opening vocal phrase, Webern established the primary intervals that he would use to articulate the stanzaic structure of the piece: the minor ninth and the major seventh. Though both intervals are commonly assumed to occur often in Webern's music, in fact the minor ninth becomes much more prominent after 1920 than it was before. In the earlier works it is used sparingly, and then for special emphasis, such as 'Mond, als träte ein *Totes*' that begins Abendland I and 'besiegelte des Freundes Um*nachtung*' that dramatically concludes 'Nachts'. In 'Die Sonne', the minor ninth is heard so often that it becomes almost interchangeable with the major seventh, although the larger interval still retains some of its extra intensity. The opening vocal line of 'Die Sonne', with its two minor ninths and two major sevenths in this phrase alone, clearly diverges from Webern's previous practice.

In the 1921 continuity draft, the minor ninth gradually becomes analogous to some of the parallel grammatical constructions in the poem. Webern first introduces this interval in the second line, at 'Schön ist der Wald' (remember that at this stage the first line had no

[13] See Valentina Cholopova, 'Chromatische Prinzipien in Anton Weberns Vokalzyklus "Sechs Lieder nach Gedichten von G. Trakl" op. 14', *Beiträge zur Musikwissenschaft*, 17 (1975), 156.

TABLE 16. 'Die Sonne': Minor 9ths in Vocal Line (Italicized): Continuity Draft and Final Version (Both 1921)

Continuity Draft	Published Version
	*1. *Täglich kommt die* gelbe Sonne . . .
	2. Schön ist *der Wald* . . .
3. Der Mensch; Jäger od*er Hirt.*	3. Der Mensch; Jäger od*er Hirt.*
*4. *Rötlich* steigt im grünen *Weiher* . . .	*4. *Rötlich* steigt im grünen *Weiher* . . .
6. *Fährt der* Fischer leise . . .	6. *Fährt der* Fischer leise . . .
*7. *Langsam* . . .	*7. Langsam reift die Traube, *das Korn.*
8. Wenn sich stil*le der Tag neigt,*	8. Wenn sich stil*le der* Tag neigt,
*10. Wenn es *Nacht wird,*	*10. Wenn es *Nacht wird,*
11. Hebt der Wanderer *leise* . . .	11. Hebt der Wanderer *leise* . . .
12. Sonne *aus fin*sterer Schlucht bricht.	12. Sonne aus finste*rer Schlucht* bricht.

* Beginnings of stanzas.

minor ninths), and then repeats the interval at the end of the stanza, at '[o]-der Hirt'. The next stanza, 'Rötlich . . .', begins with a transposition of the immediately preceding minor ninth. In the sketch, the stanza beginning 'Langsam reift die Traube' caused Webern a lot of trouble; he drafted it several times. In one of the early layers, 'Langsam' is set to a descending minor ninth, making it parallel to the first line of the preceding stanza. In another early layer, the last line of this stanza ('Ist ein Gutes und Böses bereitet') is saturated with three minor ninths. The parallelism is continued with the descending $F\sharp^6$–F^5 of 'Wenn es *Nacht wird*'.

At the end of the sketch, Webern revised the opening bars so that they too were saturated with this interval. The beginnings and endings of all stanzas except the third are now related by a kind of 'musical rhyme', similar to what we saw in the 'Verklärung' fragments (see Table 16). He also went back and revised the third stanza, 'Langsam reift . . .', taking away the intervallic parallel that he had originally conceived, creating a contrasting section for these lines instead. By doing this, he removed a musical–grammatical parallel in favour of a setting that differentiated between lines on the basis of meaning.

Proto-Serial Transformations?

The large leaps, the number of sevenths and ninths, and the pointillistic texture of the final version have led to speculation that 'Die

Sonne' foreshadows aspects of twelve-tone technique. The chrono-
logical proximity of 'Die Sonne' to the inception of the twelve-tone
method, as well as its superficial resemblance to later works, is
intriguing. Composed in August 1921, 'Die Sonne' follows by only
days Schoenberg's first twelve-tone effort, the 'Präludium' of the
Suite, Op. 25, composed in late July of that year. In July 1922, one
year after composing 'Die Sonne', Webern was to write out twelve-
tone row charts for the sacred song 'Mein Weg geht jetzt vorüber'
(Op. 15 No. 4).[14]

The 1921 version of 'Die Sonne' does feature some motivic transformations that resemble serial ones. For example, in mm. 5–7
(compared above with the early draft), the vocal line at 'oder Hirt' is
an inversion of 'ist der Wald'. If the operation of inversion takes
precedence over traditional declamation, this could explain the unusual emphasis on unaccented syllables in this phrase. In his essay
'Das Umkreisen der Sonne', Angerer argues that Webern's manipulation of small motivic cells bespeaks a kind of serial thinking before
rows were used.[15]

In order to support such a claim, however, one would have to show
that the notions of inversion and retrograde of ordered sets were
part of Webern's thinking at this point, as they clearly were to
Schoenberg.[16] In 'Die Sonne', transformations of motivic material
seem rather looser, relying on identity of diatonic interval types
rather than chromatic interval class. For example, mm. 19–20 present
several manifestations of a figure we might describe as 'third and
semitone'. The voice at 'stille der' presents this in the form of an
ascending minor sixth and descending minor ninth. This is followed
by what is clearly a variant of this figure at 'ist ein Gutes', but here
the third is both major and minor (and is presented both as a sixth
and as a third), and the semitone occurs in the total span of the
figure, which reaches a minor ninth. The phrase ends with another
'third and semitone' figure (at 'bereitet'), here presented in the shape
minor third and major seventh. In the instruments we hear exaggerated versions of this figure (for example, the cello in m. 19).
These transformations are not exact in terms of interval size; the
third can be major or minor, and can be presented as a sixth or a
third. The semitone is usually a major seventh or minor ninth, but
can also be in close position. In Schoenberg's analysis of his songs
Op. 22, he outlines a similarly flexible technique of motivic transfor-

[14] A facsimile of this sketch page is in Moldenhauer, *Anton von Webern*, 311.
[15] Angerer, 'Das Umkreisen der Sonne', 99.
[16] See Schoenberg's Op. 23 (1920) for examples of what he called 'composing with tones', a
clear precursor to twelve-tone technique.

Ex. 11.4. (*a*) 'Die Sonne', c.d. sketch, mm. 1–2 (PSS, film 101:0554); (*b*) 'Die Sonne', Op. 14/1, final version, mm. 1–2; (*c*) 'Verklärung' No. 6, mm. 1–2 (PSS, film 101:0557); (*d*) Berg, *Four Pieces* for clarinet and piano, Op. 5/1, m. 1.

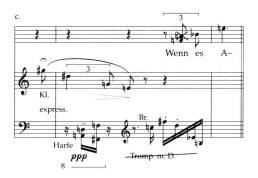

mation.[17] He identifies several motives as equivalent which do not have 'the same' intervals measured chromatically. Motivic development in Webern's songs likewise proceeds from free transformations that follow one another in a stream-of-consciousness-like fashion, rather than from strict serial operations.

That Webern's ultimate solution for 'Die Sonne' avoided serial operations does not mean that he was completely unaware of them. One of the most intriguing aspects of the 1921 sketch is that Webern initially planned quasi-serial imitations among the instruments in the opening measures, then rejected them. In the sketch, the violin's first five notes present a near-retrograde of the opening clarinet figure, transposed down a semitone (shown in Ex. 11.4a and b). Since the sequence of intervals and the contour are the same in both figures, the retrograde is easily audible. Moreover, the second and third notes of both figures (counted backwards in the violin) are D and E♭; the presence of the same notes in the same position in different transpositions anticipates the later technique of hexachordal invariance. The cello responds to the clarinet gesture with a transposed imitation, starting with its second note, B.

At some point after sketching the entire piece, Webern rewrote the opening measures, reducing the violin's gesture to three notes.[18] The final version eliminates the audible retrograde; the remaining three notes are derived from the original version, but now the gesture shares neither pitches nor intervals with the clarinet.

With the benefit of hindsight, it is tempting to see the inversion of a motive as a harbinger of twelve-tone technique. But in the sketches, obvious relationships such as retrograde or inversion occur very seldom, and when they do, they show no evidence of an a priori idea. The fact that in one sketch Webern rejected an operation similar to those found in serial pieces indicates that he was not following a system. Even when aiming for clarity, he avoided obviousness; his customary way of varying and developing motives was one of subtle references, with very few overt imitations or repetitions. In spite of the occasional presence of such imitation, the overall flexibility of the approach contradicts the basic principles of serial thinking.

Though 'Die Sonne' looks ahead in some respects to the later twelve-tone works, its language and presuppositions have a much greater affinity to Webern's earlier Trakl songs. One aspect familiar from the other songs is how the instruments restate and reflect mate-

---

[17] Schoenberg, 'Analyse der 4 Orchesterlieder op. 22', in *Stil und Gedanke*, 286–300.

[18] The rewritten version appears on the last page of the sketches. But Webern apparently intended from the beginning to revise this measure; on the first page, the violin gesture is marked by a parenthesis, one of Webern's signs for deletion.

rial in the vocal line. In 'Die Sonne', these reflections exist, albeit disguised to the point where they often cannot be heard as vocal references any more. Another feature that 'Die Sonne' shares with its predecessors is the succession of strophes, corresponding to stanzas of text, which are related by recurring intervals and pitches but have fundamentally contrasting characters. At the second stanza, 'Rötlich steigt . . .' (m. 8), the tempo and metre change from a 'Ruhig fließend' 3/4 to a 'Sehr fließend' 3/8. This new strophe is characterized by ländler-type gestures, such as dance-rhythms and glissandos, that we saw in Op. 14 Nos. 2 and 3. The third strophe is marked by a decisive slowing of tempo and return to the 3/4 metre (m. 17). In the voice the note-values slow, while the instruments are frozen into near-immobility, reflecting the sense of the text: 'Langsam reift die Traube'. The final gesture of the piece is a rapid accented outburst (m. 25), reminiscent of a similar outburst that ended 'Abendland I'. This is also text-driven: the music at 'Sonne aus finsterer Schlucht bricht' contrasts abruptly with the slower, quieter setting of the previous line, 'die schweren Lider'.

One aspect of 'Die Sonne' that has not been noted before is the similarity of its opening gesture to the beginning of the first of Berg's clarinet pieces. (Ex. 11.4b and d display the final version of 'Die Sonne' and Berg, Op. 5.) Berg's Op. 5, though written in 1913, was not performed until October 1919, the year in which Webern wrote most of his Op. 14 Trakl songs. With this quote from Berg, Webern pays discrete homage to his friend. In the original 1921 sketch, the 'Berg' figure is echoed by the violin and is therefore more prominent than in the final version, in which the allusion is confined mainly to the first two notes. Webern has however included the rest of the pitches from Berg's opening gesture without retaining their contour and register. (On the verso of the 'Die Sonne' continuity draft, Webern sketched the beginning of Trakl's 'Verklärung' using a similar opening figure: see Ex. 11.4c.)

Though forward-looking, 'Die Sonne' is also firmly imbedded in the context of the other Trakl songs. Like them, No. 1 is 'about' the free interplay of rhetorical gestures in a contrapuntal texture. Paradoxically, as Webern's language became limited to fewer intervals, he cultivated a greater variety of mood and texture within a piece. After 'Abendland III' (1917), which one could almost describe as 'monothematic', 'Die Sonne' (1921) contains an extremely wide range of gestures. One could not imagine something so continuous as an ostinato in this piece; rather its short punctuating outbursts give the piece a disjunct quality, especially compared to the more immediately 'lyrical' Trakl settings that preceded it. As minor ninths and larger intervals permeate the vocal line, and as the instrumental allusions to it become more and more distant, No. 1 continues the process of 'objectification' begun earlier. Yet the evidence of Webern's sketches for 'Die Sonne' indicates that the piece was not a proto-serial attempt. Rather, for all its newness, 'Die Sonne' has clear roots in the past, drawing in particular on a 1918 draft with the same text.

Afterword: Webern's Op. 14 as Modernist Work

When Webern warned his friend Josef Humplik that 'My Trakl songs are pretty well the most difficult there are of this type',[1] he was referring not only to difficulties of performance, but to difficulties of apprehension and perception as well. The music's complex atonal language is played out in a contrapuntal texture, which results in a correspondingly dense network of motivic connections. Webern's settings do not iron out the fractured syntax and multiple meanings of the Trakl texts; instead these ambiguities are multiplied further. Webern's Trakl songs Op. 14, which form a kind of summa of his atonal techniques, are remarkably thorny for a composer who was later to stress so much the importance of *Fasslichkeit* (comprehensibility).

This 'difficulty' is an essential aspect of Webern's atonal technique, in which 'condensation of expression and technique work together with a greatly extended force of expression, strengthened by the well-suited poems: returning without retreating [Rückkunft ohne Zurückweichen]', as Adorno, the Trakl songs' first advocate, put it.[2] Adorno also alludes to the performing difficulties of Webern's vocal music:

Not only is it difficult for the ear to synthesize the different notes of the [vocal] melody, but also, because of the amount of careful attention required to get the right notes, the singing is in danger of lapsing into nervous tightness and even shrillness. . . . The maturation of these pieces [middle-period vocal works] is a function of the progress made in their performance; only when they can be done without fear and bravura will their content be truly apparent.[3]

Schoenberg, Berg, and Webern acknowledged that their music was difficult to perform, and therefore tried to control the conditions

---

[1] 'Meine Trakl-Lieder sind so ziemlich das Schwerste, was es auf diesem Gebiet gibt.' Letter from Webern to Josef Humplik, in Moldenhauer, *Anton von Webern*, 269 (Ger., 243).

[2] 'Kondensation von Ausdruck und Verfahrungsweise treten zusammen mit einem Expansionsdrang des Ausdrucks, der an den kongenialen Gedichten sich kräftigt: Rückkunft ohne Zurückweichen.' Adorno, 'Anton von Webern', 119.

[3] 'Nicht nur ist dem Ohr die Synthese der disparaten Töne zum Melos schwierig, sondern der Gesang ist in Gefahr, durch die vordringliche Sorge um die jeweils richtige Note ins unfrei Ängstliche und zugleich Schrille zu geraten. . . . Die Entfaltung dieser Stücke ist eine Funktion des Fortschritts ihrer Wiedergabe; erst wenn sie ohne Angst und ohne Bravour übermittelt werden, dürfte ihr Gehalt sich recht manifestieren.' Adorno, 'Anton von Webern', 119–20.

surrounding a performance as much as possible. This sometimes led
to a certain unmistakable reluctance to have their works done at all.
On at least one occasion Webern vetoed a possible performance because he did not have a competent singer and there was not enough
time for rehearsals: 'Innumerable rehearsals would be necessary. . . .
A thing like a performance of a work of mine requires the fulfilment
of a host of conditions, and in this case they simply do not exist. . . .'[4]
On another occasion, when Jalowetz had offered to perform some of
Webern's orchestra songs, Webern responded with very guarded
enthusiasm. Though he provided Jalowetz with a list of his songs, he
alluded again and again to their difficulty, suggesting that only two
songs (of the eleven proposed) could possibly be prepared.[5] His
hesitation could have stemmed from knowing the pool of possible
singers (mentioned are Max Klein and Hans Nachod), of whose
abilities and limitations he was quite aware.

The huge amount of preparation time normally allotted to all
performances supervised by Schoenberg and his followers can be
seen (paradoxically) as another manifestation of their reluctance.
Though the music's unfamiliar tonal patterns and rhythms certainly
required a lot of rehearsal, the practice grew into a kind of 'cult of
rehearsal', which was actually used to limit outside performances. In
a telling anecdote, Stuckenschmidt relates how angry Schoenberg
became upon hearing that Varèse planned to programme *Pierrot
Lunaire* in New York. Varèse, who no doubt thought he was doing
Schoenberg a favour, must have been surprised to receive this
response:

In Vienna with everyone starving and shivering, something like a hundred
rehearsals were held and an impeccable ensemble achieved with my col-
laboration. But you people simply fix a date and think that's all there is to it!
Have you any inklings of the difficulties; of the style; of the declamation; of
the tempi; of the dynamics and all that? . . . What I want to know is: 1. How
many rehearsals? 2. Who is in charge of the rehearsals? 3. Who does the
speaking voice? 4. Who are the players? If all this is to my satisfaction, I
shall give my blessing.[6]

This obsessive attitude was not entirely to the composers' disadvantage; even though they lost a wider circulation of their works
(which they probably would not have had anyway), they gained total
artistic control over the product, and their works received an aura of

---

[4] *Letters to Hildegard Jone and Josef Humplik*, 13.
[5] 'Ich möchte dir raten: mache lieber nur 2 Lieder. Es ist sicher alles sehr, sehr, schwer.'
Letter to Heinrich Jalowetz, 8 Nov. 1921 (PSS, Jalowetz Collection).
[6] Stuckenschmidt, *Arnold Schoenberg*, 284.

belonging to a hermetic club of initiates.[7] These rehearsal practices were continued in the United States by émigrés; the most extreme case was the Kolisch quartet, which performed everything—including works of Schoenberg, Webern, Berg, and Bartók—from memory. As a student of Rudolf Kolisch at the New England Conservatory in Boston, I remember him saying on many occasions, 'You don't really know a piece until you have performed it from memory at least two hundred times.' This almost proprietary stance certainly served to magnify the differences between 'insiders' and 'outsiders'.

Complexity, for the Second Viennese School, was not an end in itself but resulted from their desire to achieve the maximum possible non-redundancy and compression of musical material. Berg's essay 'Warum ist Schönbergs Musik so schwer verständlich?' is a case in point.[8] Berg answers the question posed by his title by evading it. By pointing out how the 'difficult' aspects of Schoenberg's music are different only in degree from similar types of complexity in music of earlier composers, he exalts 'difficulty' as a compositional and historical necessity and places the burden of understanding on the informed listener. The 'difficulty' of Webern's Op. 14 songs is likewise intrinsic to their technique and expressive powers. Like the intentionally revolutionary first atonal pieces, Webern's Op. 14 songs are supremely—and paradoxically—comprehensible only through their 'difficulty'; at this historical moment, free atonality reached a stage where its expressivity depended upon the interaction of many musical features. This necessary complexity is also true of Trakl's poetry. In neither's work can one extract a simple underlying structure; every element is necessary in order to realize the full range of possible relationships. A similar emphasis on surface complexity is also characteristic of much abstract art of the early twentieth century, notably the work of Paul Klee, an artist whose technique and aesthetic have often been compared to Webern's.[9]

For Op. 14 Webern fashioned a powerful musical language whose primary strength is flexibility; a motive can be repeated, modified slightly, or recalled by its intervals, its pitches, its contour, its rhythm, or all of these in any combination: I have called this technique

---

[7] See Robert Morgan, 'Secret Languages: The Roots of Musical Modernism', *Critical Inquiry*, 10/3 (1984), 442–61.

[8] Reprinted in Willi Reich, *Alban Berg: Leben und Werk* (Zurich: Atlantis, 1963), 179–93.

[9] In works such as 'Pastorale (Rhythms)' (New York, Museum of Modern Art), the painting's total content has been brought forward to the front of the viewing space; there is no background or perspective in which to place the series of shapes. See Adorno, 'Anton von Webern', 123–5, and Nancy Perloff, 'Klee and Webern: Speculations on Modernist Theories of Composition', *Musical Quarterly*, 69 (1983), 180–208.

multiple reference.[10] Verbal language, with its denotative powers, is
not as pliable, but its greater concreteness enables it to refer simultaneously to more than one image, or even to refer outside the poem.
In each of the Op. 14 songs, Webern captures the non-narrative or
lyric aspect of Trakl's syntax through the use of a highly mutable
collection of motives. Even the instrumentation he chose—a small
group of melody instruments, not his previously favoured chamber
orchestra with percussion—lends itself to counterpoint rather than
colouristic effects.

The multiple motivic references are not all equal, since the singing
voice is the *Hauptstimme.* The vocal line provides the motivic material
for the piece, which the instrumental parts can then imitate and
develop. The instruments derive their motivic sustenance from the
voice, freely drawing upon it for their music. This vocal primacy has
implications for the interpretation of the text. When a given instrumental motive is first presented in the voice, it becomes associated
with particular words. Though varied or transformed, a motive can
recognizably recall the words originally associated with it. Therefore
an instrument can take on vocal capabilities, and can reminisce,
foreshadow, or reinterpret material presented in the voice, including
the words.

Schoenberg described something like multiple reference in his
analysis of his *Four Songs,* Op. 22: 'one must, as in an aphorism or
also/even in the lyric, invest every smallest component with such a
great richness of relationships to all the other components that the
minutest change of position allows as many new shapes to be seen as
do the richest working-out and development in other contexts. The
shapes are then situated as in a cabinet of mirrors and can continually
be seen simultaneously from all sides and display relationships in all
directions.'[11] Schoenberg's comments on his music could also, with
only slight modifications, describe the ambiguities and complexities

---

[10] Though I arrived at the term 'multiple reference' empirically from study of Webern's
Trakl settings, it is similar to notions used by other authors to describe Modernist works of
literature and art. See for example Malcolm Bowie, 'A Message from Kakania': 'The idea of
the unconscious . . . invites the critic to make connections between the finite array of structural
elements spread out upon the canvas and the indefinite array of drives and impulses that those
elements activate in the spectator.' In Peter Collier and Judy Davies (eds.), *Modernism and the
European Unconscious* (New York: St Martin's Press, 1990), 15. See also Astradur Eysteinsson,
'The Other Modernity: The Concept of Modernism and the Aesthetics of Interruption' (Ph.D.
diss., University of Iowa, 1987).

[11] '. . . man muß, wie im Aphorismus oder auch in der Lyrik, jedem kleinsten Bestandteil
einen so großen Reichtum an Beziehungen zu allen anderen Bestandteilen mitgeben, daß die
geringste Lagenveränderung so viel neue Gestalten sehen läßt wie andernorts die reichste
Durchführung und Entwicklung. Wie in einem Spiegelkabinett befinden sich dann die Gestalten und sind stetig von allen Seiten gleichzeitig zu sehen und zeigen Beziehungen in allen
Richtungen.' Schoenberg, 'Analyse der 4 Orchesterlieder op. 22', in *Stil und Gedanke,* 293.

of Trakl's poetry. Walther Killy, in his discussion of Trakl's 'Passion', remarks on the musical nature of the poem: 'The ear probably recognizes certain changes and motives, which—as in music—return and are transformed as the verses progress.'[12] Later he comments,

The ambiguity of changes, ellipses, and figures, the abundance of different possible meanings, is not a flaw—nor a lack of precision—but the true aspect of this kind of discourse. . . . This touches the deeper principle of the kaleidoscopic nature of a poetry that, with a few original images, always makes them new by variation, juxtaposition, and playing them off against each other.[13]

While the multi-referential, non-developmental nature of Trakl's poetry has been recognized, similar qualities in Webern's atonal music have not. Though atonal music possesses elements of disruption and discontinuity, in analytical discourse its continuous and developmental qualities have received much more attention. Theories of atonal music developed during the 1960s and 1970s have attempted to construct models that describe works as unified systems.[14] The adaptation for atonal music of terminology and concepts developed for twelve-tone music means that it has been very difficult to describe the open-ended, interruptive qualities of the much less systematic atonal repertory.

Perhaps atonal music is better perceived as the 'juxtaposition of the diverse', as Arnold Whittall has suggested; he also offers the term *symbiosis* ('contrasting events coexisting') as a more accurate model than the prevailing one of *synthesis*.[15] In a similar vein, Kathryn Bailey's study of Webern's *Symphony*, Op. 21, concludes that the traditional elements of sonata form are indeed present in the first movement, but they are presented simultaneously instead of in sequence.[16] The complex forms that result border on irrationality and prove resistant to analysis; this is something we should celebrate, according to Robert Morgan, not try to iron out into a smooth system.[17] Rather than searching for unifying background structure or

[12] 'Das Ohr erkennt wohl einige Wendungen und Motive, die—wie in der Musik—wiederkehren und sich im Fortschritt der Verse wandeln.' Walther Killy, *Über Georg Trakl*, 23.
[13] 'Das Ambiguose der Wendungen, Ellipsen und Figuren, die Fülle der Deutungsmöglichkeiten sind kein Mangel—auch kein Mangel an Präzision—sondern das eigentliche Element dieser Art von Rede. . . . Damit ist der tiefere Grund berührt des kaleidoskopischen Charakters einer Poesie, die immer aufs neue wenige ursprüngliche Bilder variiert, gegeneinandersetzt, gegeneinanderspielt.' Killy, *Über Georg Trakl*, 36.
[14] The best-known examples are George Perle, *Serial Composition and Atonality*, and Allen Forte, *The Structure of Atonal Music*.
[15] Arnold Whittall, 'Webern and Atonality: The Path from the Old Aesthetic', 734.
[16] Bailey, *The Twelve-Note Music*, 163–71.
[17] Morgan, 'Secret Languages: The Roots of Musical Modernism', 458.

functioning 'organic' process (or substitutes for them), one should explore the richness of the associations that result.

Webern's atonal language, with its capability of multiple reference, recreates the interconnected web of images in Trakl's poetry. The relationship between music and text is therefore not mimetic; it does not simply 'reflect' the text, but rather the two are analogous. The music must be complex to accomplish this. The 'difficulty' of Op. 14, especially its increasingly jagged and wide-ranging vocal lines, has however led many to conclude that the music has nothing to do with the poems, but instead uses it as a mere vehicle for vocal and instrumental display.[18] Even the earliest commentary on Op. 14, by Egon Wellesz in 1921, reinforces this view. Wellesz points out how much Webern's text-setting differs from that of traditional Lieder: 'the voice is handled like an instrument, free from every connection to the word. One can hardly imagine a stronger contrast to the Lied tradition of earlier times than in "Abendland" [I] by Georg Trakl; its closing recalls an instrumental cadenza, light and delicate, without attempting to paint the meaning of the individual words.'[19] I hope to have shown that the free atonality Webern used in the 1910s is not only suitable for Trakl's poetry, but is perhaps an ideal vehicle for his fractured syntax.

In each song of Op. 14, moreover, the poem was central to the compositional process and remains significantly involved with the development of the music. Webern's sketches show that his compositions grew out of encounters with a text; the music sets up a dialogue with the poem, reacting in different ways to its structure, images, and meanings. In all of his completed Trakl settings, he achieved a balance between setting a poem's individual images and its larger shape that sometimes eluded him in the fragments. At first, Webern struggled to illustrate each of Trakl's images separately; in fragment after fragment, phrases such as 'Dunkler Odem', 'Blaue Blümchen', or 'ein kleiner Vogel' receive their own impressionistic setting. Later he attempted a larger view, realizing the poem's whole shape in music, at the same time allowing the individual images to be freely expressed through a flexible interplay of motivic connections.

---

[18] For example, Zoltan Roman maintains that the music of Op. 14, not responding to Trakl's colour imagery, presents 'a profusion of hard surfaces antithetical to the colour-drama of Trakl's mysterious and morbid vision.' See 'From Congruence to Antithesis: Poetic and Musical *Jugendstil* in Webern's Songs', *Miscellanea Musicologica* (Adelaide), 13 (1984), 196.

[19] 'Auch die Singstimme ist, der letzten Bezüglichkeiten zum Wort ledig, wie ein Instrument behandelt. Es läßt sich kaum ein stärkerer Kontrast zur Liedbehandlung der früherer Epoche denken, als in dem "Abendland" von Georg Trakl, dessen Schluß wie eine Instrumental-Kadenz anmutet, leicht und zart, ohne den Sinn der einzelnen Worte mit Tönen untermalen zu wollen.' Egon Wellesz, 'Anton von Webern: Lieder', 40.

When the song is finished, the poem exists no more as a verbal text. What Trakl experienced as 'ein infernalisches Chaos von Rhythmen und Bildern'[20] while writing a poem was replaced by Webern's own rhythms and images. A musical setting may well rob the poem of its own rhythmic force and metrical shape; Webern's settings of Trakl, by eschewing the recitative-like writing that would let the words have some independence, are especially coercive. While Schoenberg's songs feature a fluid, prose-like delivery of the sung lines, Webern's settings replace the poems' verse-structure and metres with analogous musical ideas. Even the celebrated musical features of Trakl's poetry have been rendered inaudible and replaced by sounding music. But the musical ideas into which the poem is transformed—or translated—are themselves informed at every level by words and verbal gestures. By this means Webern achieves a musical analogue to Trakl's juxtaposed *Zeichen*.

Webern's use of multiple reference works analogously to Trakl's imbedded overlapping images because, at the core, both Webern's and Trakl's works are founded on the same principle. Adorno has suggested that Webern, of all composers, comes the closest to the immediate expression possible in the lyric poem, which music can even surpass in immediacy:

A lyric poem . . . has always come up against a limit: the objective concept, never completely translatable into pure expression, on which language is based. . . . Music too has been held back by its architecture and the givens of traditional form. [Music] cannot avoid the articulation of time; it dares not shorten [time] without regard; must devote itself to [time] for the sake of intensity in order to control extensive length. Therefore music has never completely realized the idea of the lyric, which is nevertheless irrevocably present within it. Webern—one might almost say: only Webern—achieved this.[21]

Through the use of self-referential images, Trakl's poetry approaches the limits that Adorno claims hold the lyric poem back from 'pure expression'. As an image, like 'die Amsel', recurs from poem to poem in different contexts, it loses its connection with a real bird and

---

[20] Letter from Trakl to Buschbeck, in *Erinnerung an Georg Trakl*, 138.

[21] 'Die lyrische Dichtung . . . stieß von Anbeginn auf eine Grenze: die des objektiven, in reinen Ausdruck nie vollends übersetzbaren Begriffs, an den die Sprache gebunden ist. . . . Musik aber stand im Bann ihres architektonischen Wesens, der überlieferten Vorstellung von Form. Sie möchte nicht darauf verzichten, Zeit zu artikulieren; sie wagte nicht, sie ohne Rücksicht zu verkürzen; was als extensive Größe gemeistert werden wollte, um der Intensität willen dranzugeben. Darum hat Musik niemals die Idee von Lyrik vorbehaltlos realisiert, die doch in ihr selbst unabdingbar gegenwärtig ist. Webern—fast möchte man sagen: Webern allein—ist es gelungen.' Adorno, 'Anton von Webern', 112.

begins to function like a musical gesture. Adorno's concept of the absolute lyricism (*absolute Lyrik*) of Webern's music is analogous to the absolute metaphors in Trakl's poetry. Sometimes Webern's motivic connections link parts of a poem that remained separated in the text, other times a gesture intensifies a single word or phrase. The interaction of motives linked to the text allows various instrumental 'subtexts' to comment on the vocal delivery. Still other times, the music pulls back from 'expressing' the passage and may even contradict it. It is difficult to speak any more of 'setting' a poem to music; this would be better described as 'recreating' or 're-enacting' the text. Webern's 're-enactment' of Trakl's poetry enabled him to develop his atonal language to its highest levels of complexity and subtlety; the 'difficulty' that results is essential to its expression.

Even in their 'difficulty', the six songs of Webern's Op. 14 remain in many ways quite traditional. Apart from their atonal language, Webern's pre-twelve-tone songs operate on assumptions that would have been familiar to Wagner or Wolf. The words of the text, delivered syllabically by a prominent vocal line, are presented in full without repetitions or interpolations. The voice's rhythm is for the most part consistent with the verbal accents. Stanzaic divisions and punctuation (and sometimes even rhyme) are reflected in the musical division of sections and phrases. The intelligibility (though not necessarily simple audibility) of the text is the supreme goal. Eighty years after Schumann's *Dichterliebe*, there are no extensive introductions, interludes, or postludes. The instrumental parts complement the voice; though they articulate independent contrapuntal lines, they do not function on their own. The harmonic vocabulary is small, overwhelmingly emphasizing a few favourite set-classes. The limited harmonic palette is balanced by a wide variety of gestural types, which change to reflect different moments in the text. All of these features point even beyond Webern's immediate predecessors Wolf and Mahler, back to Schubert, the first master of the German Lied.

Yet Webern's Trakl songs make an essentially modernist statement precisely through their reinterpretation of tradition. The complex motivically based atonal language transforms the traditional features, requiring them to function in a new way. Instead of having a specific role, each previously conventional unit—theme, phrase, motive, section, reprise, development—now has multiple functions. For example, a figure may refer to a previous one by pitch or pc identity, and at the same time to another place by intervallic similarities. Through an allusion to a previous vocal phrase it can recall some words of text while simultaneously alluding to a previous (or future) instrumental gesture. We have seen in 'Abendland III' how the notion of 'reprise' is modified when the recapitulation folds together earlier material at pitch and transposed at the same time. In 'Abendland I', audible sectional divisions are blurred when gestures from the 'wrong' section are interjected or occur too early. In Webern's hypercondensed language, two or three notes can refer to a much longer previous gesture. These ambiguities do not create imprecision, but rather the opposite. The multi-referent possibilities of every gesture create a wide network of precise relationships; this multiplicity results in complexity, to be sure, but not amorphousness. As in the poetry of Mallarmé or the paintings of Kandinsky, there is a rejection of monolithic linearity.

Although Webern, as well as Schoenberg and Berg, used explicitly organic metaphors to justify the strange new disjunctions in their music,[22] their writings are deeply contradictory on this issue. Schoenberg, for example, sometimes emphasized the organic qualities of post-tonal music to validate its historical continuity, and at other times proclaimed its revolutionary newness.[23] Peter Collier has suggested, in connection with Modernist literature, that both tendencies can coexist in a different relationship than before: 'there is a moment when the aesthetic of the "organic" image in Romantic and Symbolist literature tends to give way to a Modernist image, which is "organic" in some respects, but which differs in two key respects. Firstly, it accommodates the idea that the mind is split against itself. Secondly, it regards and expresses itself as process.'[24]

Collier's two 'key ways' in which the 'Modernist image' differs from past ones have parallels in atonal music. The second point is the most immediately relevant: without rhetoric, repetition, or signals such as cadences characteristic of tonal music, atonal music unfolds completely through process, its interest lying primarily in the transformation of its materials. The composer's mind can also be seen as 'split against itself'. Writing atonal music required at least at first a self-conscious avoidance of certain patterns. In order to create the illusion of organic development without the organizing power of a tonal centre, composers had to superimpose the metaphors of two different ways of thinking about music, at some level a conscious and intellectual act.

---

[22] See in particular Webern's analogy of the twelve-tone method to Goethe's 'primeval plant' ('Urpflanz') in *The Path to the New Music*, 40–1.

[23] See Joseph Auner, 'Schoenberg's Compositional and Aesthetic Transformations 1910–13: The Genesis of *Die Glückliche Hand*' (Ph.D. diss., University of Chicago, 1991); an unpublished essay by Jonathan Cheskin, 'Schoenberg's *Harmonielehre*: An Avenue Toward the Author's Pre-Twelve-Tone Personal Identity', also cogently addresses this point.

[24] Collier, 'The Unconscious Image', in Peter Collier and Judy Davies (eds.), *Modernism and the European Unconscious* (New York: St Martin's Press, 1990), 18.

At the end of a German Lieder tradition that had become increasingly text-centred, Webern brought this tendency to a rarefied
extreme. Though his radicalism lay in heightening tradition, not
eliminating it, Webern's followers paradoxically took his vocal music
as an invitation to shift the balance away from the verbal to the
musical. After Webern, works such as Boulez's *Pli selon pli* and
Stockhausen's *Gesang der Jünglinge* deconstructed words by enfolding
them more completely into the musical process. Webern's Trakl
settings lie at the juncture of this shift. As such they represent a
unique historical moment in the long association between poetry and
song.

Works Cited

ADORNO, THEODOR W., 'Berg and Webern—Schönberg's Heirs', *Modern Music*, 8 (1931), 29–38.

—— 'Anton von Webern', in *Klangfiguren* (Berlin and Frankfurt am Main, 1959), 110–25.

—— 'Zur Aufführung der fünf Orchesterstücke in Zürich', in Heinz-Klaus Metzger and Rainer Riehn (eds.), *Musik-Konzepte Sonderband: Anton Webern I* (Munich, 1983), 269–71.

ANGERER, MANFRED, 'Das Umkreisen der Sonne: Zu Anton Weberns Trakl-Lied, op. 14/1', *Melos*, 49 (1988), 94–117.

AUNER, JOSEPH, 'Schoenberg's Compositional and Aesthetic Transformations 1910–13: The Genesis of *Die Glückliche Hand*' (Ph.D. diss., University of Chicago, 1991).

BAILEY, KATHRYN, *The Twelve-Note Music of Anton Webern: Old Forms in a New Language* (Cambridge, 1991).

BASIL, O., *Georg Trakl in Selbstzeugnissen und Bilddokumenten* (Reinbek bei Hamburg, 1965).

BENJAMIN, WILLIAM, review of Forte's *Structure of Atonal Music*, *Perspectives of New Music*, 13 (1974), 170–90.

BOWIE, MALCOLM, 'A Message from Kakania', in Peter Collier and Judy Davies (eds.), *Modernism and the European Unconscious* (New York, 1990), 3–17.

BRINKMANN, REINHOLD, 'Schoenberg und George: Interpretation eines Liedes', *Archiv für Musikwissenschaft*, 26 (1969), 1–28.

—— 'Die George-Lieder 1908/9 und 1919/23—ein Kapitel Webern-Philologie', in *Österreichische Gesellschaft für Musik, Beiträge '72–73: Webern-Kongress* (Kassel, 1973), 40–50.

BROCH, HERMANN, *Hugo von Hofmannsthal and His Time: The European Imagination, 1860–1920*, trans. and ed. Michael P. Steinberg (Chicago and London, 1984).

BUDDE, ELMAR, *Anton Weberns Lieder Op. 3 (Untersuchungen zur frühen Atonalität bei Webern)* (Wiesbaden, 1971).

—— 'Metrisch-rhythmische Probleme im Vokalwerk Weberns', in *Österreichische Gesellschaft für Musik, Beiträge '72–73: Webern-Kongress* (Kassel, 1973), 52–60.

BUSCH, REGINA, 'On the Horizontal and Vertical Presentation of Musical Ideas and on Musical Space', *Tempo*, 154 (1985), 2–10, and 156 (1985), 7–15.

CHESKIN, JONATHAN, 'Schoenberg's *Harmonielehre*: An Avenue Toward the Author's Pre-Twelve-Tone Personal Identity', unpub. paper.

CHOLOPOVA, VALENTINA, 'Chromatische Prinzipien in Anton Weberns Vokalzyklus "Sechs Lieder nach Gedichten von G. Trakl" op. 14', *Beiträge zur Musikwissenschaft*, 17 (1975), 155–69.

COLLIER, PETER, 'The Unconscious Image', in Peter Collier and Judy Davies (eds.), *Modernism and the European Unconscious* (New York, 1990), 18–43.

CONE, EDWARD T., *The Composer's Voice* (Berkeley, Calif., 1974).

COX, GARETH, *Anton Weberns Studienzeit: Seine Entwicklung im Lichte der Sätze und Fragmente für Klavier* (Frankfurt am Main, 1992).

CULLER, JONATHAN, *The Pursuit of Signs: Semiotics, Literature, Deconstruction* (Ithaca, NY, 1981).

DAHLHAUS, CARL, 'Musical Prose', in *Schoenberg and the New Music*, trans. Derrick Puffett and Alfred Clayton (Cambridge, New York, [etc.], 1978), 105–19.

DANUSER, HERMANN, *Musikalische Prosa* (Regensburg, 1975).

DETSCH, RICHARD, *Georg Trakl's Poetry: Toward a Union of Opposites* (University Park, Pa., and London, 1983).

DOPPLER, A., '"Der Brenner" als Kontext zur Lyrik Georg Trakls', in Kurt Bartsch (ed.), *Die andere Welt, Festschrift für Hellmuth Himmel zum 60. Geb.* (Berne and Munich, 1979), 249–59.

DÜMLING, ALBRECHT, *Die fremden Klänge der hängenden Gärten: Die öffentliche Einsamkeit der neuen Musik am Beispiel von Arnold Schönberg und Stefan George* (Munich, 1981).

DUNSBY, JONATHAN, and WHITTALL, ARNOLD, *Music Analysis in Theory and Practice* (London and Boston, 1988).

Erinnerung an Georg Trakl (Innsbruck, 1926).

EYSTEINSSON, ASTRADUR, 'The Other Modernity: The Concept of Modernism and the Aesthetics of Interruption' (Ph.D. diss., University of Iowa, 1987).

FICKER, LUDWIG VON (ed.), *Der Brenner* (Innsbruck, 1910–54). Repr. edn. by Kraus Reprint (Nendeln, Liechtenstein, 1969).

FIEDLER, THEODORE, 'Hölderlin and Trakl's Poetry of 1914', in Emery E. George (ed.), *Friedrich Hölderlin: An Early Modern* (Ann Arbor, Mich., 1972), 87–105.

FISCHER, KURT VON, 'A Musical Approach to Georg Trakl (1887–1914): A Study of Musical Settings of German Twentieth-Century Poetry', in Claus Reschke and Howard Pollack (eds.), *German Literature and Music: An Aesthetic Fusion: 1890–1989* (Munich, 1992), 1–25.

FORTE, ALLEN, *The Structure of Atonal Music* (New Haven, Conn., 1973).

—— 'A Major Webern Revision and its Implications for Analysis', *Perspectives of New Music*, 28/1 (1990), 224–55.

GERLACH, REINHARD, 'Die Handschriften der Dehmel-Lieder von Anton Webern: Textkritische Studien', *Archiv für Musikwissenschaft*, 29 (1972), 93–114.

GOEHR, ALEXANDER, 'Schoenberg and Karl Kraus', *Music Analysis*, 4 (1985), 59–72.

GOSSETT, PHILIP, *Anna Bolena and the Artistic Maturity of Gaetano Donizetti* (Oxford, 1985).

GRIFFITHS, PAUL, 'Webern', in *The New Grove Second Viennese School: Schoenberg, Webern, Berg* (London and New York, 1983), 87–134.

HAMBURGER, MICHAEL (ed. and trans.), *Friedrich Hölderlin: Poems and Fragments* (Ann Arbor, Mich., 1967).

HASTY, CHRISTOPHER, 'Composition and Context in Twelve-Tone Music of Anton Webern', *Music Analysis*, 7/3 (1988), 281–312.

HILMAR, ERNST (ed.), *Anton Webern 1883–1983* (Vienna, 1983).

HOFMANNSTHAL, HUGO VON, 'Der Brief des Lord Chandos', in *Gesammelte Werke in zehn Einzelbänden*, vii (Frankfurt am Main, 1979), 461–72.

JANIK, ALLAN, and TOULMIN, STEPHEN, *Wittgenstein's Vienna* (New York, 1973).

JOHNSON, DOUGLAS, 'Beethoven Sketches and Beethoven Scholars', *Nineteenth-Century Music*, 2 (1978–9), 3–17.

JOHNSON, PETER, 'Studies in Atonality: Non-Thematic Processes in the Early Atonal Music of Schoenberg and Webern' (D.Phil. thesis, Oxford, 1978).

KABBASH, PAUL ANDREW, 'Form and Rhythm in Webern's Atonal Works' (Ph.D. diss., Yale University, 1983).

KERMAN, JOSEPH, 'Sketch Studies', in D. Kern Holoman and Claude V. Palisca (eds.), *Musicology in the 1980s: Methods, Goals, Opportunities* (New York, 1982), 53–65.

KILLY, WALTHER, *Über Georg Trakl* (Göttingen, 1960).

KLETTENHAMMER, SIEGLINDE, and WIMMER-WEBHOFER, ERIKA (eds.), *Aufbruch in die Moderne: Die Zeitschrift 'Der Brenner' 1910–1915* (Innsbruck, 1990).

KRAUS, KARL (ed.), *Die Fackel* (Vienna, 1899–1936).

LEWIN, DAVID, 'Inversional Balance as an Organizing Force in Schoenberg's Music and Thought', *Perspectives of New Music*, 6 (1968), 1–21.

—— 'Auf dem Flusse: Image and Background in a Schubert Song', *Nineteenth-Century Music*, 6 (1982), 47–59.

LINDENBERGER, HERBERT, *Georg Trakl* (New York, 1971).

LOCKWOOD, LEWIS, 'On Beethoven's Sketches and Autographs: Some Problems of Definition and Interpretation', *Acta Musicologica*, 42 (1970), 32–47.

—— 'The Beethoven Sketchbooks and the General State of Sketch Research', in William Kinderman (ed.), *Beethoven's Compositional Process* (Lincoln, Nebr. and London, 1991), 6–13.

LYNN, DONNA, 'Twelve-Tone Symmetry: Webern's Thematic Sketches for the Sinfonie, Op. 21, 2nd Movement', *Musical Times*, 131 (1990), 644–6.

—— 'Genesis, Process, and Reception of Anton Webern's Twelve-Tone Music: A Study of the Sketches for Opp. 17–19, 21, and 22/2 (1924–1930)' (Ph.D. diss., Duke University, 1992).

METZGER, HEINZ-KLAUS, 'analyse des Geistlichen Liedes op. 15 nr. 4', *Die Reihe*, 2 (1955), 80–4.

MEYER, FELIX, 'Im Zeichen der Reduktion: Quellenkritische und analytische Bemerkungen zu Anton Weberns Rilke-Liedern op. 8', in Hans Oesch (ed.), *Quellenstudien I* (Winterthur, 1991), 53–100.

—— and SHREFFLER, ANNE, 'Webern's Revisions: Some Analytical Implications', *Music Analysis*, 12 (1993), 355–80.

—— and STAMPFLI, SABINE (comps.), *Anton Webern Musikmanuscripte* (Inventare der Paul Sacher Stiftung, 4; Winterthur, 1988).

MOLDENHAUER, HANS, 'Excelsior! Die Genese des Webern-Archivs', in Hans Jörg Jans (ed.), *Komponisten des 20. Jahrhunderts in der Paul Sacher Stiftung* (Basel, 1986), 131–5.

—— (ed.), *Anton von Webern: Sketches (1926–1945)* (New York, 1968).

—— and MOLDENHAUER, ROSALEEN, *Anton von Webern: A Chronicle of His Life and Work* (New York, 1979). German version: *Anton von Webern: Chronik seines Lebens und Werkes*, trans. Ken W. Bartlett (Zurich, 1980).

MORGAN, ROBERT, 'Secret Languages: The Roots of Musical Modernism', *Critical Inquiry*, 10/3 (1984), 442–61.

MURRAY, EDWARD, 'New Approaches to the Analysis of Webern' (Ph.D. diss., Yale

University, 1979).

NOLAN, CATHERINE, 'Hierarchic Linear Structures in Webern's Twelve-Tone Music' (Ph.D. diss., Yale University, 1989).

OESCH, HANS, 'Webern und das SATOR-Palindrom', in Hans Oesch (ed.), *Quellenstudien I* (Winterthur, 1991), 101–56.

PERLE, GEORGE, 'Webern's Twelve-Tone Sketches', *Musical Quarterly*, 57 (1971), 1–25.

—— *Serial Composition and Atonality: An Introduction to the Music of Schoenberg, Berg, and Webern*, 3rd edn. (Berkeley, Calif., 1972).

—— *The Operas of Alban Berg*, i (Berkeley, Calif., 1980).

PERLOFF, NANCY, 'Klee and Webern: Speculations on Modernist Theories of Composition', *Musical Quarterly*, 69 (1983), 180–208.

PHIPPS, GRAHAM, 'Tonality in Webern's Cantata 1', *Music Analysis*, 3 (1984), 125–58.

POLNAUER, JOSEF (ed.), *Anton Webern: Letters to Hildegard Jone and Josef Humplik*, trans. Cornelius Cardew (Bryn Mawr, 1967).

POUSSEUR, HENRI, 'Strukturen des neuen Baustoffs', *Die Reihe*, 1 (1955), 42–6.

—— 'Weberns organische Chromatik (1. Bagatelle)', *Die Reihe*, 2 (1955), 56–65.

PREISENDANZ, WOLFGANG, 'Auflösung und Verdinglichung in den Gedichten Georg Trakls', in W. Iser (ed.), *Immanente Ästhetik/Ästhetische Reflexion: Lyrik als Paradigma der Moderne* (Munich, 1966), 227–61.

REICH, WILLI, *Alban Berg: Leben und Werk* (Zurich, 1963).

REINHARDT, LAURIEJEAN, '"Ich und Du und Alle": Hildegard Jone, Ferdinand Ebner, and Webern's Drei Gesänge Op. 23', unpub. essay.

RINGGER, ROLF URS, 'Sprach-musikalische Chiffern in Anton Weberns Klavierliedern', *Schweizerische Musikzeitung*, 106 (1966), 14–19.

RODE, SUSANNE, *Alban Berg und Karl Kraus* (Frankfurt am Main, 1988).

ROGNONI, LUIGI, *The Second Vienna School: The Rise of Expressionism in the Music of Arnold Schoenberg, Alban Berg, and Anton von Webern*, trans. Robert Mann (London, 1977).

ROMAN, ZOLTAN, *Anton von Webern: An Annotated Bibliography* (Detroit, 1983).

—— 'From Congruence to Antithesis: Poetic and Musical *Jugendstil* in Webern's Songs', *Miscellanea Musicologica* (Adelaide), 13 (1984), 191–202.

SCHOENBERG, ARNOLD, preface to score of Webern's *Six Bagatelles for String Quartet*, Op. 9 (Vienna, 1924).

—— *Stil und Gedanke: Aufsätze zur Musik*, ed. Ivan Vojtech ([Frankfurt am Main], 1976).

—— *Style and Idea: Selected Writings of Arnold Schoenberg*, ed. Leonard Stein, trans. Leo Black (Berkeley and Los Angeles, 1984).

SHACKLETON, NICHOLAS, 'Bass Clarinet', in *The New Grove Dictionary of Musical Instruments*, i (London, 1984), 170.

SHARP, FRANCIS M., *The Poet's Madness: A Reading of Georg Trakl* (Ithaca, NY, 1981).

SHREFFLER, ANNE, 'Webern's Trakl Settings' (Ph.D. diss., Harvard University, 1989).

—— 'Webern's Compositional Process: Origins of "Gesang einer gefangenen Amsel"', in *Atti del XIV Congresso della Società Internazionale di Musicologia*, iii (Turin, 1990), 369–80.

—— 'A New Trakl Fragment by Webern: Some Notes on "Klage"', in *Mitteilungen der Paul Sacher Stiftung*, 4 (Jan. 1991), 21–6.

—— 'Webern, Trakl, and the Decline of the West: Webern's Setting of "Abendland III"', in Claus Reschke and Howard Pollack (eds.), *German Literature and Music: An Aesthetic Fusion: 1890–1989* (Munich, 1992), 145–57.

—— '"Mein Weg geht jetzt vorüber": The Vocal Origins of Webern's Twelve-Tone Composition', *Journal of the American Musicological Society*, 47 (1994), 275–338.

SMALLEY, ROGER, 'Webern's Sketches', *Tempo*, 112 (1975), 1–12; 113 (1975), 29–40; 114 (1975), 14–22.

STEPHAN, RUDOLPH, 'Zu einigen Liedern Anton Weberns', in *Österreichische Gesellschaft für Musik, Beiträge '72–73: Webern-Kongress* (Kassel, 1973), 135–44.

STIEG, GERALD, *Der Brenner und die Fackel: Ein Beitrag zur Wirkungsgeschichte von Karl Kraus* (Salzburg, 1976).

STINCHCOMBE, J., 'Trakl's "Elis" Poems and E. T. A. Hoffmann's "Die Bergwerke zu Falun"', *Modern Language Review*, 59 (1964), 609–15.

STRAVINSKY, IGOR, preface to *Die Reihe*, 2 (1955), p. vii.

—— 'Introduction: A Decade Later', in Demar Irvine (ed.), Hans Moldenhauer (comp.), *Anton Webern Perspectives* (Seattle and London, 1966), p. xxiv.

STUCKENSCHMIDT, H. H., *Arnold Schoenberg: His Life, World and Work*, trans. Humphrey Searle (New York, 1977).

SUBOTNIK, ROSE R., *Developing Variations: Style and Ideology in Western Music* (Minneapolis and Oxford, 1991).

TEITELBAUM, RICHARD, 'Intervallic Relations in Atonal Music', *Journal of Music Theory*, 9 (1965), 72–128.

TODD, R. LARRY, 'The Genesis of Webern's Op. 32', *Musical Quarterly*, 66 (1980), 581–91.

TRAKL, GEORG, *Gedichte* (Leipzig, 1913).

—— *Sebastian im Traum* (Leipzig, 1915).

—— *Twenty Poems of Georg Trakl*, trans. James Wright and Robert Bly (Madison, Minn., 1961).

—— *Dichtungen und Briefe: Historisch-kritische Ausgabe*, ed. Walther Killy and Hans Szklenar (2 vols.; Salzburg, 1969).

—— *Poems*, trans. Lucia Getsi (Athens, Oh., 1973).

—— *Das Dichterische Werk* (Munich, 1987).

VOJTECH, IVAN (ed.), 'Arnold Schoenberg, Anton Webern, Alban Berg, Unbekannte Briefe an Erwin Schulhoff', *Miscellanea Musicologica* (Prague), 18 (1965), 31–83.

WEBERN, ANTON, 'Schönbergs Musik', in *Arnold Schönberg: Mit Beiträgen von Alban Berg* [et al.] (Munich, 1912), 22–48.

—— *Briefe der Freundschaft*, ed. Heinrich Lindlar (Rodenkirchen, 1958).

—— *The Path to the New Music*, ed. Willi Reich, trans. Leo Black (London and Vienna, 1975). Original German version: *Der Weg zur neuen Musik*, ed. Willi Reich (Vienna, 1960).

—— *Letters to Hildegard Jone and Josef Humplik*, ed. Josef Polnauer, trans. Cornelius Cardew (Bryn Mawr, Pa., 1967).

WELLESZ, EGON, 'Anton von Webern: Lieder opus 12, 13, 14', *Melos*, 2 (1921), 38–40.

WESTERGAARD, PETER, 'On the Problems of Reconstruction from a Sketch: Webern's

Kunfttag III and *Leise Düfte*', *Perspectives of New Music*, 11 (1973), 104–21.

WETZEL, HEINZ, *Klang und Bild in den Dichtungen Georg Trakls* (Göttingen, 1972).

—— (ed.), *Konkordanz zu den Dichtungen Georg Trakls* (Salzburg, 1971).

WHITTALL, ARNOLD, 'Webern and Atonality: The Path from the Old Aesthetic', *Musical Times*, 124 (1983), 733–7.

—— 'Webern and Multiple Meaning', *Music Analysis*, 6 (1987), 333–53.

WILDGANS, FRIEDRICH, *Anton Webern: Eine Studie* (Tübingen, 1967).

WOLF, JANET, 'The Ideology of Autonomous Art', in Richard Leppert and Susan McClary (eds.), *Music and Society: The Politics of Composition, Performance, and Reception* (Cambridge, 1987).

WOODWARD, GREGORY, 'Non-Pitch Aspects as Structural Determinants in the Atonal Works of Anton Webern' (Ph.D. diss., Cornell University, 1986).

ZENCK, MARTIN, 'Indifferenz von Ausdruck und Konstruktion in Anton Weberns Trakllied "Gesang einer gefangenen Amsel" (Op. 14, nr. 6)', in *Kunst als begriffslose Erkenntnis: Zum Kunstbegriff der ästhetischen Theorie Theodor W. Adornos* (Munich, 1977).

Index of Names and Works